Guide to Joining the Military

Military

SCOTT A. OSTROW

AIR FORCE · ARMY · COAST GUARD · MARINE CORPS · NAVY

www.petersons.com/arco

ARCO
THOMSON LEARNING

Australia · Canada · Mexico · Singapore · Spain · United Kingdom · United States

About Peterson's

Founded in 1966, Peterson's, a division of Thomson Learning, is the nation's largest and most respected provider of lifelong learning online resources, software, reference guides, and books. The Education Supersite^{SM} at petersons.com—the Web's most heavily traveled education resource—has searchable databases and interactive tools for contacting U.S.-accredited institutions and programs. CollegeQuest^{SM} (CollegeQuest.com) offers a complete solution for every step of the college decision-making process. GradAdvantage^{TM} (GradAdvantage.org), developed with Educational Testing Service, is the only electronic admissions service capable of sending official graduate test score reports with a candidate's online application. Peterson's serves more than 55 million education consumers annually.

Thomson Learning is among the world's leading providers of lifelong learning, serving the needs of individuals, learning institutions, and corporations with products and services for both traditional classrooms and for online learning. For more information about the products and services offered by Thomson Learning, please visit www.thomsonlearning.com. Headquartered in Stamford, Connecticut, with offices worldwide, Thomson Learning is part of The Thomson Corporation (www.thomson.com), a leading e-information and solutions company in the business, professional, and education marketplaces. The Corporation's common shares are listed on the Toronto and London stock exchanges.

For more information, contact Peterson's, 2000 Lenox Drive, Lawrenceville, NJ 08648; 800-338-3282; or find us on the World Wide Web at: www.petersons.com/about

COPYRIGHT © 2000 Peterson's, a division of Thomson Learning, Inc.
Thomson Learning^{TM} is a trademark used herein underlicense.

The information, opinions, suggestions and comments contained in this book are those of the author and are not endorsed by the Department of Defense or any of the branches of the Armed Forces of the United States or any other Government Agency.

For permission to use material from this text or product, contact us by
Phone: 800-730-2214
Fax: 800-730-2215
Web: www.thomsonrights.com

Photography Credits:

MEPS photos in Chapter 4 courtesy of U.S. MEPCOM.
Air Force photos in Chapters 1 and 6 courtesy of U.S. Air Force.
Army photos in Chapters 1 and 6 courtesy of U.S. Army.
Coast Guard photos in Chapter 6 courtesy of U.S. Coast Guard.
Marine Corps photos in Chapter 6 courtesy of U.S. Marine Corps.
Navy photos in Chapter 6 courtesy of U.S. Navy.

Library of Congress Cataloging-in-Publication Data

Ostrow, Scott A.
  Guide to joining the military / Scott A. Ostrow.
    p.cm.
  ISBN 0-7645-6189-8
    1. United States—Armed Forces—Vocation guidance. I. Title.

  US147 .O68 2000
  355'.002373—dc21

                                                              00-048519

Printed in Canada

10 9 8 7 6 5 4 3 2 1

A Note to Parents

Although this book was written to be used by individuals who are trying to decide whether or not to join the military, it can also be used by parents to help their kids make the right decision. If you are a concerned parent reading this book because your child is interested in joining the military, I urge you to read on.

It is not the intent of this book to persuade or dissuade your child from joining the military. Rather, its primary purpose is to give you and your son or daughter an honest look at the "enlistment process." In addition, there is an entire chapter dedicated to an inside look at Basic Training (or what you might know as Boot Camp).

Your child has probably seen recruiting commercials on television and received several colorful brochures that are designed to show the benefits of joining the military. While this book covers the many benefits of life in the military, it also separates the hype from the reality of enlisting.

Although I've made the military my career (a career I wouldn't trade for anything else in the world), I must admit that life in the military, while exciting and rewarding, isn't always quite the same "As Seen on TV." But even though those burgers you get at fast food restaurants somehow don't look exactly like the photo up on the menu board, they still taste good.

I don't have to tell you that your job as a parent is to offer guidance to your children and help them make the right decisions in planning their futures. However, if your child is old enough to be considering a military enlistment, the one thing you cannot do is mandate what decision your child makes.

If your child is under 18, he or she cannot enlist without your consent, so if you hold back your consent, your child will not be able to enlist—for now. My experience has been, however, that in the rare occasions when parents have not given permission for their child to enlist, the individual will wait until he or she turns 18 and will enlist anyway. Holding back consent just causes resentment.

Instead of creating animosity, you should use this book and work with your child to determine whether or not the military is the right choice for him or her. Remember that you don't necessarily have to agree with your child's decision—you just have to support it.

If you wish, you might want to meet with the recruiter to discuss the options available to your son or daughter. I would not, however, recommend that you attend the first meeting your child has with the recruiter. During the first meeting, the recruiter will ask your child some very personal questions and will expect some very honest answers in return. No matter how close a child is to his or her parents, there are things the child may not want his or her parents to know. Also, whatever information your child has given to the recruiter is protected by the Privacy Act of 1974. Therefore, you shouldn't ask the recruiter for details of the information provided to him by your child; he is forbidden by law to discuss that with you.

The prospect of their child serving in the military scares most parents (especially mothers) at first. It is a natural reaction for parents to be distrustful of military recruiters. For some parents, this distrust is based on a personal experience; for others, it comes from the "bad press" that military recruiters and the military itself have gotten over the years.

Instead of discouraging, or worse forbidding, your child from pursuing enlisting in the military, you should be proactive in gaining as much information as possible about the opportunities available to him or her in the military.

The computer-literate parent will find a wealth of information on the Internet. Some useful links are listed in Appendix E, "Contact Information." I would like to forewarn you, though, that most of these Web sites (either branch-specific or Department of Defense)—while offering valuable information—are focused on encouraging their visitors to enlist in the military. Knowing that, you should use the information they provide and the information contained in this book to help your child make an informed decision. But remember that, ultimately, it is your son's or daughter's decision to make, not yours.

As a postscript, I would like to address those parents who are trying to encourage a child to enlist who has no interest in the military. You may feel that your child needs to "grow up" or "get her act together."

While many young military members do a lot of "growing up" and maturing in Basic Training, that will never occur if your child was forced into the decision to join the military. The military is not a "scared straight" program to help troubled youths solve their behavioral problems. If, however, you feel that your child needs some direction in his or her life and think that the military could provide that direction, you may want to do some additional research and use this book to show your child the opportunities the military has to offer.

Good Luck!

Scott A. Ostrow

Dedication

In memory of my father, Artie Ostrow, who fought proudly in the European Theatre during World War II.

Acknowledgments

To acknowledge all the people and organizations that assisted me in the research for this project would double the number of pages contained in the book! Many people throughout the Department of Defense and elsewhere provided guidance, information, inspiration and encouragement to ensure that this project turned out to be a success.

Some of the organizations I'd like to thank include

Air Force Recruiting

Marine Corps Recruiting

Army Recruiting

Navy Recruiting

Coast Guard Recruiting

and their respective Reserve and Guard Recruiting counterparts.

I would also like to thank:

The Public Affairs (PA) officials of all the military services

PA officials of each of the services' Basic Training sites

USMEPCOM (especially its PA staff)

Air Force Reserve PA officials

A special thank you goes out to all the recruiters from all the military branches who took time from their busy schedules to answer questions and share their insights. Besides offering information, most also provided words of encouragement and told me that it was about time a book like this was published and that they wished they had come up with the idea themselves.

Thank you to the men and women of Air Force Reserve Recruiting, especially the Headquarters staff members who have supported this project 100 percent. And a very special thank you to my father-in-law (John) Warren Ewald, who saw the value of this project and supported and encouraged me along the way.

Thanks also to Colonel David Richards, Lt Col Dirk Palmer, Lt Col Kevin (Joe Miller) Reinert, 2Lt Brian Yoh, SMSgt Dave Schoch, SMSgt Loren Wright, and MSgt Cheri Johnson. Also, thank you to my editor, Kristi Hart, who has helped this first-time author make this book "be all it can be." Her guidance and support have truly made this book a better tool for the reader.

Most of all, I want to thank my family for their continual support and understanding during the writing of this book. My children: Scott II, Matthew, Brittany, Corey, Jennifer and Mary; and, of course, my wife Susie for her support, help and encouragement—although at times I am certain that she wished I'd never started this project in the first place!

There is one last acknowledgment I'd like to make, and it concerns the Internet. Although some would disagree, the invention of the Internet was, and continues to be, a wonderful thing. Without it, I think this book would have been impossible for me to write—or if not impossible, it would have taken me years and miles of red tape to compile all the data necessary to complete it.

The Internet (which was an invention of the United States Military) made available to me documents, forms and data that would have required me to file request after request with the appropriate agencies in the past.

CONTENTS

In this chapter you will learn about military recruiters, their training, their tactics and their procedures. You'll also learn what a recruiter can and cannot promise you.

This chapter will discuss the factors that must be considered in order to make an informed decision on whether or not to join the military. It will include a needs assessment to determine whether or not the military can fulfill your needs.

This chapter will not prepare you for the ASVAB; however, it is a general overview of the exam and its parts and contains some helpful hints.

Perhaps the most traumatic—and memorable—experience in the entire enlistment process is the applicant's first trip to the MEPS. This chapter will outline the purpose of the MEPS and reassure you that it is not an indicator of what life in the military is like.

Many, if not most, applicants wind up in a Delayed Entry Program (DEP). In this status, the applicant has already been sworn in and is awaiting his or her "ship date" to Basic Training. The enlistee can remain in DEP status for up to a year. A lot can happen between the day you swear in and the day you ship. This chapter will discuss things to avoid as well as keeping in shape and keeping the recruiter informed.

Chapter 6. Basic Training and beyond:
Early to bed, early to rise, makes a man or a woman
This chapter will outline the Basic Training of each military branch. Sample schedules are included as well as some basic advice for getting through the hell that is boot camp.

"How can I use my military experience to get an education?"

Find out with the **QuickStart Counselor**–
real-time, online education advice you can trust.

Are you looking for

• An alternative to expensive independent counseling?

• Personalized attention from a qualified professional?

• Valuable advice to help you reach your educational goals?

Chat online with a trained education counselor!

• 60 minutes of unlimited sessions

• Immediate feedback from an actual human being

• Access to high-quality educational resources from the leader in education information

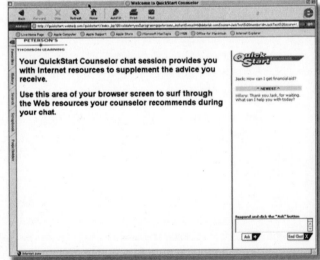

Register today at www.petersons.com/counselor

Introduction

As the largest employer in the country, the United States military offers its members high-tech training and experience—with pay— and even helps finance a college education. Indeed, every year thousands of young people pursue a military career and enjoy the benefits it offers. Yet thousands more consider joining the military and decide against it. The reasons why vary, but many choose not to enlist because they lack knowledge of the benefits a career in the military can offer, while others simply mistrust recruiters based on the horror stories they've heard from acquaintances. Sadly, many make the decision against joining the military without ever setting foot in a recruiting office.

In the past, military recruiters have been compared to used-car salesmen—and we all know what kind of bad reputation used-car salesmen get. Despite the stereotype, however, we still buy automobiles from salesmen. But the smart shopper arms herself with knowledge before going to a used-car lot. She prepares herself with information about the car that she wants to buy—what the car should cost, the available options, and its safety record. Most importantly, she determines whether the car of her dreams will suit her needs.

The main thrust of this book will be to transform you into an educated consumer. In the chapters to follow, you will learn how to determine if the military is the right choice for you. After that, you will learn how to deal with that salesman they call a recruiter. Just as the car buyer does his homework so he can get the best deal from the salesman, you will learn how to do the homework necessary to get what you want from your recruiter.

For the most part, military recruiters are highly trained and skilled salespeople. Their job and sole purpose in life is to find, qualify and, ultimately, enlist people for military service. Although the training and education benefits are excellent in the military, recruiters are not in the business of college counseling, nor are they employment agents. The bottom line is that we need a military to defend our country and her allies. As an Airman, a Soldier, a Coast Guardsman, a Marine, or a Sailor, that is your primary reason for being. Military recruiters are employed to ensure that only the best (mentally, physically and morally) individuals join our nation's military.

Despite what you may have heard, most military recruiters have a high degree of integrity. Why then all those horror stories of "how my recruiter lied to me"? In most cases, it's a matter of "selective listening" on the part of the applicant. This book will help you understand the enlistment process and keep you from being a selective listener.

Another purpose of this book is to dispel some of the myths about recruiters and life in the military. Things have changed quite a bit from the time when your Uncle Joe served in Vietnam, yet many times we rely on stories from friends and relatives to get our information about the military. Just as you would probably turn to the Internet to research a school paper and not your Uncle Joe's outdated encyclopedias, you should turn to someone who has up-to-date information about military benefits—your recruiter.

This book will walk you step by step through the enlistment process; you will know what to expect at every turn. From the initial interview, through testing and the physical exam, and ultimately to taking the oath of enlistment, you will be prepared. Could you get through the enlistment process without this book? Of course you could. Millions have. But just as you wouldn't think of planning a trip without a good road atlas to guide the way, why would you want to take this journey without some sort of guidance? Think of this book as your roadmap to joining the military. There may be some detours along the way, but ultimately you will arrive at your destination a lot better off than if you hadn't used this valuable tool.

Take the time to read this entire book, to study and to prepare for the meetings with your recruiter and your trips to the Military Entrance Processing Station (MEPS) just as you would for any test or job interview. The key to the entire enlistment process is preparation. Given the proper preparation, you will succeed in getting what you want. While you won't become an expert on the military enlistment process overnight, it is my sincere hope that this book will help you become familiar enough with the process so that your decision to join the military will be an educated one in which you are knowledgeable enough to get what you want from it.

This book is separated into six chapters. Each will cover a specific aspect of the enlistment process. So, without further introduction, let's get started on the adventure that is joining the military. Let the journey begin. (Where have I heard that one before?)

1 YOUR FIRST MEETING WITH A RECRUITER: FACING THE BEST-TRAINED SALESPERSON ON THE FACE OF THE EARTH

In this chapter, you will learn about military recruiters, their training, their tactics and their procedures. You'll also learn what a recruiter can—and cannot—promise you.

How can you tell if a military recruiter is lying to you? His lips are moving!

Is that what you think of military recruiters? If so, I hope you will feel differently by the time you've finished reading this chapter.

If you are reading this book, you probably have either been contacted by a recruiter or seen some sort of advertisement that interested you or perhaps someone you know has suggested that you explore a military career. Notice I've used the term "military career," instead of a "military job." The reason is simple. Although the military is a place to get a start and to learn a skill, it is also a way of life, not a job. And the opportunities (for those who pursue them) are endless.

You are now at the crossroads of a journey that may change your life. Do you make an appointment to see the recruiter, or do you pass? Many have come before you and have chosen not to talk to a military recruiter; many others have chosen to give the recruiter a chance to make his pitch. Many of those who chose to take the chance have joined the military. The ones who chose not to take that chance will never know what might have been.

Enough with the melodrama! If you're having doubts about whether or not to meet with a recruiter, I'm sure you have your reasons. Some common reasons why people are reluctant to meet with a recruiter are:

- I'll be pressured into joining—I just can't say no to any salesman.
- I don't think I'll like the military; I don't like rules and regulations.
- My friend's dad was in the Army (I think), and he hated it.
- I don't like getting up early in the morning.
- They wouldn't want me; I've got nothing to offer them.
- They've got nothing to offer me.

When I was younger, I used to get calls constantly from life insurance agents. They were relentless in their pursuit of getting me to make sure I had the peace of mind of knowing my family would be taken care of in the event of my untimely demise.

After the millionth telephone call I'd received, and after the millionth time I repeated, "I'm sorry, I'm not interested," I decided I'd take a different approach. I started inviting them to my house.

1

Before I did that, however, I did my homework. Yes, they were right: I needed supplemental life insurance, for my family's sake, but were they giving me the best deal I could get? After listening to sales pitch after sales pitch, I finally agreed to buy a life insurance policy. But it was on my terms, and I believe I got the best deal I could. More importantly, every time I received a telephone call from a life insurance salesman after that, I was able to say, "I've checked all of my available options, and I am certain that I have made the right decisions." Pretty soon, most of the phone calls ceased.

Before I decided to explore the possibility of supplemental life insurance, I had my reasons why I didn't need it. Just like the reasons why some people won't meet with a military recruiter, my reasons were unfounded, based on my lack of knowledge about life insurance and on my mistrust of insurance salesman. The main reasons were:

- I'm never going to die.
- My wife has my military life insurance policy. When she's done with that, she can go out and get a job!
- I'll be dead; who cares what happens after that.
- I can take the money I'd spend on insurance and invest it.

Sure, they weren't very good reasons not to see the insurance agent, but they were my reasons; and they were all I had.

The moral of this story? Do your homework, meet with the recruiters and make an informed decision. You, too, will be able to say, "I've checked all of my options, and I am certain I have made the right decision."

So, how do you decide which recruiter you meet with first? That's an easy question to answer: Meet with the one that you've already had some contact with or the one that is listed first in the telephone book. It doesn't really matter, because if you take my advice, you'll eventually speak with recruiters from all of the services.

Why the Military Needs Recruiters

Although the military, as a whole, went through a massive drawdown during the 1990s, it still must recruit an approximated 353,000 new people each year just to keep pace with the number of people leaving its ranks. People leave the military for a variety of reasons: Some retire after twenty years of service, some get out to pursue a civilian occupation (most times using the skills they learned in the military) and others leave to pursue higher education. Whatever their reasons for leaving, the fact is they leave and need to be replaced.

The military must be able to attract enough qualified individuals each year to maintain a high level of readiness and be able to perform its mission. This is where the recruiter comes in. It is not enough to advertise an "800-number" on television and wait for the calls to come flooding in (that only works for Ginsu knives and the exercise videos). No, the military must depend on their recruiters to get out into the communities, schools, youth groups and wherever else they can reach America's youth in order to keep their numbers strong.

Who Is "The Recruiter?"

At this point, all recruiters may look the same to you. You may not be able to distinguish an Army recruiter from an Air Force recruiter. In fact, unless you've done some research, you probably don't know much about the differences between the missions of the Army and the Air Force.

Although I will refer to all recruiters in the generic sense by calling them "military recruiters," or just "recruiters," make no mistake about it: Each recruiter works for his branch of the service and does not represent any other branch.

Why do I tell you this? Sometimes a recruiter will speak to an applicant about the opportunities that are not available from another branch. Don't let an Army recruiter tell you what an Air Force recruiter can't offer you. Instead, let him tell you what the Army can give you, and then let the Air Force recruiter tell you what he can and cannot offer you.

Each branch of the armed forces uses different criteria in the selection of its recruiters. However, they all have one thing in common: They employ experienced enlisted personnel from within their ranks to sell their product. It is this fact that sets military recruiters apart from the vast majority of "salespeople."

Recruiters know what they are selling; they lived and breathed the military long before they started selling it. The military recruiter is both an expert on, and an advocate of, his product. As such, he is able to provide information, guidance, opinion and an occasional story or two.

Recruiters do not start their military careers as salespeople; they come from all walks of military life. They are mechanics, cooks, administrators, electricians, and just about anything else you can think of. They come to recruiting, most often, with no sales background at all. So, you may ask, how does a cook become so good at selling? The answer is a simple one: recruiting school.

"Live from New York, it's . . . an Air Force recruiter."

WHAT RECRUITERS ARE TRAINED TO DO

Each branch of the military runs its own unique recruiting school whose primary mission is to turn "cooks" into highly effective salespeople in a matter of weeks. In that short amount of time, they must learn not only how to sell but also how to complete all the paperwork necessary for enlistment. It doesn't end there, though. They must also learn and become familiar with all the enlistment criteria, such as what makes someone physically unfit to enlist. They must learn how to be public speakers, how to deal with school and community officials, how to be job counselors, and a myriad of other things. This is somewhat amazing considering that most have had little, or no, formal civilian education since high school. What they learn in weeks would take months, or even years, of training elsewhere.

Although recruiters learn a multitude of things in recruiting school, the primary focus is sales: how to contact (prospect for) potential applicants and then convince them to join their particular branch of the military.

Prospecting for Applicants

Unless you took the first step and made the initial contact, your recruiter somehow got your name and contact information. In fact, if the recruiter made the initial contact by telephone, you may have even asked him, "How did you get my phone number?" Military recruiters have many ways to get your name, and here are just a few:

- A list provided by your school
- Referral from a friend, family member, classmate or coworker
- In response to your request for information
- Your high school yearbook and a little investigative work
- You took the Armed Services Vocational Aptitude Battery (ASVAB) exam at school
- He got a wrong number, but you were home, so why waste the call?

Selling the Interview

Once he has made contact, it is the job of the recruiter to get you to come in for an interview. As with any job, you can't be hired without a formal interview. Depending on your level of interest, you may or may not agree to the interview. If you don't agree, it is up to the recruiter to sell the interview.

Sure, you may use excuses for not meeting with the recruiter. You may say "Can you mail me some information?" Or maybe you'll say "I'd like to think about it some more." Or maybe you'll use my favorite, "I don't have time for an interview." Believe me, if you've got a reason (or an excuse) for not meeting with the recruiter, he has at least one response to overcome that reason. Take my advice, if you're reading this book, you already have some level of interest in at least checking out what the military has to offer. Make the appointment, and show up for it! Don't agree to an appointment that you have no intention to keep. Not keeping appointments speaks volumes about your character.

Selling "The Military"

Later in this chapter, I'll discuss your first meeting with the recruiter and how to handle yourself during the initial interview. I'll cover the actual sales pitch and how to respond to it. At this point, a simplified outline of the sales process is provided in the following figure. As you review it, keep in mind that you will probably spend an hour or more with the recruiter during your first interview.

It is the recruiter's job to find your primary motivator for joining the military. It may be money for education, desire for technical training or having secure employment. This is where the comparison of a recruiter's methods to a car salesman's methods begins. When you walk into that car dealership, the conversation would probably sound something like this:

Salesman: "What are you looking for in a car?"

Customer: "I need a seven-passenger minivan to transport my family."

If the salesperson doesn't sell minivans and only has five-passenger sedans, it is unlikely that he will get you to buy a sedan. It is difficult to sell a product that just can't fit the needs of the customer. The recruiter must not only sell you a product that meets your needs, but he must first determine your needs. This can be extremely difficult, especially if you don't express those needs to him or if you are unsure of those needs. The following conversation rarely, if ever, occurs in a recruiting office:

Recruiter: "What are you looking for from an enlistment in the military?"

Applicant: "I want to complete a degree in biology at XYZ University and have enough leisure time to go bowling with the guys, and can you throw in good pay, too?"

WHAT THE RECRUITER CAN AND CANNOT PROMISE YOU

As a recruiter, one of the lines I heard more often than most when trying to get a prospective applicant in for an interview was, "I'll come in tomorrow for an interview, but I won't sign anything." My response to that was always along the lines of "I wish it were that simple to enlist someone." Just as you wouldn't expect to be hired on the spot after your first job interview with a civilian company, the same is even more true with the military. You must get over many hurdles before you can qualify to wear a military uniform.

When you spoke to the recruiter to make an appointment for an interview, she probably asked you some preliminary questions concerning your health, your education, and any involvement with law officials. If you passed this initial inquiry, you made it over the first hurdle. When you meet the recruiter for the first time, she will probe even deeper into these areas to determine whether or not you initially qualify for enlistment. Assuming that you agree to enlist after listening to the recruiter's sales presentation, here is a list of the hurdles that you must get over in order to eventually enlist:

- Questions regarding your medical history to ensure that you do not have (or have not had) a medically disqualifying condition
- Questions regarding any involvement with law officials, including traffic tickets and arrests as an adult or juvenile
- Questions regarding illegal drug usage
- The Armed Services Vocational Aptitude Battery (ASVAB)
- A complete (and I do mean complete) physical examination
- A background check

A more detailed explanation of these hurdles is presented later in this chapter. However, as you can see from this list, you are in no danger of being whisked off to Basic Training after your initial interview.

So what can the recruiter promise you after all is said and done? The answer is simply this: not much! What the recruiter can promise is that you will be treated fairly throughout the enlistment process. He can ensure that you fully understand the steps to enlistment; that he doesn't lie, or misrepresent, anything to you; and that you are fully prepared for enlistment. The recruiter should be your advocate, not your babysitter. Do not expect the recruiter to hold your hand during the process. You are expected to be responsible for your own actions because you will be expected to do so when you are on active duty.

COMMON MISCONCEPTIONS ABOUT RECRUITERS

There are some common misconceptions that people have about recruiters and recruiting. Here are a few:

- Recruiters are on quotas and receive a "bonus" for every new recruit they enlist.
  The fact is that recruiters are paid their regular military pay plus a standard "professional pay" every month. They are paid the same whether they enlist one, two or twenty people every month. Of course, if they want to keep their jobs, they'll try to enlist as many people as possible.

- Recruiters will lie, cheat and steal to get you to enlist.
  As I mentioned earlier, there are some recruiters who would do whatever it takes to get someone to enlist. So be careful, but not cynical. The majority of the recruiters will not misrepresent themselves or their service. Most successful recruiters rely on referrals from satisfied applicants— if you are unhappy with your experience with your recruiter, you won't refer others to him, and he knows that.

- They'll trick me into signing a contract, and then it's too late.
  Remember that enlisting in the military is a long and involved systematic process that consists of many steps. It is the job of the recruiter to get you ready for each of the steps.

Now that you have a better understanding of who the recruiter is, it is almost time to meet with him, but not before you read the rest of this chapter. It will better prepare you for this first meeting. Although the recruiter is your advocate and not your opponent, you should do your homework to make sure you are ready for the "battle." Just as you would prepare for a visit to the local car dealership to buy that new car, you should prepare for your first meeting with your recruiter.

Your Responsibilities during the Recruiting Process

During the recruiting process, you have several responsibilities. They include:

- Keeping all your appointments and arriving on time for them
- Studying for the Armed Services Vocational Aptitude Battery (ASVAB)

- Getting enough sleep before the ASVAB and physical examination
- Being open and honest with your recruiter and the Military Entrance Processing Station (MEPS) staff
- Being an active—not selective—listener

PRIORITY ONE: BE HONEST

Of all your responsibilities, being honest with your recruiter is paramount. Telling white lies and half truths will eventually catch up to you—maybe not at first, maybe not while you are at Basic Training, but some day. Not telling the truth about past physical problems or past involvement with law enforcement officials are the fastest ways to find yourself in a heap of trouble. Remember these simple rules:

- Divulge all involvement with law enforcement even if you weren't convicted or even if the court told you your records would be closed and eventually expunged.
- Tell about all medical conditions that you have been diagnosed with. Do not conceal anything that you didn't think was important. Conversely, do not make anything up. If you were never diagnosed with asthma, even though your mother told you that you had it, you never had it! I cannot tell you how many people who never had asthma disqualify themselves.
- Do not, under any circumstances, lie because someone has told you to do so. This includes your recruiter, your brother and your mother.

PRIORITY TWO: BE AN ACTIVE—NOT SELECTIVE—LISTENER

Do recruiters lie? There are good and bad people in just about all professions, and military recruiters are not excluded. Aside from those few bad apples that give recruiters a bad name, most misunderstandings attributed to "my recruiter lied to me" come down to a phenomenon called selective listing.

Selective listening occurs when an applicant (or, using the car dealership example, the customer) hears only the parts of the recruiter's (salesperson's) presentation that interests him. For example, a customer leases a car for three years, and at the end of the lease he's ready to trade the car in for a new one. He works out the deal for his new vehicle and notices an additional charge of $1,000. Of course, he questions the charge and is given the following response: "Your three-year lease allowed for a maximum of 30,000 miles (an average of 10,000 miles per year), and your vehicle's odometer reads 40,000 miles. Your contract states that you will be charged ten cents per mile for every mile exceeding 30,000. At ten cents per mile, 10,000 miles equals $1,000." The customer leaves the car dealership $1,000 poorer, totally disgusted and in search of a car salesman that won't "lie" to him. Isn't it ironic that when he first leased the vehicle, he didn't "hear" the part of the sales presentation that talked about exceeding the mileage, yet when he found out it was going to cost him $1,000 he heard loud and clear?

Sometimes salespeople do their best to gloss over these "minor details," helping the customer to be a selective listener. "The maximum mileage allowed is 30,000. I've never seen anyone exceed that mileage after only three years." Is the salesperson in this example lying? Maybe not, but it's only a matter of semantics.

Be an active listener, not a selective one. Make sure you understand everything that is presented to you. Do not be afraid that you will appear stupid if you ask for clarification. Remember that the recruiter is the expert; you are not. If you think you don't understand something, you're probably correct in that assumption. Ask your questions and listen to the answers.

Setting up the Interview

Most appointments to meet with a recruiter are made over the telephone, although you may have met the recruiter somewhere in person, such as at your school or at a job fair. No matter how the first contact is made, it all comes down to your committing to an appointment.

NEGOTIATING THE APPOINTMENT DATE AND TIME

If you have decided to meet with a recruiter (and I'll assume you have based on the fact that you are reading this book), all that remains is deciding on a good time to meet with him. Because you are the customer, the recruiter should accommodate your schedule and meet with you when it is convenient for you. Most recruiters will use some variation to the following tried-and-true method of giving a prospective applicant an "option" of when to meet for an interview. It goes something like this:

Recruiter: "I am glad you decided to investigate the opportunities the [insert service name here] has to offer. The next step is a face-to-face interview so we can determine if we'll be able to meet your needs."

Applicant: "Sounds good to me. When can we meet?"

Recruiter: "I've got openings on Monday and Wednesday. Which is better for you?"

Applicant: "Wednesday would be better."

Recruiter: "Great! What's better for you, mornings or afternoons?"

Applicant: "Afternoons are generally better."

Recruiter: "Okay, I have an opening at three and another at five. Which is better for you?"

Applicant: "Five would be better."

Recruiter: "Good. I'll see you on Wednesday afternoon at five, then."

Who was in control of the conversation? Although it seemed like the recruiter was being very accommodating, in reality she was in total control of the situation. When you take a closer look at the conversation, you can see that the applicant was given only a few choices of interview times. What if the applicant was available only on Thursdays and only between two and four in the afternoon?

Although recruiters do spend some time in actual face-to-face contact with applicants, most of their time is spent doing other activities, such as making appointments over the telephone. This gives recruiters some flexibility in their daily schedule and allows them to switch activities around to accommodate the applicants.

In the above example, there is no problem if it is convenient for the applicant to meet with the recruiter when the recruiter states she is available. But if the applicant isn't available, then what?

The answer is simple. The applicant should just say, "I'm sorry, but I have a pretty full schedule during the week. I am available on Thursday afternoons between two and four and also any time on Saturday."

At this point, the recruiter will either agree to an appointment that is in line with the applicant's schedule or he will offer an alternative. It is important to note that recruiters do have lives outside of their jobs, so don't be unreasonable. Don't insist on meeting on Sunday afternoon at two (although some recruiters may take you up on it if that is truly the only time you have free). However, if your free time is indeed that limited, how will you get the time off to do the actual processing for enlistment (such as testing and taking the physical examination)?

If you make a reasonable request for a time to meet with the recruiter and he tells you he can't make it, ask about the following week, or perhaps the week after that. Most recruiters (the good ones anyway) will want to get you into the office as soon as possible and will rearrange their schedule, if possible, to accommodate you.

The following true story is an example of an inflexible recruiter who focused more on his needs than on those of his applicants.

After determining that an applicant could not meet at a time convenient for the recruiter, the following conversation ensued:

Applicant: "I'm in school all week, but I can meet you any weekday after five or any time on Saturday."

Recruiter: "Sorry, but my last appointments are at 3:30, and I don't work Saturdays."

Applicant: "Well, okay, maybe we'll be able to meet in a few months when I'm on summer vacation."

Two things resulted from this conversation. First, the prospective applicant never contacted the recruiter again and never enlisted. Second, this particular recruiter was not happy when his supervisor found out about what had happened. One thing is for certain: This recruiter would never survive in a commission-based sales environment where the customer always comes first.

If you find yourself in a similar situation with a recruiter who is unwilling to be flexible after you make reasonable demands concerning when to meet for your interview, find yourself another recruiter. If he doesn't have the time for you now when you represent new business, how will he treat you once you've already made the purchase (that is, enlisted)?

Unfortunately, finding another recruiter may not be that easy. Depending on the service, recruiters may be spread over a wide geographical area. Also, most branches have rules against their recruiters "poaching" applicants from other recruiters' zones—that is, enlisting applicants who live in an area covered by another recruiter. Most recruiter supervisors, however, would probably make an exception if an applicant were having a problem with a particular recruiter.

If it isn't feasible for you to seek out another recruiter, you have three choices. First, you go to another branch of the military. Second, you can change your schedule to accommodate the recruiter. Third, you can forget the whole thing.

Of the three choices, the first one is probably your best. I would not, however, recommend that you forget about enlisting because of a bad experience with one recruiter.

THE WALK-IN APPLICANT

Often when people take the initiative to see a recruiter, they will simply walk in to a recruiter's office without an appointment. While this may seem like a good idea, it isn't.

Would you ever consider walking in to the corporate office of a large company and demand an interview or ask for information about the company? Probably not. The same holds true for your recruiter's office. Most successful recruiters rely on a schedule to get all of their planned daily activities accomplished. By walking in without an appointment you may throw a wrench into the recruiter's entire work schedule for that day. In addition, he may be in the middle of an interview with a prospective applicant. How would you feel if you were the person being interviewed and you found yourself being ignored while the recruiter dealt with someone else?

Perhaps a recruiter told you to "stop by anytime." If he did, he more than likely told you that because you couldn't take time out of your schedule to set up an appointment and he thought an open invitation may result in your wandering into the office someday. Or maybe you've been thinking about enlisting for a while when you just happen to walk by a recruiting office and decide to stop in for some information—like I did.

If being a walk-in applicant is the only way you can find the time to see a recruiter, then I would recommend it. If, however, you can make an appointment with a recruiter, I suggest you do that instead. By dealing with walk-in applicants, the recruiter is forced to meet with someone he knows nothing about, so he is flying blind until he can ask you some questions and establish a rapport with you.

INTERVIEW SETTINGS

Although most initial interviews with recruiters take place in the recruiter's office, there may be an occasion when the recruiter might suggest another setting for the meeting. The two most popular alternatives are the applicant's residence and the applicant's school.

Although the alternative settings may be more convenient for the applicant, I suggest that the recruiter's office is the best setting for the initial interview. Just as it is possible to be treated for an injury out on the street by an ambulance crew, I would much rather be treated by a doctor in a hospital. An ambulance crew has limited resources "out in the field," and so does the recruiter. If given the choice, meet the recruiter in his office.

This will also give you the advantage of seeing your recruiter in his environment. During your interview, your recruiter will undoubtedly be interrupted several times, usually by telephone calls from other applicants. How he handles those interruptions will tell you a lot about your recruiter.

Does your recruiter take the time to speak to the person on the other end of the telephone? Does he politely dismiss the caller with a sincere promise to call back? Or is he very short and impolite with the caller and doesn't even write a note so he can remember to call back? Remember that you may some day be the person on the other end of the telephone. Is he the kind of salesperson who will treat you well while you're thinking about buying and then forget about you once the sale has been made?

Preparing for the Interview

Once you have an appointment date set, if you think that all you have to do now is sit back and wait for your alarm clock to buzz that morning, think again. You need to prepare for your interview.

OBTAIN THE NECESSARY PAPERWORK

The recruiter may have asked you to bring along some documents to your appointment. Although some (if not most) people are put off by this, it will save you from having to make multiple trips to the recruiter's office if you decide to proceed in the enlistment process.

The documents requested will probably include:

- Social Security card
- Birth certificate (usually the one issued by the state or county, not by the hospital)
- Driver's license
- High school diploma (if applicable)

Although you will eventually need a copy of your birth certificate in order to enlist, you may begin the process as long as you have your Social Security card. The other documents can be furnished later, although doing so will slow the enlistment process.

If you cannot locate your birth certificate, your recruiter may be able to assist you in either getting a new one or by verifying your birth certificate information by telephone.

STUDY FOR YOUR INTERVIEW

Besides dressing appropriately, the one thing that the experts will tell you about preparing for an interview is to do your homework and find out as much as you can about the company you are interviewing for. Meeting with a military recruiter is no exception.

In addition to reading this book to prepare you to deal with the recruiter, you should review any literature you may have received from that service and also visit recruiting and other Web sites. After you've reviewed all the material, get out a pencil and paper and write down any questions you may have. You should also talk to any friends who have either recently enlisted in that particular military branch or have been interviewed by that particular recruiter.

The smart recruiter will try to learn as much about you as he can before the initial interview; this gives him a competitive edge when dealing with a new applicant. I can assure you that he is doing his homework prior to the interview.

When I dealt with new applicants, they were amazed at how much I knew about them. It was as if I should have been working for one of those psychic networks. In reality, I would do a little investigative work prior to the interview. This was particularly easy when dealing with high school seniors. Since I had several seniors from each of the local high schools in my Delayed Entry Program (DEP) waiting to leave for Basic Training, I was able to get information from them. Also, I would have them bring in their yearbook so I could get information about a potential applicant's school activities.

As you'll see in a later section, the first thing a recruiter will do when meeting a new applicant is gain rapport. That is, he will try to "connect" with the applicant by putting him or her at ease and at the same time by showing interest in the applicant's accomplishments, hobbies and other interests.

What I have just described will occur if you are dealing with a professional, successful recruiter. If the recruiter has not done his investigative work, or has tried and was unable to gather any information about you, he will spend more time establishing rapport.

Discussing test results.

The Interview Session—An Overview

You will probably spend an hour or more with the recruiter during your first interview, and every interview follows the same basic plan. Your recruiter will, in the following order:

- Establish rapport with you
- Determine your eligibility for enlistment
- Ask you questions to find your primary motivator(s) for enlisting
- Determine whether the military can meet your needs/wants
- Make his closing sales pitch

Each of these phases is described in detail in the following sections.

GUIDELINES FOR PROPER DRESS: APPEARANCE AND INTERVIEWING PROTOCOL

The following rules apply to the meeting with your recruiter—as well as most job interviews you may find yourself going to.

Dress Appropriately

While it is not necessary (or even advisable) to wear a suit, or equivalent attire for women applicants, you should dress neatly.

Be on Time

Ensure that you have accurate directions to the recruiter's office, and then allow yourself plenty of time to get there. Take into account the usual traffic conditions at the time of your interview. If you are going to be late for any reason, make sure you call to let the recruiter know.

Be Mentally Alert

Make sure you get plenty of rest before an early appointment; if you are meeting in the afternoon or evening, don't schedule an appointment after a big track meet or a final exam. It is important that you have the ability to give your recruiter your undivided attention.

Be Polite

Even if you've determined that you are not interested in what the recruiter has to say, remain polite and give her the respect you would expect in return. Most importantly, don't use foul language.

Don't Smoke, Chew Gum or Eat Anything during the Interview

Do I need to say any more about this?

Remember to Bring the Required Documents

Bring all the documents described earlier (if the recruiter requested you to do so). Also, don't forget to bring your notepad with the questions you've written down.

Establishing Rapport

As I mentioned earlier, the first step the recruiter will take when meeting you face-to-face is establish a rapport with you. He will hopefully have done his homework and will be ready for you.

Most recruiters will use the first few minutes of the interview to put you at ease and, at the same time, learn a little more about you. The recruiter will, more than likely, also spend some time talking about his favorite subject: himself!

The first reaction most applicants have when meeting their recruiter for the first time is one of intimidation. Most of us equate someone in uniform as an authority figure, especially if he is wearing a chest full of medals. Do not let this make you feel uneasy; although you do need to treat your recruiter with respect, do not allow him to dominate you because of his appearance and demeanor.

Allow the recruiter to get to know you a little better. At the same time, you will get to know the recruiter somewhat better. You will also know by this point if the recruiter has been doing his homework or not.

The recruiter may start rattling off some names of your classmates or friends. He will do this in order to prove to you that he has dealt with people you know and that they are satisfied with the way he has treated them.

At some point in your conversation, your recruiter will ease out of the rapport step and start asking some specific questions about your medical and criminal history. He will also ask some questions about the use of illegal drugs. These questions will allow the recruiter to make some preliminary decisions regarding your eligibility for enlistment.

Determining Your Enlistment Eligibility

Unlike most employers, the military can—and does—impose stringent eligibility requirements on its applicants. These requirements include mental, physical and moral standards. Your recruiter's job at this point is to ensure that you, at least tentatively, meet these standards.

Depending on your answers, your recruiter will either proceed with the interview process or inform you of your ineligibility for enlistment and tactfully dismiss you.

MORAL REQUIREMENTS

Your recruiter may or may not have asked you some questions about law violations when she called to set up the interview. Even if she did, she will ask you again during the interview. Despite what you might have heard, enlisting in the military is not an option for criminals facing jail time—although I've heard stories that many years ago it was common for a judge to allow offenders to enlist in the military instead of going to jail.

Meeting the moral requirements for enlisting is not difficult for the average law-abiding citizen. Even minor indiscretions may not disqualify you for enlistment. As you'll see later in this section, certain law violations may even be waived in order to let some individuals who have made mistakes in the past get a fresh start in the military.

Your obligation is to tell your recruiter the truth, not the truth as you see it. Although your recruiter is pretty much taking you at your word to determine your eligibility at this point, what you tell him will eventually be verified before you enlist.

Your recruiter will more than likely check with local and state law enforcement agencies to search for any involvement you may have had with the law. Later on in your processing, the investigation will be more in-depth. The section in Chapter 4 entitled "Background Screening" further explains this process. One important fact to remember at this time is that you must divulge information about all law violations no matter when they happened—this includes crimes or offenses committed as a juvenile, no matter what you were told by your attorney or the court.

Your recruiter will probably stress this point and impress on you the importance of revealing all past law violations. Sometimes, for one reason or another, a recruiter may not stress the significance of telling the entire truth. She may not want to go through the "hassle" of submitting a morals waiver, or your offense may not be waiverable, and she doesn't want to lose you as an applicant. Whatever the reason, this behavior is unacceptable. It is unlikely that your recruiter will come straight out and tell you to lie, but it may come in the form of, "that's really not important to mention," or something similar. If this happens, find yourself another recruiter; if she can ask you to lie, what lies is she capable of telling you? Remember that you alone are responsible for any false statements that you make.

Each military branch has its own set of standards concerning disqualifying law violations. In some cases, even small offenses such as traffic violations can be disqualifying if there are enough of them in a short period of time.

MORALS WAIVERS

It is possible that you may become eligible to enlist in the military even if you were convicted of a law violation that has made you ineligible. Depending on the circumstances, you may be granted a morals waiver.

Waivers are not automatically granted; in fact, in most cases, a recruiter will not even offer a disqualified applicant the possibility of a waiver. It is up to the applicant to initiate the conversation concerning a waiver. The conversation may go something like this:

Recruiter: "I'm sorry, but based on what you have just told me about your law violations, I am afraid that you are ineligible for enlistment."

Applicant: "Isn't there anything I could do to enlist? It was a stupid mistake I made two years ago. Can't you do anything for me?"

Recruiter: "Since you asked, and you sound so sincere, there is a possibility that we can get you a waiver for enlistment."

Since the applicant in this example has initiated the conversation, the recruiter was free to offer him the option of a morals waiver. Usually, however, the recruiter also has the option of using his discretion if he does not want to offer the applicant that option. If a particular recruiter does use his discretion and refuse to run a waiver, find another recruiter who will. In addition, what may require a waiver with one branch of the military may not require one with another; so, if necessary, try another branch.

Who Can Grant a Morals Waiver?

A recruiter is not authorized to grant morals waivers at his level. The level at which the waiver is granted depends on the severity of the crime. The time it takes for an approval decision to be made, one way or the other, depends on the level of the approval authority.

Increasing Your Chance of Getting Your Waiver Approved

There are several ways to increase your chances of getting your waiver approved; there are also mistakes you can make that will more than likely result in a disapproved waiver. First, though, here is the number one rule regarding morals waivers: In most cases, you must divulge the information about the law violation yourself before a waiver will even be considered. In other words, if you told the recruiter that you had no law violations and then something came up on a police check, you would automatically be disqualified without the chance for a waiver. The same offense may have been waived had you disclosed it to your recruiter. The bottom line is this: Tell the truth.

You will be required to write a statement concerning the law violation that led to your disqualification. It is important that your letter is well-thought-out and sincere because, in most cases, it is the only way you can tell the waiver-granting authority about yourself. Here are some tips for writing your statement:

- Take responsibility for your own actions—do not blame others for what you've done. If you were convicted of assault, don't say, "I was an innocent bystander. He walked into my fist." If you were in a fight, even if you didn't start it, take responsibility for your part in the fight.
- Tell the waiver authority how much out of character this behavior was. If you had never been in a fight before and have never been in trouble with the law, write that in your statement.
- Take your time, write neatly and, if allowable, type the statement, proofreading for spelling and grammar. The waiver authority will be looking at the whole person when determining whether or not to grant a waiver.
- Be polite in your writing; use sir or madam in addressing the waiver authority. Use words like please and thank you.
- Do not make derogatory comments about the police, the courts, the judge, etc. This shows how well (or badly) you deal with authority figures.
- Stress what you can offer the military (such as skills or work ethic) and not what you want from the military.
- Request a face-to-face interview to discuss your waiver request.

The statement does not have to be long; it just has to be accurate and cover the details about the law violation. A good example of a well-written letter requesting a waiver appears on the next page.

Notice how the applicant takes full responsibility for his actions and doesn't place blame on others, although he could have. Although a letter like this will not guarantee that this applicant's waiver will be approved, the chances are very good that it will.

Law Violations

This section lists examples of law violations. I would warn you not to use these examples to disqualify yourself before you even talk to a recruiter. Although no list can be totally complete, this one comes very close. If, by chance, you have been convicted of a violation not listed in your recruiter's recruiting regulation, he probably will make a determination as to what violation on his list most closely matches yours. If he is smart, he will not make the determination himself but will ask for guidance up his chain-of-command.

This list is divided into different levels of violations; all military branches use a similar method to determine level of waiver approval. The level in which the law violation is placed depends on the individual branch.

Level One Offenses

These offenses are very serious in nature and require the highest level of waiver approval.

- Aggravated assault with a dangerous weapon, intentionally inflicting great bodily harm with intent to commit a felony
- Bribery

August 19, 2000

Dear Sir:

I am requesting a waiver in order to enlist in the United States Army. I believe that it would be in the best interest of the Army to grant this request.

On August 1, 1998, a group of my friends and I decided to go to the beach for the day. We were there for about an hour when we decided to go for a swim. When we returned about 15 minutes later we found another group of teenagers on our blankets.

When we asked them to get off our blankets, they started cursing at us and one of them started pushing one of my friends. Before I knew what was going on, everybody was fighting, and someone pushed me to the ground.

The fight lasted about 5 minutes, until the police arrived. We were all taken to the Main Street police station and later released to our parents.

I went to court on October 1, 1998, and was found guilty of disturbing the peace and unlawful assembly. I paid a $50 fine, and because of my age (16) I received 30 hours of community service, which I completed on January 15, 1999.

I have never been in trouble before this incident and feel very ashamed because of it. I should have contacted the police or the lifeguard when we found the other teenagers on our blankets. That would have solved the whole problem without fighting.

I hope that this one isolated incident does not keep me from enlisting in the Army. I am a good student and a trustworthy person. I believe the Army could use someone like me.

Thank you for the opportunity to apply for enlistment in the Army. If you wish, I am available to meet with you in person to discuss this matter.

Very Respectfully,

Joe Applicant

- Burglary
- Carnal knowledge of a child under 16 years of age
- Draft evasion
- Extortion
- Indecent acts or liberties with a child under 16 years of age, molestation
- Kidnapping, abduction
- Manslaughter
- Murder
- Perjury
- Rape
- Robbery

Level Two Offenses

These offenses, although serious, are less serious than Level One offenses and usually require approval at a level above the local waiver approval authority. Level Two contains some of the same offenses found in Level One, but they are considered at the lesser level if adjudicated when the applicant was a juvenile.

- Arson
- Aggravated assault with a dangerous weapon, intentionally inflicting great bodily harm with intent to commit a felony
- Attempting to commit a felony
- Breaking and entering a building with intent to commit a felony
- Breaking and entering a house
- Bribery
- Burglary
- Carrying a concealed firearm or unlawful carrying of a firearm
- Carrying a concealed weapon (other than a firearm), possession of brass knuckles
- Child pornography offenses
- Conspiring to commit a felony
- Criminal libel
- DUI/DWI (Driving under the influence of, while intoxicated or impaired by, alcohol or drugs)
- Embezzlement
- Extortion
- Forgery: Knowingly uttering or passing a forged instrument (except for altered identification for purchase of alcoholic beverages)
- Grand larceny
- Grand theft
- Indecent assault
- Involuntary manslaughter
- Leaving the scene of an accident (hit-and-run) involving personal injury
- Lewd, licentious or lascivious behavior
- Looting
- Mail or electronic emission matters: abstracting, destroying, obstructing, opening, secreting, stealing or taking
- Mail: Depositing obscene or indecent matter (includes electronic or computerized e-mail/bulletin board systems and files)
- Maiming or disfiguring
- Marijuana: simple possession or use
- Negligent homicide
- Pandering
- Perjury
- Prostitution or soliciting to commit prostitution
- Public record: altering, concealing, destroying, mutilating, obliterating or removing
- Riot
- Robbery
- Sedition or soliciting to commit sedition

- Selling, leasing or transferring a weapon to a minor or unauthorized individual
- Sexual harassment
- Willfully discharging firearms so as to endanger life, or shooting in a public place

Level Three Offenses

Less serious than Levels One and Two, yet more serious than a traffic ticket, Level Three offenses can usually be waived at the local level.

- Adultery
- Assault (simple)
- Breaking and entering a vehicle
- Check—insufficient funds (amount more than $50, worthless, or uttering with intent to defraud or deceive)
- Conspiring to commit a misdemeanor
- Contempt of court (includes nonpayment of child support or alimony required by court order)
- Contributing to the delinquency of a minor (includes purchase of alcoholic beverages)
- Desecration of a grave
- Discharging a firearm through carelessness or within municipal limits
- Drunk in public, drunk and disorderly, public intoxication
- Failure to stop and render aid after an accident
- Indecent exposure
- Indecent, insulting or obscene language communicated directly or by telephone
- Killing a domestic animal
- Leaving the scene of an accident (hit-and-run) with no personal injury involved
- Liquor or alcoholic beverages: unlawful manufacture or sale
- Malicious mischief
- Resisting, fleeing or eluding arrest
- Removing property under lien or from public grounds
- Slander
- Shooting from highway or on public road
- Shoplifting, larceny, petty larceny, theft or petty theft (age 14 or older or stolen goods valued over $50)
- Stolen property: possession of, or knowingly receiving stolen property
- Unlawful or illegal entry
- Unlawful use of long distance telephone lines or any electronic transmission method
- Use of telephone or any electronic transmission method to abuse, annoy, harass, threaten or torment another
- Wrongful appropriation of motor vehicle, joyriding or driving without owner's consent

Level Four Offenses

Approved at the local level, these offenses are not usually disqualifying unless you've committed more than one of them.

- Abusive language under circumstances to provoke breach of peace
- Altered identification when intent is to purchase alcoholic beverages
- Careless or reckless driving
- Check—($50 or less, insufficient funds or worthless)
- Curfew violation
- Committing or creating nuisance
- Damaging road signs
- Disorderly conduct, creating disturbance or boisterous conduct, disturbing the peace
- Failure to appear, comply with judgment, answer or disobey summons
- Failure to comply with officer's direction
- Fare evasion
- Fighting, participating in a brawl
- Illegal betting or gambling: operating illegal handbook, raffle, lottery, punch board, or watching a cockfight
- Juvenile non-criminal misconduct: beyond parental control, incorrigible, runaway, truant or wayward
- Liquor or alcoholic beverages: unlawful possession or consumption in a public place
- Littering or dumping refuse near highway or other prohibited place
- Loitering
- Possession of indecent publications or pictures (other than child pornography)
- Purchase, possession or consumption of alcoholic beverages by a minor
- Racing, drag racing
- Shoplifting, larceny, petty larceny, theft or petty theft (committed under age 14 and stolen goods valued at $50 or less)
- Trespass on property
- Unlawful assembly
- Vagrancy
- Vandalism, defacing or injuring property
- Violation of fireworks law
- Violation of fish and game laws

Level Five Offenses

Consideration for waivers is given at the local level for multiple convictions of Level Five violations.

- Blocking or retarding traffic
- Crossing yellow line, drifting left of center
- Disobeying traffic lights, signs, or signals
- Driving on shoulder
- Driving uninsured vehicle
- Driving with blocked or impaired vision
- Driving with expired plates or without plates
- Driving without license in possession
- Driving without registration or with improper registration

- Driving wrong way on a one-way street
- Failure to display inspection sticker
- Failure to have vehicle under control
- Failure to keep right or in proper lane
- Failure to signal
- Failure to stop or yield to a pedestrian
- Failure to yield right-of-way
- Faulty equipment
- Following too close
- Improper backing
- Improper blowing of horn
- Improper passing
- Improper parking
- Improper turn
- Invalid or unofficial inspection sticker
- Leaving key in ignition
- License plates improperly or not displayed
- Operating overloaded vehicle
- Playing vehicle radio/stereo too loud
- Speeding (does not include racing)
- Spinning wheels, improper start
- Seatbelt violation
- Zigzagging or weaving in traffic

Morals Waiver Summary

Morals waivers may be granted on a case-by-case basis to applicants who are ineligible for enlistment. Being granted a waiver depends on the circumstances surrounding the law violation(s), your age at the time of the incident(s), your current level of maturity and your level of sincerity.

Although you may be granted a morals waiver, you are, essentially, still not technically "qualified" for enlistment. Because of this, you must be flexible when it comes time to choose a military career field (job). You will read more about this in Chapter 4.

PHYSICAL REQUIREMENTS

Although some branches of the military will require you to meet some physical fitness requirements prior to enlistment (most people of enlistment age are in good enough physical condition to meet those standards), they rely on Basic Training to get you in the proper physical conditioning for military service.

The physical requirements that will be of concern to your recruiter during your initial interview will be your overall health and medical history. As you'll see in Chapter 4, you will be subjected to a very thorough physical examination.

In addition to the physical examination, you will be "grilled" for information concerning your medical history at the Military Entrance Processing Station (MEPS).

As with law violations, your recruiter may or may not press you to reveal details concerning your medical history. And just as with the law violations, you may be told that certain things are best left undisclosed. I will give you the same advice as I have previously given: If you are asked to conceal or withhold information, find yourself another recruiter.

Your recruiter should have asked some preliminary medical history questions over the telephone before the initial appointment was made. The recruiter made a determination of your eligibility based on your answers to those questions.

Unless there is something visibly wrong with you, your recruiter will have to take your word on your present health and your medical history. The one exception to this is your weight. You will be required to get on the scale so your recruiter can determine if you are within weight standards.

On a lighter note (no pun intended), there is an urban legend involving recruiters who convince female applicants that they must get undressed in order to get an accurate reading on the scale. At no time should any applicant (male or female) remove any clothing as part of the interview process with the recruiter. Of course, you will be required to get undressed at the MEPS for your physical exam.

Divulging Medical History Information

The rule is very simple when it comes to divulging information about your medical history: Divulge everything!

Although you should disclose all information about your medical history, make sure that you divulge information about problems that have actually been diagnosed by a physician. All too often applicants will disqualify themselves by telling their recruiter that they had an illness that they were never diagnosed with. A popular example of this is asthma.

Many times applicants are intimidated by the strong wording about what can happen to you if you lie on the application forms. If you are unsure about a particular question, inform the recruiter that you must confirm the information before answering it. That might mean you could resolve it right away by making a telephone call or you may need to get back to your recruiter at a later time. In no case, however, should you feel compelled to answer a question you are uncertain about.

Chapter 4, which deals with MEPS processing, contains more information on this subject.

Just as it is possible to be granted a morals waiver for disqualifying law violations, you may be granted a medical waiver for certain disqualifying medical conditions. Unlike morals waivers, however, the recruiting chain-of-command has no control of waiver approval.

Medical Waivers

As with a morals waiver, it is up to the applicant to request a medical waiver. You may be told, however, that no waivers may be granted for your disqualifying condition. While this might be true, ask to see it in writing (if possible). Some recruiters just don't want the hassle of bothering with medical waivers because, in most cases, they are too time consuming and many times are not granted, leaving the recruiter with nothing to show for his efforts.

If your condition is truly not waiverable, try another branch of the military; although very similar, the standards are not 100 percent the same for all services.

Two recruiters discuss an applicant's qualifications.

Initiating a Medical Waiver

Most times a medical waiver may be initiated by getting all the documentation concerning an applicant's disqualifying condition and forwarding it to the MEPS for determination. The MEPS Chief Medical Officer (CMO) may then take one of several options. He may

- request that the applicant come to the MEPS to process and then make a final determination (sometimes a waiver may not even be required).
- ask for further tests to be accomplished.
- disapprove a waiver (at his level).

If the CMO wants you to process at the MEPS, he will evaluate you at that time and make a determination. If you pass your physical at that time, you are on your way to enlisting.

If he requires further tests, the results of those tests will be evaluated by the CMO. Then he may either ask you to come to the MEPS for further evaluation or he may deny you a waiver based on the information you provided.

If the CMO disapproves your waiver request (either initially, after reviewing the additional tests or after evaluating you at the MEPS), you may request (through your recruiter) that your waiver request be up-channeled (that is, sent to a higher authority for review).

The level at which a waiver must be approved depends on the service. However, one thing is true of all military branches: The further a medical waiver has to be up-channeled, the more likely it will be disapproved and the longer it will take for a final decision to be made.

Disqualifying Medical Conditions

Remember, at this stage, you are being evaluated solely by the information you have provided to the recruiter. For instance, if you were epileptic, the recruiter would have no idea of that, unless you had a seizure in his office.

Therefore, the recruiter can only find you tentatively physically qualified for enlistment. Final determination on your fitness for enlistment will be made at the MEPS. The waiver process may also begin at that time if a disqualifying condition is found at the MEPS.

The following disqualifying conditions are typical for all branches of the military. Do not use this list to disqualify yourself for enlistment but rather as a guide to make you aware of the physical standards criteria. If you are completely healthy and have never been hospitalized, I would advise you not to review the disqualifying conditions below. I found myself getting sick just writing about them!

Waiver approval procedures differ between services and change from time to time, so it is important to get up-to-date information from your recruiter.

MEDICAL CONDITIONS THAT MAY RESULT IN DISQUALIFICATION

Category	Condition
Abdomen and Digestive System	
	Abdominal surgery within sixty days
	Cirrhosis
	Colon, megacolon, diverticulitis, regional enteritis or ulcerative colitis—spastic colon if more than moderate
	Fistula in anus
	Gallbladder removed and symptoms continue—special diet required
	Gallstones—current
	Hemorrhoids—symptomatic
	Hepatitis—within six months
	Hernia—if present
	Intestinal obstruction—within five years
	Pancreas—any acute or chronic disease
	Rectum—stricture or prolapse
	Resection of any portion of the digestive tract
	Scars that show bulging or herniation, prevent full activity or cause pain
	Splenectomy (except for trauma)
	Tumors
	Ulcer

Category	Condition
Allergies	Allergic manifestations—a reliable history of life-threatening generalized reaction with anaphylaxis to stinging insects or reliable history of moderate to severe reaction to common foods, spices or food additives
	Asthma, including reactive airway disease, exercise-induced bronchospasm, or asthmatic bronchitis—at any age
	Hay fever and skin allergies
Blood and Blood-Forming Tissue Disease	
	Anemia (unless permanently corrected by therapy)
	Bleeding and clotting disease
	Enlarged spleen
	Immunodeficiency diseases
	Leukemia
	Low white count
	Myeloproliferative disease or Myelodysplactic disease
Dental	
	Diseases not easily corrected
	Inability to eat an ordinary diet
	Orthodontic appliances (acceptable to enter Delayed Entry Program (DEP) but must be removed before going on Active Duty)
Ears and Hearing	
	Acute or chronic otitis media of any type
	Infection of canal—if acute or chronic
	Loss of ear
	Mastoidectomy
	Mastoiditis—if acute
	Menieres syndrome
	Middle ear infections—if acute or chronic
	Perforated eardrums
	Severe scarring of eardrums—with associated hearing loss of more than 20 dB
	Smallness or closing of ear canal
	Tumors of canal
Endocrine and Metabolic Disorders	
	Most disorders, except simple low thyroid that is being controlled medically, are disqualifying.
	Hypothyroidism, symptomatic or uncontrolled by medication, is disqualifying.

Category	Condition
Extremities (Orthopedic)	

Amputation of:
  Big toe
  Hand, foot, arm, leg
  More than one third of distal portion
    of thumb
  One joint on two or more fingers
    (except little finger)
  One or more small toes if it interferes
    with function
  Two joints of index, middle, or ring
    finger

Fractures:
  Bones (major) within six months
  Healed improperly
  Injury (bone)—without fracture
    disqualified for six weeks
  Metal retained for repair of fracture

Joints:
  Arthritis—other than very mild
  Cartilage (knee)—torn, unless surgically
    repaired, more than six months since
    surgery and rehabilitation completed
  Deranged joint (unstable)
  History of anterior cruciate ligament knee
    or posterior cruciate ligament injury
  Ligament (knee) surgery
  Significantly impaired joint function

Muscles—weakness, paralysis, contracture
Neuroma—refractory to medical treatment
Osteomyelitis—in past two years or if extensive or
  recurrent
Plantar fasciitis—refractory to medical treatment
Retropatellar knee pain syndrome (chronic)
Scars—if extensive, deep, adherent or painful
Silastic or other devices implanted to correct
  orthopedic abnormalities
Soft bones (such as osteoporosis)
Un-united fractures—except ulnar styloid process

Category	Condition
Back, Spine and Sacroiliac Joints	
	Congenital deformities
	Curvature of the spine—if more than moderate
	Infections
	Recurrent back pain
	Ruptured disc
	Spondylolisthesis
	Symptomatic healed fractures
Eyes	
	Absence of lens or lens implant
	Blind in one eye
	Corneal scars or ulcers
	Double vision
	Glaucoma
	History of surgery to modify the refractive power of the cornea
	Night blindness
	Nystagmus
	Opacities of cornea or lens
	Refractive error of 8.00 diopters or more
	Torn or diseased retina
	Vision requiring contact lens for correction
Genitourinary System (Males)	
	Absence of both testicles
	Hydrocele or left varicocele—if painful or any right varicocele unless urological evaluation reveals no disease
	Undescended testicle
	Urethritis—acute or chronic
Genitourinary System (Females)	
	Congenital absence of uterus
	Infections—if acute or recurrent
	Irregular periods or no periods
	Menopausal symptoms if caused by surgery—thirteen-month waiting period
	Painful periods
	Pelvic inflammatory disease—acute or chronic
	Vagina—congenital abnormalities that interfere with physical activities
	Vulva—condyloma accuminatum and dystrophic conditions

MEDICAL CONDITIONS THAT MAY RESULT IN DISQUALIFICATION

Category	Condition
Kidneys	
	Albuminuria (protein in the urine)
	Bed-wetting
	Kidney disease (absence of one kidney)
	Kidney stones—if in past year, or more than twice, or on both sides at any time, or present now
Head and Neck	
	Concussions—more than mild within three months
	Depressed fractures of the skull
	Loss of portion of the skull—larger than the size of a quarter
	Severe contusions or lacerations within three months
	Unsightly deformities, scars, etc.
Heart and Vascular System	
	High blood pressure is usually disqualifying, especially if it requires medication or dietary restriction.
	Usually any heart disease is disqualifying.
Lungs and Chest	
	Acute disease of the lungs, pneumonia, bronchitis, etc.—chronic lung disease if more than mild
	Asthma—at any age
	New growth of breast
	Removal of any part of the lungs
	Removal of breast (females)
	Tuberculosis—within two years, or active two or more times
Mouth	
	Harelip—unless repaired
	Mutilations
	Perforation of hard palate
Nose	
	Chronic rhinitis (allergy)
	Hay fever—if not controllable
	Perforated nasal septum
	Sinusitis—acute or chronic (if more than mild)
Neurological Disorders	
	Arteriosclerosis
	Brain hemorrhage

Category	Condition
	Congenital malformations
	Degenerative and hereditodegenerative disorders
	Disturbances on consciousness—head injury resulting in unconsciousness or amnesia
	Early post-traumatic seizures—occurring within one week of injury (five-year waiting period)
	Embolism
	Incoordination
	Intellectual deficit
	Late post-traumatic epilepsy—occurring more than one week following injury
	Multiple sclerosis
	Muscular atrophies and dystrophies
	Organic personality disturbances
	Paralysis
	Paroxysmal convulsive disorders—epilepsy, seizures, fits, etc. (except fever fits before age five)
	Recurrent headaches—when interferes with normal function, or history of such headaches within three years
	Sensory disturbance
	Severe head injury with associated abscess or meningitis (within five years)
	Sleep disorders
	Tremors
Psychiatric	
	Alcohol or drug dependence (or history of)
	Anabolic steroids requiring professional care within one-year period before examination or if it is determined that the applicant has accepted their use as a pattern behavior
	Character and behavior disorders, manifested by: Dependency Homosexual conduct Immaturity Instability Personal inadequacy Repeated inability to maintain reasonable adjustment at school, work or with family

Category	Condition
	Chronic history of academic skills or perceptual defects secondary to organic or functional mental disorders that interfere with work or school after age 12. Current use of medication to improve or maintain academic skills is disqualifying.
	Personality disorders, manifested by:
	Chronic alcoholism
	Drug addiction
	Repeated and frequent encounters with law enforcement
	Sleepwalking or eating disorders that are habitual and persistent—since age 12
	Stammering or stuttering—unless mild
	Psychoneurosis—if hospitalization required
	Psychosis at any time
	Suicide attempts—history of suicidal behavior
Skin	
	Acne—severe
	Any skin condition aggravated by sunlight, high humidity or extreme heat or cold
	Contact dermatitis involving rubber or other materials used in protective equipment
	Cysts, pilonidal, if evidenced by the presence of a tumor mass or a discharging sinus—history of pilonidal cystectomy within one year before examination
	Eczema—if chronic and resistant to treatment
	Fungus infections—if extensive and resistant to treatment
	Lupus erythematosus
	Psoriasis
	Scars—if extensive, deep, or adherent and may interfere with wearing military clothing or equipment
	Urticaria (hives)—if chronic
Tumors	
	Any tumor or history of benign tumors of:
	Anywhere—if large
	Auditory canal
	Bone, if subject to trauma

Category	Condition
	Brain, spinal chord or central nervous system
	Eye
	Kidney, bladder, testicle or penis—uterus, ovary or breast
	Tongue, if interferes with function
	Any tumor if malignant (even if removed and cured), with exception of small, early, basal cell carcinoma of skin
	Benign tumors of the peripheral nerves that interfere with function, have malignant potential or interfere with military duty or the wearing of the uniform or military equipment
Miscellaneous Conditions	
	Cold urticaria and angioedema, hereditary angioedema
	HIV/AIDS—tested positive for HIV/AIDS-related complex
	Malignant hypothermia
	Motion sickness—frequent, incapacitating after 12th birthday
	Organ transplant recipient
	Residual of tropical fevers and various parasitic or protozoal infections that prevent the satisfactory performance of military duty
	Rheumatic fever within two years—history of recurrent attacks
	Sydenham's chorea at any age

I realize that the temptation is just too much for most people, so you probably read the entire table of disqualifying conditions. Hopefully you didn't pick up any new diseases as you read it.

USE OF ILLEGAL DRUGS

The military has a zero-tolerance policy for drug use among its members. Therefore, all applicants are required to be drug-free. Besides illegal drugs, the abuse of prescription drugs is also disqualifying.

Each branch has its own policy on granting waivers for past drug usage, and because policy changes often, the specifics are not listed here. Like the other waivers, the applicant must initiate the request for a drug waiver. In determining whether or not to grant a waiver, the following will be considered:

- The type of drug
- The number of times used

- Your age at the time of use
- Length of time since you used the drug
- Any law violations connected to your drug use (this, of course, would require a double waiver—one for the law violation and one for the drug use)
- Your sincerity about any future drug use

As with the initial morals and physical qualifications, your recruiter must take your word concerning your involvement (past and present) with drugs. One thing for certain, though, if you get to MEPS and are found to have drugs in your bloodstream, there will be no waivers granted.

OTHER ELIGIBILITY REQUIREMENTS

There are a few more qualification areas that will be covered by the recruiter, such as citizenship and whether or not you have any dependents.

Citizenship

Certain military occupations require United States citizenship. Your recruiter will determine your status by reviewing your birth certificate, naturalization documents and the like.

Dependency

Dependency does not refer to your dependency on someone else; it refers instead to others' dependency on you. This includes single parents, spouses of military members with minor children and married applicants with multiple dependents.

If you have dependents, you will more than likely be told that you are ineligible for enlistment. However, as with other criteria, you may be able to obtain a waiver. As with other types of waivers, a dependency determination can only be made if the applicant asks for one; it will not be offered. Each dependency waiver is looked at on a case-by-case basis.

Isn't it discriminatory to make an applicant with dependents ineligible for enlistment? The answer is no. Consider the following:

- Because military members are sometimes deployed away from home for extended periods of time, single parents may be required to make semi-permanent arrangements for the care of their children.
- If both parents are military members, a military deployment may turn one of the spouses into a temporary single parent. What happens if that remaining parent is then deployed?
- Considering the salary of a person just starting out in the military, it would be irresponsible for the military to allow someone with many dependents to enlist and try to support a family.

MENTAL REQUIREMENTS

Perhaps the only part of the qualifications for enlistment that cannot be waived, the mental requirements begin with the Armed Forces Aptitude Battery (ASVAB) examination.

If you've already taken the ASVAB (at school or for another recruiter), your recruiter will have you complete a form called the 714A. Signing this form does not obligate you to anything, but it does allow your recruiter to gain access to your ASVAB scores.

If you haven't taken the ASVAB, your recruiter may ask you to take the Enlistment Screening Test (EST). This short exam, administered by your recruiter, will give him an idea of how you'll do on the actual ASVAB.

Based on the results of the EST, your recruiter will either proceed with the interview or inform you that additional study will be needed in order for you to pass the ASVAB.

Chapter 3 covers the ASVAB exam, includes a few sample questions and provides some common sense test-taking techniques. If you are serious about getting yourself more prepared for the ASVAB, however, I suggest that you purchase a study guide like one of the books available from ARCO.

If you've passed all the preliminary qualifications hurdles, it will be time for the recruiter to get down to the real nitty-gritty of the interview.

Probing to Find Your Primary Motivator(s)

I enjoy cop shows on television, especially detective shows. As a matter of fact, I'm usually pretty good at solving the crime before the end of the show. There is always a common thread between all the detective shows I've ever watched—usually the first thing all the detectives look for before anything else is motive!

The reason is simple; nearly all crimes are committed for a reason. Maybe the motive is money, maybe it's revenge or perhaps it's hatred. Whatever the reason, it all comes down to motive.

The same is true of sales (or recruiting): Every buyer (or applicant) has at least one motive for buying (enlisting). In the case of military recruiting, it is up to the recruiter to uncover your motives for enlisting. It helps, of course, if you know your own motives.

STATE YOUR MOTIVES

For one reason or another, some applicants feel that they need to conceal their motives for enlisting from their recruiter. Often applicants will force a situation where the recruiter must coerce the applicant to reveal his true motive(s) for enlisting.

Consider the example of the police detective trying to establish a motive for a crime. The conversation might go something like this:

Detective: Why did you kill him?

Suspect: I didn't!

Detective: Didn't you discover that the victim was stealing from your company bank account?

Suspect: Yes, but why would I kill him for that?

Detective: Maybe it's because you were listed as the beneficiary on his life insurance policy and you wanted to get back the money that he stole from you and more.

Suspect: Okay, okay, you got me; that was my motive.

(I'm sure it's clear why I'm not writing detective novels—but even this illustration will serve my purpose.)

In the case of a detective questioning a suspect, the suspect has everything to gain by not revealing his motive. In fact, he will do everything in his power to prevent the police from finding it.

In sales, the exact opposite is true. Take a car buyer, for example. Suppose you want to buy a car that will serve your needs. You stroll down to the dealership looking for a small, fuel-efficient car with a hatchback, so you can easily load the gear you use on your frequent camping trips. In most cases, you would probably tell the salesman, up front, what you are looking for so that he could show you the right vehicle to meet your needs. Rarely would you play the detective-suspect game with a salesman.

The same holds true for dealing with your recruiter. You need to let him know, up front, what it is you expect from an enlistment in the military. Don't worry that your motives may appear totally selfish, or maybe even weird, because seasoned recruiters have heard them all. Some common motives include:

- Money for college
- Technical training
- Security of steady employment
- Travel
- Patriotism
- Discipline
- Pride

Your motives may be many or just one—one of those listed above or one completely different. Be sure you know what your motive or motives are before you meet with your recruiter so you can be straightforward with him.

Have you ever purchased something and then later said to yourself, "Why on earth did I ever buy this?"

The reason this happened is because you had no clear motives in mind when you purchased the item. Or, you had clear motives in mind and then purchased something that did not meet what motivated you to go to the store in the first place.

Motives can also translate to "needs" and "wants." Showing you how the specific branch of the military can meet these needs and wants is the job of the recruiter. Once your motivators are on the table, your recruiter will move on to the next step, which is showing you how his service is the one that can best meet those needs and wants.

Meeting Your Needs (Wants)

This is where the sales (recruiting) process starts to get tricky. What if, after finding your primary motivation for enlisting, the recruiter realizes that the service he represents is not the best to meet your needs? In most cases, the answer is easy: He will force a "fit," and someday in the future you'll find yourself saying, "Why on earth did I ever buy into this?"

Just as you wouldn't expect a car salesman to say, "You know, it doesn't appear that a Chevy will meet your needs, so why don't you try Ford?" rarely will you hear a recruiter say, "The Army doesn't seem to be the best solution to your needs, but I'm sure the Navy can meet them." The recruiter that can admit that you might be better off shopping elsewhere is saying a lot about himself and the service he represents.

THE BENEFITS DUMP

The approach your recruiter takes in demonstrating how his service can meet your needs will vary from recruiter to recruiter. Generally, though, recruiters will engage in what is known as a "benefits dump"; that is, they will throw all the benefits their service has to offer at you and hope some of them are of interest to you. Here's a little secret that I'll share with you that they probably won't: The basic benefits of military service are the same for all branches of the military:

- The same pay scales
- Medical care
- Dental care
- GI Bill for higher education
- Housing allowance
- 30 days of vacation with pay, per year
- Privileges at base stores
- Availability of recreational activities such as golf courses and swimming pools
- Retirement plan

(These and other basic benefits will be covered in more detail in Appendices B and D.)

After you've been subjected to the deluge of benefits, your recruiter will more than likely try to sell you on the "exclusive" benefits of his particular service.

THE PRESSURE IS ON

Although the actual "sale" has already begun, it is now that the real pressure will begin. And it is at this point that you must be on the offensive.

During the benefits dump, most recruiters will make it sound as if they have an exclusive on the basic benefits, but now you know better! If the recruiter can satisfy your needs (motivator) with the basic benefits, he will more than likely try at this time to make the sale. If, however, he doesn't feel that he has satisfied your needs, he will employ his skills to convince you that his service is the one to get what you want.

THE ART OF PERSUASION

Recruiters, just like any well-trained salespeople, are trained on the art of persuasion. That is, they are taught to get people to agree with them and ultimately to buy their product.

They will use all sorts of tactics and techniques in order to convince you to agree to enlist. At this stage of the game, most recruiters will try to match your wants with the benefits of their particular service. The recruiter will make everything make sense and lead you down a path that comes to only one conclusion: enlist in her particular branch!

The typical recruiter will give what amounts to a sales pitch and will ask feedback questions along the way to ensure that you are on track and following her down the path she is creating for you. Here's how part of the conversation may go:

Recruiter: "Okay, Sue, from what you told me, your primary interest is to get some training in the area of computers. Is that correct?

Applicant: "Yes, that's correct."

Recruiter: "Well, Sue, the Navy has many jobs that are directly related to computers. We have computer programming jobs, computer repair jobs and data processing jobs. In addition, Sue, many Navy jobs require sailors to work directly with computers. Does that sound interesting to you?"

Applicant: "So far, yes. But how much training will I get to prepare me for my job?"

Recruiter: "I'm glad you asked that, Sue, because I want to tell you that the Navy has some of the best computer training you'll find anywhere. In addition, we do it all at an accelerated pace because, for the time you'll be in school, that's your only job. You'll be focusing on your studies and won't have any other duties to worry about. Add to that the fact that you'll be receiving your full pay the entire time. This is starting to sound better and better, isn't it?"

Applicant: "Yes, it is!"

Recruiter: "Great, Sue. I'm sure we'll be able to find you a Navy job that meets your needs of providing computer training. Let me ask you this: If I could guarantee you computer training, would you be ready to take the next step?"

Applicant: "I think so. What is the next step?"

Recruiter: "The next step is to take the ASVAB and then the physical."

Applicant: "When can I take the ASVAB and physical?"

Recruiter: "Sue, I know you're busy, so I'd suggest that you do one-stop processing. You'll take the ASVAB on Tuesday evening at the MEPS, stay at a hotel overnight at our expense and then take your physical the next day. How does that sound?"

Applicant: "Sounds great."

Recruiter: "Good, before we arrange the ASVAB and physical, we need to complete some paperwork. Are you ready to get started?"

Applicant: "Sure, let's get started."

Notice how the recruiter laid a path for the applicant to follow. The recruiter asked a number of feedback questions to ensure that the applicant was still on the path and not getting lost. Also, like many salespeople, recruiters tend to use the applicant's name a lot (a trait that I never liked). Good recruiters will also look for nonverbal cues to make sure their applicants are following them down the path. Positive body language and an applicant nodding in agreement are signs that he or she is on the way to enlistment.

My advice at this stage of the game is to keep 'em guessing; it's not time to buy quite yet. Don't get overly enthusiastic about anything your recruiter has presented. Answer her feedback questions matter-of-factly, not emotionally.

When my wife and I went looking for a house to buy, I gave her the following instructions when we pulled up in front of each house: "Show no emotion, don't say anything positive about the house while we're inside and definitely don't start telling them where you would put your furniture or what color you'd paint each of the rooms."

Why did I give such explicit instructions? The answer is simply that I didn't want the seller to know I was eager to buy. I wasn't rude to the seller, but I also wasn't giving her signals that I had already made up my mind.

Unfortunately for recruiters, conversations with applicants rarely go as smoothly as the example given here. Most times, applicants will respond negatively to feedback questions:

Recruiter: "Great, Sue, I'm sure we'll be able to find you a Navy job that meets your needs of providing computer training. Let me ask you this: If I could guarantee you computer training, would you be ready to take the next step?"

Applicant: "No, I don't think so."

In this situation, the recruiter is met with an objection. It is up to him at this time to identify and overcome it.

OVERCOMING OBJECTIONS

Part of a recruiter's training deals with overcoming applicant objections. Before he can overcome it, however, he must identify it.

The true objection in the example is not, "No, I don't think so." Rather, it is whatever motivated the applicant to say "No." What the applicant may have been trying to say was:

- "No, I don't think so. You haven't told me enough about the training I'll receive."
- "No, I want to know more about the jobs I might be doing after the training."

Or there may be other concerns holding the applicant back. It is the recruiter's job to identify them. Once the recruiter has identified the objections by asking probing questions, he can begin to overcome them. In the above scenarios, he would probably give Sue more information to answer her concerns and continue to ask feedback questions like, "How does that sound?" or "Does that answer your question?" in order to get Sue to agree to continue processing for enlistment.

Sometimes, however, the objection may not be that the applicant needs more information; rather, it may be that the applicant doesn't think that proceeding is the right choice. For example, "No, I don't think so. I'm not ready for a commitment to the Navy."

There are as many objections as there are applicants, and it is up to the recruiter to probe deeper to overcome every objection.

There are several methods a recruiter can use to try to overcome an objection such as fear of commitment. One of the most popular methods is the "feel, felt, found" approach. For example:

Applicant: "No, I don't think the Army is right for me because I don't think I'd make it through Basic Training."

Recruiter: "I understand how you feel; many people have felt the same way. This is what they've found: Basic Training was not as hard as they thought it would be. They found that Basic Training actually helped them realize just how much they could accomplish if they put their mind to it."

Recruiters may use variations of "feel, felt, found" and may also just come out and ask you, "Why do you feel that way?" or "What makes you say that?" or something else along those lines.

The bottom line is that the recruiter will make sure all your objections are uncovered and put to rest so that he can close the sale and get you to commit.

What if I Have Objections?

If you have any objections, make them known to the recruiter. By hiding objections, you may be sending a signal to the recruiter that you are ready to buy, when in fact you are not. Give the recruiter every opportunity to answer your concerns, and then let him know if he has answered your questions to your satisfaction.

Sometimes the objection may be that you have heard what the recruiter has to offer and you are just not interested. If this is the case, let the recruiter know that, and tell him matter-of-factly that you are just not interested in proceeding.

Of course, at this time any good recruiter will say something to the effect of "I understand why you would say that. Many people have felt the same way, this is what they have found . . ."

If this is the case, end the conversation right there. Do not feel pressured or obligated to continue. The most important thing is not to continue in the enlistment process if you don't intend to enlist. There is nothing worse for a recruiter than having an applicant complete all the paperwork, take the ASVAB and physical, and then not enlist. Believe me, despite how he feels at the time, a recruiter would much rather you be up front with him in the beginning than go through all the steps of enlistment and lose you in the end.

If you just need more time to think things through, let the recruiter know that. If, however, you've already made up your mind not to enlist, don't tell him you'll think about it.

Assuming that your recruiter has satisfied all your questions and you are still interested in enlisting, the recruiter will no doubt move to the next step of closing the sale.

Closing the Sale

A recruiter will usually wait until he is sure that he has overcome all your objections and has sold you on all the benefits of enlisting in his particular service before trying to close the sale. However, sometimes recruiters may notice certain buying signals from an applicant during the interview and may try closing during an earlier step of the process (this is called a trial close).

Consider the car dealership example again for a moment. Most salespeople will tell you all about the features of the car, will answer all your questions, will allow you to test drive the car and may even talk about financing options before asking you, "Would you like to buy this car?"

On the other hand, if you walk into the dealership, tell the salesman how much you love the car, how you've always wanted one, and rave on about the car's features, chances are he will say at the first opportunity, "So when will you be ready to take delivery of the car?"

In this case, you've sold yourself; the salesman has no need to sell you any further. How easy would it be for you to negotiate a better price in such a situation? The same is true for applicants; that's why it is so important for you to maintain a "poker face" when dealing with your recruiter. Let him know you are interested, but don't make it too easy for him and don't get emotional about the sale (remember my example of looking for houses).

THE CLOSING PITCH

Recruiters have been taught many techniques for closing the sale. They range from impending doom ("You've got to make up your mind right now or the offer will expire") to making a list of the pros and cons (remarkably, the pros always seem to win out). Some recruiters may close by painting a mental picture of life in the military and then paint you into the picture. Some are more subtle: They may just say, "Okay, if you don't have any other questions, let's get started" or "Is there any reason we shouldn't get started with the paperwork?"

If you are ready to proceed at that point, then, by all means, do so. If you have doubts or there are still unanswered questions, stop the process right there. It's okay to go home and think about it. Do not agree to proceed with the enlistment processing if you are not ready to do so. Believe me, the recruiter and the service he represents will be there in a week, a month, or whenever you eventually make up your mind.

Although recruiters are taught to sell their particular service branch, they are also taught to sell the "enlistment process" piece-by-piece. In other words, they sell the initial interview, and then they sell the Armed Services Vocational Aptitude (ASVAB) exam and the physical. The reason for this is they believe that the further you get into the process, the more committed you will become to enlisting—and they are right.

Almost no one wants to go home after they've told all their friends and family members that they are processing for enlistment in the military and have to say, "I didn't enlist."

What makes matters even worse is that some recruiters will encourage applicants that aren't 100 percent sold on enlisting to continue processing. The conversation may go something like this:

Applicant: "I'm not sure if the Air Force will be right for me. I may want to attend college in the fall."

Recruiter: "No problem, I understand that, but let's get you tested and get your physical so that if you decide later on that you want to join, they'll be out of the way."

This type of behavior is one of a weak recruiter, one who throws as many applicants as he can against the wall to see which ones stick. Again, my advice is that if you aren't sure that enlisting is what you want to do, don't do it! The ASVAB and physical examination can be accomplished when you make up your mind to enlist.

Along similar lines, sometimes a recruiter will tell you to enlist just in case the college thing doesn't come through. Then, you'll at least have the military to fall back on, and if you do wind up going to college, he'll eventually get you out of the Delayed Enlistment Program (DEP). If your recruiter does this, get yourself another recruiter (if possible). This behavior is not only the sign of a weak recruiter but also a desperate one!

What am I trying to say with all of this? Proceed only when you—not the recruiter—are ready to.

Gathering Your Thoughts

At this point you've decided on one of the following courses of action:

- You have a strong desire to enlist and will proceed with enlistment processing.
- You have an interest in enlisting, but you are not fully committed and you want to think about it some more before continuing with the enlistment process.
- You have no desire to enlist and will not proceed with the enlistment process.

IF YOU HAVE A STRONG DESIRE TO ENLIST

If, after your initial interview, you have a strong desire to enlist and want to proceed with the enlistment process, I caution you to proceed with care. Gather as much information and literature as you can from the recruiter, and make sure you've asked all the questions that you want answers for.

After you've gathered all the data, go home and read through Chapter 2 of this book. Once you've done that, if you still fit in the "strong desire" category, I suggest that you go for it!

IF YOU HAVE SOME INTEREST IN ENLISTING

If you are unsure how to proceed, don't commit to further processing. Again, although your recruiter may push you into further processing, you need to insist on putting off continuing until you've made up your mind.

Do not agree to further processing just to pacify a pushy recruiter. This happens quite often, unfortunately; an applicant is not committed to enlisting but will continue in the enlistment process because it is easier than saying no to the recruiter. Some recruiters may even tell you that you can take the ASVAB and physical for their particular service, and if you decide to join another branch you'll already have them done and won't have to go through it again. While that may be true, it's complete nonsense. Wait to take the ASVAB and physical until you are sure that you want to enlist and you are certain of the branch you want to join.

Before you leave the recruiting office, let the recruiter know that you would like some time to think things over. Set a time for the recruiter to contact you (usually one to three weeks) for a decision. The reason you should do this is because the recruiter will probably start calling you (sometimes the day following the interview), and you need to let her know that you want some time to seriously think about it without being hounded by her.

Don't give the recruiter the old, "Don't call us, we'll call you" line. That just shows the recruiter you are probably not interested and, once again, you will start receiving persuasive telephone calls from her.

If your recruiter hasn't offered any names and phone numbers of people he's enlisted that you can talk to, ask her for some. Recruiters will often encourage members of the Delayed Entry Program (DEP) to talk with applicants. This enables the applicant to talk with people who have recently gone through the enlistment process.

If you do get some names and telephone numbers, make the phone calls! Here are some of the things you may want to ask:

- What job did you enlist for?
- Was it the job you originally wanted?
- Why did you join?
- Why did you choose this particular branch over the others?
- Did you have any problems with the recruiter?
- Was the recruiter honest with you?
- How was MEPS? Are there any surprises I should look out for?
- How was the ASVAB? Any tips on taking it?
- If you had to do it all over again, would you?

And of course, you should ask questions about anything else that may concern you.

Finally, you should obtain as much literature as you can, ensure that all your questions have been answered, go home and review all the material and read through Chapter 2 of this book.

IF YOU HAVE NO DESIRE TO ENLIST

If, after your initial interview, you find you have no desire to enlist, be up front with the recruiter and tell him so. Do not make another appointment, do not tell him to call you, do not tell him that you will call him and definitely do not agree to further enlistment processing!

Recruiters can be persuasive, and people sometimes will agree to things to appease the recruiter. If after looking at a car in a dealer's showroom you find you have no intention of buying the car, would you have the salesman work out the financing for you just because he was pushy? Although it sounds ridiculous, people do it every day with recruiters; unable to say no, they continue with the enlistment process with no intention of ever enlisting.

Ask the recruiter not to call you (this may or may not do any good), but thank him for his time. Do take some literature with you; review it when you get home and, even though you've decided not to enlist, read Chapter 2 of this book anyway.

REPEAT AS NECESSARY

Because you should talk with recruiters of most (if not all) of the military branches, you should fit into one of the three categories for each of the services.

Also, the "some desire" category will need to be turned into either "strong desire" or "no desire." Once you've narrowed down the branches to those for which you have a strong desire, it will be time to choose the right branch for you. Of course, you may find that none of the branches meet your needs. In that case, the military is not the right option for you. If that is the case, you have some options of what to do with this book:

- Pass it along to someone else.
- Try to sell it at a garage sale.
- Put it on a shelf and leave it there.
- Use it to level out an uneven table.

What's Next

If you agree to proceed with the enlistment process, your recruiter will schedule you to take the ASVAB (if you haven't already taken it) and the physical examination.

The paperwork will begin at this point, but don't worry; you aren't committed to anything until you raise your right hand and take the oath of enlistment (see Chapter 4).

FILLING OUT THE PAPERWORK

You will be asked to complete forms about your health, law violations and involvement with drugs. Your recruiter will also complete the actual application for enlistment (the DD Form 1966). You will be asked to sign this form and attest to its accuracy, so make sure that it is accurate before signing. An example of the DD Form 1966 can be found in Appendix G. The actual form will, more than likely, also contain additional comments that you will be asked to initial. Each service has special requirements concerning Basic Training, certain policies, and so on, that they want you to be aware of, so they are listed on the DD Form 1966. One such policy is the requirement for applicants to view certain videotapes dealing with Basic Training. Review the sample form so that you can become familiar with it before you see the real thing. Pay particular attention to the statements on page 3 and the certification on page 4. To use the car dealership example: Imagine being able to take the time to read an application for a loan or lease before being asked to sign on the dotted line. Well, here's your chance!

SCHEDULING THE ASVAB AND PHYSICAL EXAMINATION

Chapter 3 will cover specific details about the ASVAB and where to take it; information concerning the physical examination is contained in Chapter 4.

Your recruiter will encourage (and some will almost insist) you to take the ASVAB and physical as soon as possible. Although this is not necessary, by taking the two as soon as possible, you are showing a commitment to enlisting. However, if you are being pushed to get them done by some deadline, I can assure you that the deadline is an arbitrary one created by your recruiter.

Chapter Summary

The purpose of this chapter was to get you better prepared to meet with your recruiter for the first time and to give you some insight into what to expect from your initial interview. If you take nothing else away from this chapter, take these key points:

- Do your homework before the initial interview.
- Be honest with your recruiter.
- Be polite but firm.
- Do not allow anyone (including your recruiter) to get you to lie.
- Do not feel pressured or obligated to continue with the enlistment process.
- Continue at your own pace, but remember that the enlistment process has a logical flow that should not be unnecessarily prolonged.
- Remember that there are rarely any "special, limited-time offers" that won't be available next week (after you've had some time to think it over).
- If you are told you are ineligible for enlistment, ask for a waiver.
- If you are told that a waiver cannot be granted, ask to see it in writing.

You should now be well on your way to making a decision that may change your life. Chapter 2 will help you with that difficult task.

2 GETTING THE FACTS TOGETHER: SHOULD I OR SHOULDN'T I ENLIST?

This chapter discusses the factors that must be considered in order to make an informed decision on whether or not to join the military. It includes an assessment to help you determine if the military can fulfill your needs.

Facts or Emotion?

Once you have met with your recruiter(s) and have received some basic information, you will need to decide whether or not to proceed with the enlistment process. Your decision must be based on facts and whether or not your needs can be met by enlisting in the military.

People rarely buy anything based on their needs; instead, they buy based on their emotions. We see it on a daily basis in advertising, from automobiles to soft drinks. We rarely see an automobile commercial that gives statistics about how the car is engineered, how long it will last, the gas mileage and other technical specifications. Instead, we see people driving around having a good time, without a care in the world. And it seems as though snowboarding, skydiving and mountain climbing are used to sell soft drinks, not details about the product's nutritional value.

The reason for this is that advertising agencies know that you will buy based on how you feel rather than what you think. Because of this tendency to buy with emotion rather than reason, it is important to separate the feelings from the facts so that you can base your decision primarily on the facts.

The reason I said primarily on the facts and not solely on the facts is quite simple: We are all human and cannot be totally without emotion. For instance, you may decide that joining the military is the right choice and so you narrow your decision down to two services. After comparing the two, you may not be able to choose based on the facts, so the decision may come down to which service has the better-looking uniform.

The First Decision Point

There are two big questions that you must answer. First, is the military right for me, and second, if the first answer was yes, which branch is right for me?

Consider the car analogy again for a minute. Suppose that you have to decide whether to buy a new car or repair your current car. The first choice you make will determine your next course of action. You will have to weigh the facts to determine if you will purchase a new car or not. Once you've decided to buy a car rather than repair your old one, you must then decide exactly what make and model will best meet your needs.

The next section, "Choosing the Military (Needs Assessment)," will help you decide whether or not the military is the right choice for you. If you decide it is, the following section, "Choosing the Branch to Join," will help you in determining which branch of the military will best meet your particular needs.

In the previous chapter, you learned about your "primary motivators" for contacting a military recruiter (or agreeing to an interview) in the first place. You'll use these primary motivators to determine whether or not enlisting in the military is the right thing for you to do.

Choosing the Military (Needs Assessment)

You should have made a list of your primary motivators before you ever set foot in the recruiter's office. Whether your list was long—containing such items as money for college, job security, opportunity to travel, technical training and good pay—or contained only one item, such as having full-time employment, the number of items on your list is not what's important. What is important is that you are able to satisfy those motivators.

Whatever your list contains, the first course of action is to collect your list of primary motivators and put them in order of importance to you. This process, known as rank-ordering, will help you determine if you should proceed with the enlistment process.

It should be noted, however, that at this time you may not have all the information necessary to determine whether or not you should enlist. For instance, if your most important primary motivator is receiving technical training, you will not know if the military can meet this motivator unless you have taken the Armed Services Vocational Battery (ASVAB) and physical examinations. If this is the case, you must make the assumption that you will qualify for technical training and base your decision on the information provided to you by your recruiter. It will then be necessary for you to return to this chapter later on and reevaluate your situation if needed.

RANK-ORDERING YOUR LIST

Rank-ordering your list is a simple process of deciding which motivators are most important to you and then listing them in order of importance. List your most important motivator as number one, your next most important as number two and so on.

If we apply the car-buying scenario here, your primary motivators may be finding a car that costs under $20,000, has a four-cylinder engine, gets at least 30 miles to the gallon, has leather interior, is available in blue and has a sunroof. If you put those motivators in rank order, your list might look something like this:

1. Costs under $20,000
2. Gets at least 30 mpg
3. Has a sunroof
4. Has leather interior
5. Available in blue

You'll notice that the number one, or most important, motivator in this case is cost, while the last, or least important, motivator is color. The more important the motivator, the less likely you'll be willing to settle for something different or to live without it altogether.

MEETING YOUR NEEDS (MOTIVATORS)

After you've rank-ordered your motivators, proceed to the simple process of going down your list and determining whether or not those motivators can or cannot be met by enlisting in the military. Simply write "yes" next to those that can be fulfilled by enlisting and "no" next to those that cannot be fulfilled by enlisting.

If you find that all your motivators can be met by enlisting, that's great; but even if only some of your motivators can be met, you may still want to consider it. Seldom does a product meet all our needs and wants, and you may be able to make satisfactory compromises and still be happy with the outcome.

For instance, in the car-buying scenario, you may find that a particular car meets all of your needs but is not available in blue. Although the color of the car was important, it was the least important of all your motivators. For this reason you may decide to purchase the car despite the fact that it isn't available in blue. Or suppose you could get all your motivators met (even the color), but instead of $20,000 you would have to pay $21,000? You might decide that you're willing to compromise on the cost to get the car of your dreams.

If you were buying a car, however, you probably would compare several makes of cars to see if any of them could meet all your motivators before buying one that just met some of them. The same applies when determining whether or not to enlist. You should compare all the alternatives to enlisting—gather all the facts—before making a final decision.

COMPARING THE ALTERNATIVES

Several alternatives to enlisting may be available to you, such as going to work at a local company, attending college or attending a local vocational school. You should perform the "yes/no" test on each of your motivators as they pertain to each of the available alternatives.

For example, let's assume that one of your alternatives is a job at the local factory and your primary motivators are (in rank order):

1. Money for college
2. Technical training
3. Job security
4. Opportunity for travel

Let's further assume that the local factory offers its employees tuition assistance for college similar to that offered by the military. It also has an on-the-job technical training program and a great track record when it comes to keeping employees. However, since this is a local company, your opportunity for travel will be nonexistent.

You may need to modify your approach to your motivator list depending on the alternative. For instance, job security really does not apply when you are talking about attending college as an alternative.

You might, however, consider things like the job security of people in occupations related to your intended major or even the graduation rate of the college you are thinking about attending.

Although you are well on your way to making a decision, there is still one very important piece of the puzzle that must be considered—the negative aspects of each alternative.

NEGATIVE ASPECTS

Returning to the car-buying scenario, let's assume that you have found a car that matches all of your motivators. But the closest dealership is 100 miles away, the particular make of car has a terrible maintenance record, and after looking at the car you just don't like the style. These are the "negative aspects" that must be considered.

When you go out to purchase your car armed with your motivator (or needs) list, you should have (at least in your mind) a list of negative aspects that you just can't live with when considering a new vehicle.

The same applies to enlisting in the military: There may be certain things about military service that would conflict with your desires. For instance, if you wanted to stay in the local area, you would probably not want to enlist for Active Duty, although you might want to consider enlisting in the Reserve or Guard.

PUTTING IT ALL TOGETHER

Once you have gotten all of your lists together, it is time to make a decision. At this point the decision can be whether or not to continue processing (i.e., take the ASVAB), or it could mean making the decision to enlist.

Whatever your decision, it should be made based primarily on the facts, with very little emotion as part of the equation. That said, I must also say that although I am "preaching" about keeping emotion out of the decision process, there may be times when emotion may be the one thing that will sway your decision. In fact, emotion may actually be your primary motivator.

EMOTION AS A PRIMARY MOTIVATOR

When I enlisted, I met several people who joined the military for primarily emotional reasons. For instance, there was one who had immigrated to the United States with his family. He lived very well here (better than he could ever have hoped for in his home country), received a very good education and genuinely loved the United States. In his words, he wanted to pay something back to the country that had given him so much. His way of doing that was to enlist in the military. He didn't base his decision on the facts; he was motivated solely by emotion.

In other cases, individuals enlisted because they wanted to keep a family tradition alive. They joined because their fathers and grandfathers had joined, and they wanted to follow in footsteps of their forefathers.

The emotional reasons people have for enlisting in the military are many and aren't necessarily bad. However, as a word of caution, be very careful of making any "buying" decision based on emotion alone.

THE NEXT STEP

If you've gotten this far, the next step may be very easy or it may be extremely difficult. It all depends on the amount of homework you've done on each of the military branches you are considering.

Choosing the Branch to Join

If you are seriously considering joining the military, you probably have checked out at least two of the branches. I advise you to check them all out, even if it means just requesting literature and reviewing it. Although I was not interested in joining the Army, I did look at its brochures first to find out a little about its programs before I made my final decision.

A word of caution though: Sometimes (in reality, most times) brochures do not tell the complete story, and it is very difficult to base your decision either for or against on the contents of a brochure. When I was a recruiter, people were always telling me that they weren't interested because of what they had read about it in a brochure. I'd usually say something like, "I understand why you wouldn't be interested in joining, but how could you be interested in something you know very little about? That's why I'd like to take a few minutes to meet with you in person and tell you a little more about your opportunities."

Smooth sales talk? Perhaps, but it was the truth. Would you buy a car based solely on the information contained in a brochure? Probably not! And unless you **totally** hated the car based on the information in the brochure, you would probably not completely dismiss it as an option.

MAKING A CHOICE

If, after checking into the military branches that interest you, there is clearly only one choice, then your decision has already been made (although I would have to question what you have based your decision on). But, if you are like most people (most people, that is, who have read this book and are taking my advice), you will have at least two branches in mind, so read on!

The process of choosing the right branch of the military for you is basically the same process that you used to determine if joining the military was right for you. You should start with your list of primary motivators and use the "yes/no" method to determine whether each branch can meet all or some of those motivators. Once you've determined which branch or branches can best meet your motivators, it's time to compare those branches. What the first branch meets, the second may not; but what the first branch doesn't, the second one might meet in a big way. Remember to look for the negative aspects as well as the motivators of each of the branches as you compare.

After making your comparisons, you may still find yourself with more than one choice. What do you do then? You could flip a coin, but I wouldn't advise it. Instead, you may want to look at some of these factors:

- Length of enlistment—Some branches may require a longer term for offering the same benefits that you could receive from another branch.
- Advanced pay grade—You may be entitled to an advanced rank in some branches based on certain enlistment options.

- Length and type of training—How long will the training you'll receive take? Usually the longer the training, the more in-depth and useful it is. You'll also want to consider how useful the training will be once you've left the military.
- Enlistment bonuses—I caution you about using an enlistment bonus as the only factor in deciding which branch to choose. If it comes down to a tie between two branches and only one offers a bonus, it's not a bad reason to choose that branch.
- Additional pay and allowances—There may be additional pay you'd be entitled to that can only be offered by a particular branch. For instance, if you join the Navy, you may be entitled to Sea Pay and Submarine Pay, something obviously not available if you join the Air Force.
- Ability to pursue higher education—While all the military branches offer educational benefits, you must consider when you will be able to take advantage of these benefits. If you are in a job requiring 12-hour shifts and being out in the "field" a great deal, when will you be able to attend classes?

Once you have considered these factors, and perhaps some of your own, you should be able to decide which branch is right for you. If you still haven't been able to select one branch over another, though, consider the following:

- Ask your recruiter if you can speak to someone who has recently joined.
- If there is a base nearby, you may be able to get a tour to get a look at its facilities.
- If you are well versed in Internet chat rooms, you may want to look for ones that cater to military members—then ask a lot of questions.
- Talk to friends and family members who are currently serving in the military. Be careful, however, not to talk to individuals who have been out of the military for a while as they probably do not have an understanding of "today's" military. Also avoid individuals who left the military under less-than-desirable conditions (for example, someone who was discharged from basic training for noncompatibility).

If you still are having problems deciding, maybe you should choose the service with the best-looking uniform!

Guard and Reserve Opportunities

Other alternatives that may be available to you are the Air National Guard, the Army National Guard and the Reserve components of the Air Force, Army, Coast Guard, Marine Corps and Navy. More information about the Guard and Reserve is provided in Appendix C. However, at this point it is important to mention that, depending on your primary motivators, the Guard and Reserve may be a more viable option for you than Active Duty.

You should seriously consider the Guard and Reserve if

- you have "deep roots" in your local community and you do not desire to leave home;
- you are attending college full-time and wish to continue at your current school;
- you currently have a full-time career and are only looking for additional income or some additional skills that you can apply to your full-time job.

The Guard and Reserve would probably not be an option for you if

- you are looking for full-time employment;
- you desire to leave your current surroundings.

When choosing between Active duty and the Reserve, apply the primary motivator principles to help you decide your course of action.

Job Selection

You'll learn about the job selection process later, in Chapter 4, when I cover the Military Entrance Processing Station (MEPS).

I bring this up now, however, because you may wish to utilize the primary motivator—needs assessment principles—when selecting the right military job. Keep in mind, however, that, depending on your motivators, the job you wind up with might not play such a major role in your decision-making process.

For instance, if your primary (and perhaps only) motivating factor is getting money for college, your choice of jobs may be secondary to getting into the branch that can offer you the most money to pay for college. On the other hand, if your primary motivator is getting high-tech training, the job you choose would probably take precedence over which branch you wound up selecting.

Chapter Summary

The decision of whether or not to join the military and then choosing a specific branch to join must be made by analyzing and applying facts, not by responding to emotions. Because most buying is done on feelings and not facts, it is important for you to determine your primary motivators, which are the needs you are looking to fulfill by joining the military.

Following the "rank-order-chart" procedure first will help you determine which of the military branches (if any) can meet your motivators. Once you have determined those branches, you must compare the military to your other alternatives, remembering to consider the negative aspects along with your motivators to get the "whole picture." You should also add the Guard and Reserve alternatives to the mix for consideration.

Joining the military is a big step, whether you go Active Duty or Reserve, and no matter which branch you choose. By following the advice offered in this chapter, you will be able to make a more informed and rational decision based on the facts.

If you choose to continue with processing for enlistment, your next step will probably be to take the Armed Services Vocational Aptitude Battery (ASVAB) (if you haven't already done so). The next chapter will familiarize you with the ASVAB and also offer some advice so that you can maximize your chances of doing well on this important test.

3 PREPARING FOR THE ARMED SERVICES VOCATIONAL APTITUDE BATTERY (ASVAB) EXAM: YIKES! DID YOU SAY EXAM? DO I NEED TO KNOW MATH?

This chapter will not prepare you for the ASVAB. However, it provides a general overview of the exam and its parts, along with some helpful hints so that you can take the necessary steps to prepare yourself for the ASVAB.

Having an understanding of the Armed Forces Vocational Aptitude Battery (ASVAB) exam will increase your chances of scoring higher and will consequently qualify you for more military occupations. If you've already taken the Scholastic Aptitude Test (SAT), you know how important it is to prepare for an exam that will, in all likelihood, shape your future. I am not comparing the ASVAB to the SAT; however, as with the SAT, you do not want to go into the ASVAB exam without preparation.

Unlike the SAT, the ASVAB is given free of charge by the military through the Military Entrance Processing Station (MEPS). There are two ways in which you can take this exam. First, many high schools sponsor the ASVAB and offer it to all interested students. This is called the "institutional" ASVAB. In fiscal year 1999, 857,456 high school students were given the institutional ASVAB examination.

If you choose to take the institutional ASVAB, you will take the exam with other students at your school. More than likely, there will be one or more military recruiters present to proctor the exam. This is their sole purpose for being there on test day; in fact, they are prohibited by regulations from actively recruiting during the ASVAB. However, when you complete the ASVAB answer sheet, you will be asked about your plans after high school—such as attending a two- or four-year college or vocational (or trade) school or enlisting in the military. If you do well on the ASVAB, military recruiters will contact you regardless of your intended plans. Of course, if you list your intention to join the military, you are a prime candidate for enlistment and will be pursued by recruiters of all services. If you choose to enlist in the military, your high school (institutional) ASVAB scores can be used for purposes of enlistment. Your ASVAB scores will remain valid for two years.

The second way that the ASVAB is given is referred to as the "production" ASVAB. This version of the ASVAB is given to individuals pursuing enlistment who either did not take the institutional version or who want to retake the exam in the hope that they will improve on their previous scores. In fiscal year 1999, 487,218 exams were administered at the 65 MEPS and more than 685 Mobile Examining Team (MET) sites. There are specific rules on how often you may take the ASVAB; these rules will be discussed later in the chapter.

The production ASVAB is given in one of two places: either at one of the 65 MEPS or at a MET site. In either place, you will be taking the exam with others who have also decided to pursue enlistment in the military. There is one main advantage of taking the ASVAB at a MET site versus one of the MEPS: the method in which the test is administered.

There's also a third way to take the ASVAB. All MEPS now administer what is referred to as the Computerized Adaptive Test (CAT) ASVAB. This version of the exam, as the name implies, is administered by computer. If you take this version of the ASVAB, you'd better be very certain of your answers because you can only move forward through the questions; you cannot return to previous questions. Because of this, many of the tried-and-true test-taking techniques go out the window. For instance, anyone who has ever taken a paper-based test knows that you should skip questions you are unsure of and return to them later. Also, most people will go back and review their answers if there is time remaining at the end of the test section. That is not possible with the CAT ASVAB. Also, the "Adaptive" part of the CAT refers to the fact that the test adapts to how well the test-taker is doing and adjusts the next question accordingly. In other words, if you are doing very well on the exam, the questions get harder; if you are not doing particularly well, the questions get somewhat simpler. Therefore, I recommend avoiding the ASVAB administered at the MEPS in favor of a MET-site administered exam.

What Is the ASVAB?

Now that you know about the different versions of the ASVAB, your next question is probably "What is the ASVAB?"

The ASVAB is the exam given by all military branches to determine your basic skills (such as verbal and math) as well as your aptitude for other skills (such as electronics and mechanics). Your overall score, known as the Armed Forces Qualification Test (AFQT), will determine whether you meet the basic qualifications for enlistment, while the specific scores in other areas will determine if you have the aptitude to qualify for certain military career fields.

The ASVAB is divided into ten subject tests, which are presented in the following table. The tests are listed in the order in which you take them.

SUBJECT TESTS FOR THE ASVAB

Subject	Total Questions	Minutes to Complete
General Science (GS)	25	11
Tests knowledge of biological and physical sciences		
Arithmetic Reasoning (AR)	30	36
Tests ability to solve arithmetic word problems		
Word Knowledge (WK)	35	11
Tests ability to select correct word definitions and synonyms		
Paragraph Comprehension (PC)	15	13
Tests ability to extract information from passages		
Numerical Operations (NO)	50	3
Tests ability to do simple math computations (very quickly)		

Subject	Total Questions	Minutes to Complete
Coding Speed (CS)	84	7
You have to see this one to understand it—tests your ability to swiftly use a key to assign code numbers to words		
Auto and Shop Information (AS)	25	11
Tests knowledge of automobiles and related tools and terminology		
Mathematics Knowledge (MK)	25	24
Tests knowledge of general mathematics, including algebra and geometry		
Mechanical Comprehension (MC)	25	19
Tests knowledge of mechanical and physical principles		
Electronics Information (EI)	20	9
Tests knowledge of electronics principles		

Example test questions in each of these subject tests follow. More examples and practice tests can be found in the ASVAB study guides published by ARCO. These guides provide excellent study tips as well as many practice problems to hone your skills and to make you more comfortable with the ASVAB.

Armed Forces Qualification Test (AFQT)

As I mentioned earlier in this chapter, the AFQT is a composite score used to determine your eligibility for enlistment. You will be placed in a "mental category" based on your AFQT score. This mental category has no real relevance and is only mentioned here so you can understand the terminology that may be used by your recruiter. For example, "mental category one" (CAT I) is a good thing to hear; conversely, "mental category four" (CAT IV) is not. Your only concern is whether or not you have a high enough AFQT (or QT) score to qualify. The formula for calculating your AFQT is based on the following ASVAB subject tests:

Arithmetic Reasoning + Mathematics Knowledge + 2X Word Knowledge + 2X Paragraph Comprehension

Preparing for the ASVAB

As discussed earlier, in order to increase your chances for success, you must prepare for the ASVAB. If you've taken the SAT and done well on it, there is a good chance that you will score high enough on the AFQT to qualify for enlistment. However, the SAT will not prepare you for some of the other ASVAB subject areas, which will determine your aptitude for specific jobs in the military. The table on page 56 estimates approximate AFQT scores based on SAT scores.

Sample ASVAB Test Questions

General Science (GS)

1. The chief nutrient in lean meat is

- 1-A fat
- 1-B starch
- 1-C protein
- 1-D carbohydrates

2. Which of the following is an invertebrate?

- 2-A starfish
- 2-B pigeon
- 2-C gorilla
- 2-D alligator

Arithmetic Reasoning (AR)

1. If three hoses of equal length connected together reach 24 feet, how long is each hose?

- 1-A 6 feet
- 1-B 7 feet
- 1-C 8 feet
- 1-D 9 feet

2. A salesperson earns 30% commission on each sale made. How large a commission would the salesperson earn for selling $160.00 of merchandise?

- 2-A $36.00
- 2-B $40.00
- 2-C $48.00
- 2-D $50.00

Word Knowledge (WK)

1. Small most nearly means

- 1-A cheap
- 1-B round
- 1-C sturdy
- 1-D little

2. The wind is variable today.

- 2-A mild
- 2-B steady
- 2-C shifting
- 2-D chilling

Paragraph Comprehension (PC)

1. In the relations of man to nature, the procuring of food and shelter is fundamental. With the migration of man to various climates, ever new adjustments to the food supply and to the climate became necessary.

According to this passage, the means by which man supplies his material needs are

- 1-A accidental
- 1-B inadequate
- 1-C limited
- 1-D varied

2. Twenty-five percent of all household burglaries can be attributed to unlocked windows or doors. Crime is the result of opportunity plus desire. To prevent crime, it is each individual's responsibility to

- 2-A provide the desire
- 2-B provide the opportunity
- 2-C prevent the desire
- 2-D prevent the opportunity

Numerical Operations (NO)

1. $3 + 6 =$

- 1-A 3
- 1-B 6
- 1-C 9
- 1-D 12

2. $60 \div 15 =$

- 2-A 4
- 2-B 5
- 2-C 6
- 2-D 7

Coding Speed (CS)

At the top of each section in this subject test, there is a key, which consists of a group of words with a code number for each word. Each question in the test is a word taken from the key. From among the 5 options (columns A, B, C, D and E) listed for each question, you must find the correct code number for that word.

Key

game	6456	hat	1413	man	3451	salt	4586
green	2715	house	2859	room	2864	tree	5972

QUESTION #		OPTIONS			
	A	**B**	**C**	**D**	**E**
1. room	1413	2715	2864	3451	4586
2. green	2715	2864	3451	4586	5972
3. tree	1413	2715	3451	4586	5972
4. hat	1413	2715	3451	4586	5972
5. game	2859	2864	4586	5972	6456

Auto and Shop Information (AS)

1. A fuel injection system on an automobile engine eliminates the necessity for

    1-A a manifold
    1-B a carburetor
    1-C spark plugs
    1-D a distributor

2. What happens if cylinder head torquing is not done in proper sequence?

    2-A It warps the piston rings.
    2-B It cracks the intake manifold.
    2-C It distorts the head.
    2-D It reduces valve clearance.

Mathematics Knowledge (MK)

1. If 50% of x = 66, then x is

    1-A 33
    1-B 66
    1-C 99
    1-D 132

2. What is the area of this square?

    2-A 1 square foot
    2-B 5 square feet
    2-C 10 square feet
    2-D 25 square feet

5 ft.

Mechanical Comprehension (MC)

1. Which post holds up the greater part of the load?

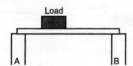

Load

    1-A post A
    1-B post B
    1-C both equal
    1-D not clear

2. If all of the following objects are at room temperature, which will feel coldest?

    2-A book
    2-B metal spoon
    2-C wooden chest
    2-D blanket

Electronics Information (EI)

1. The safest way to run an extension cord to a lamp is

    1-A under a rug
    1-B along a baseboard
    1-C under a sofa
    1-D behind a sofa

2. In the schematic vacuum tube illustrated, the cathode is element

    2-A A
    2-B B
    2-C C
    2-D D

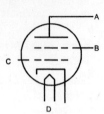

ANSWER KEY:

General Science (GS): 1. C 2. A
Arithmetic Reasoning (AR): 1. C 2. C
Word Knowledge (WK): 1. D 2. C
Paragraph Comprehension (PC): 1. D 2. D
Numerical Operations (NO): 1. C 2. A
Coding Speed (CS): 1. C2. A 3. E 4. A 5. E
Auto and Shop Information (AS): 1. B 2. C
Mathematics Knowledge (MK): 1. D 2. D
Mechanical Comprehension (MC): 1. A 2. B
Electronics Information (EI): 1. B 2. D

Comparison of SAT Scores to AFQT Scores

SAT Composite Score	Estimated AFQT Score Range
1,100–1,600	93–99
780–1090	65–92
660–770	50–64
540–650	31–49 (usual minimum for enlistment)
470–530	21–30
450–460	16–20
400–440	10–15

For those who did not do well on the SAT (or did not take it at all), and for the other subject areas of the ASVAB, the only way to ensure success is by studying! A great place to start is by using ASVAB study guides. When I say use, I don't just mean reading or browsing through them, I mean taking all the practice tests and going over them again and again. Remember, the ASVAB is a timed exam, and in certain areas, such as Numerical Operations, it's not the difficulty of the questions that will get you in trouble—it's the amount of time you're given to complete these problems.

Here are some other tips for doing well on the ASVAB:

- Read every day. Use a dictionary to look up definitions of words you don't understand.
- Read magazines dealing with mechanics, electronics and automobiles.
- Practice math problems, either from your ASVAB study guides, SAT preparation books or math textbooks.
- Attend classes in SAT preparation.
- Ensure that you get enough sleep prior to the exam.

- Show up early enough for the exam so you don't feel rushed.
- Don't schedule the exam if you cannot devote enough time to prepare for it.
- When all else fails, guess! You do not get penalized for guessing. Answer all the questions.

Of course, if you have no mechanical or automotive background, you will not become an expert in time for the ASVAB. Just remember that the ASVAB measures your *aptitude* for a certain area, not necessarily that you've mastered it.

Can you do well on the ASVAB without any preparation? The answer is a *definite maybe*! If you are a solid student who has also taken some shop classes or likes to work on cars, you will probably do okay on the ASVAB without any outside help. Keep in mind, though, that the job and the training you receive in the military is based largely on the results of the ASVAB.

Retaking the ASVAB

If you've taken the ASVAB and feel you didn't do as well as you could have, request to take it again. Just as taking the SAT more than once sometimes results in higher scores, the same can be true for the ASVAB. Here are the rules for repeating the exam:

- You may retake the ASVAB after three months from the date of your first exam.
- Subsequent exams can be taken every six months.
- Your last ASVAB results are good for two years from the test date.

If you are being pressured into using scores you are uncomfortable with, it may be because the recruiter is trying to meet his her or own goal and is more interested in enlisting you into any career field than enlisting you into a career field you are more suited for. By the same token, if you've taken the ASVAB more than once, with the same results, the recruiter is not obligated to wait for some "miracle" transformation to take place. It may be that even though you want a job in electronics, you are more suited for a position in a mechanical field.

Who Can Use My ASVAB Scores?

No matter which version of the ASVAB you take, any branch of the military can use it. You will be asked to sign a form called the 714A in order to convert your scores for use by that particular service. Even if you take the production ASVAB for the Navy, for example, and then decide you'd rather join the Marines, you do not have to take the ASVAB again.

If you have taken the institutional ASVAB, your scores can also be used by your high school guidance counselor to determine what path you may choose to follow after leaving high school.

Some high schools that offer the ASVAB to their students do not share the results, or even the names of those who took the exam, with the military. In these cases, the high school only uses the results for their own purposes in student counseling. You should, therefore, ask your school whether or not they plan to release the results to the military. If they do not, it will be up to you to contact the recruiter(s) of your choice to discuss the results, as they have no way of contacting you.

When to Take the ASVAB

You have no control of the scheduling of the institutional ASVAB, but you do have some control over when you take the production ASVAB.

Your recruiter will try to get you to take the ASVAB as soon as possible. That is understandable since there is a logical order in the enlistment process and the ASVAB is a major part of that process. But unlike a sale at your favorite store that happens only once a year, the ASVAB is given several times a week (depending on the location), and it probably will still be given next week if you decide to wait until then rather than taking it this week.

Usually, the ASVAB is administered certain days at the MEPS and other days at a MET site. Ask your recruiter when the exam is given. Also, most MEPS schedule one Saturday opening a month to accommodate those who cannot lose a day of school or work. Do not miss an important final exam or midterm in order to take the ASVAB, because you can always schedule it for another day.

Another option you may have is "one-stop" processing. This is where you spend the night at a hotel (at the government's expense) and arrive at the MEPS early in the morning to take the ASVAB and physical examination on the same day. This works very well for those who cannot miss time away from school or work.

Again, I'd like to emphasize that you should not be pressured into taking the ASVAB "as soon as possible." Take it only when you feel comfortable in doing so. Remember, however, that the recruiter has a job to do, and one of his duties is to get you tested. Therefore, be honest with him: If you have no intention of taking the ASVAB, tell him so; or if you need more time to study before you take it, tell him when you think you'll be ready.

Chapter Summary

Although this chapter has not prepared you for the ASVAB, it has served as an introduction to the test-taking process. If you take no other advice from what I've written in this chapter, please do all you can to prepare to do your best on this important examination because the job and the training you receive in the military is based largely on the results of the ASVAB.

Once you are mentally prepared for military enlistment, you must also prepare yourself for the next hurdle, the physical examination. The next chapter will help you prepare to get through this—sometimes—seemingly impossible task.

4 THE MILITARY ENTRANCE PROCESSING STATION (MEPS): DON'T THESE PEOPLE EVER SMILE?

Perhaps the most traumatic—and memorable—experience in the entire enlistment process is the applicant's first trip to the MEPS. This chapter will outline the purpose of the MEPS and reassure you that the MEPS is not an indicator of what life in the military is like.

In 1978, I was taken to a place called the Armed Forces Examining and Entrance Station (AFEES) at Fort Hamilton in Brooklyn, New York, to process for enlistment. The AFEES's mission was to determine the physical, mental and moral qualifications of each applicant. I spent the day filling out paperwork, answering questions, being probed and prodded and rushing from place to place. In the time since 1978, some things have changed at AFEES; it is now called the Military Entrance Processing Station (MEPS).

Besides dealing with a recruiter, the MEPS is the first contact most people have with the military. The MEPS is staffed by members of all the military branches, so no matter which branch you are enlisting for, you will interact with personnel from them all. At times, the MEPS may seem like an assembly plant to applicants, who go from station to station until they finally raise their hands for the oath of enlistment.

Because so many people go through the 65 Military Entrance Processing stations each year (343,041 in 1999), The MEPS system must be regimented to ensure that only qualified individuals are able to enter the armed forces. Although from time to time individuals who are not qualified "slip through the cracks," the number would be much higher if every MEPS didn't abide by a stringent routine. In 1999, 254,579 (74 percent) of those 343,041 who processed through the MEPS passed the rigid standards for enlistment.

This chapter will outline the basic processes you will encounter at the MEPS. Although all MEPS follow standard procedures, there will be some differences in the way each MEPS operates, so it is important to use this chapter as insight into the MEPS, not as a substitute for information (or instructions) given to you by your recruiter.

Preparing for MEPS Processing

After you and your recruiter have worked out a day to do your MEPS processing, he will put you on their schedule so they will be expecting you. If you have already taken the Armed Services Vocational Aptitude Battery (ASVAB) examination, chances are you will travel to the MEPS on the day you are scheduled to process. Depending on your circumstances, however, you may travel to a hotel near the MEPS the night before your processing.

TRANSPORTATION TO THE MEPS

If you are scheduled for "one-stop processing," which means taking the ASVAB and physical on the same day, you may be put up in a hotel (at government expense) near the MEPS the night before. You may also get to stay at a hotel—even if you've already taken the ASVAB—if you live a considerable distance from the MEPS; you should ask your recruiter about your options.

If you spend the night at the hotel, you will, more than likely, meet somewhere in the hotel lobby for a bus ride to the MEPS. Don't be late!

If you don't spend the night in the hotel, you'll be provided transportation (of some type) to the MEPS. The type of transportation varies from service to service and location to location. Generally there are several modes of transportation that may be provided:

- Your recruiter's government-owned vehicle
- Bus
- Train
- On rare occasions, airplane

If you are required to take public transportation, you will be provided with the appropriate tickets necessary. Because family members are permitted to witness the oath of enlistment, you may be allowed to provide your own source of transportation (at your expense).

Applicants who spend the night in the hotel may take these same modes of transportation to get to the hotel the evening prior to MEPS processing.

Words of Wisdom if You Stay at a Hotel

If you spend the night prior to your MEPS processing in a hotel, there are a few things to remember. Because this is the first time many of the applicants have spent the night away from home (other than at a slumber party), applicants sometimes get into trouble at the hotel. Unlike a sleepover, this is not a time to party. The sole purpose for your being at the hotel is so that you will be well rested when your processing begins the next day at around 5 a.m.!

In the past, I have had to deal with several applicants who did not understand—or otherwise disregarded—their reason for spending the night at the hotel. Often, those applicants were sent home without ever doing any MEPS processing and, therefore, never enlisted.

Here are a few things that will get you in trouble or cause you to be unfit to take the ASVAB and physical examination. Most of these are common sense, but for the sake of argument, I'll list them anyway:

- Alcohol usage of any kind (whether you are of legal age or not)
- Destruction of property (the hotel's or someone else's personal property)
- Loud noise of any kind
- Staying up all night (If you usually require eight hours of sleep, get to bed early enough to get it.)
- Spending the night in someone else's room (or permitting someone to spend the night in your room)
- Stealing
- Use of illegal drugs
- Any other behavior that could be classified as disorderly conduct

Besides being denied processing for the military, some actions may result in criminal prosecution.

As mentioned earlier, the government will take care of all expenses, including meals. This does not, however, include telephone calls. If the hotel allows you to make outgoing phone calls, use a calling card or prepaid phone card to avoid being presented with a large telephone bill (which you might not be prepared to pay) when you check out of the hotel.

CHECKING IN AT THE MEPS

Regardless of how you get to the MEPS, make sure you get there on time! If you are late, chances are you will not be allowed to process that day. If you are traveling by public transportation, your recruiter should be able to provide you with the best times to leave in order to get there on time.

Upon your arrival, you will report to the check-in desk where you will be signed in, and you will be asked for proof of identity. Most of the time, there will be no problem with check-in; sometimes, however (usually due to an administrative error), an applicant's name may be left off the daily processing list. If this happens to you, everything possible will be done to get you processed that day.

After you've checked in, you will be given a bar-coded label to wear that includes your name and the branch of service for which you are processing. You are now ready to begin your MEPS adventure!

THE MEPS LIAISON

Each branch of the military has one or more individuals from recruiting assigned to the MEPS. These individuals are your advocates at the MEPS. Their primary responsibilities include

- ensuring that the applicants get through all stages of processing;
- job counseling (this will be discussed later in this chapter);
- working through problems that applicants may encounter during processing;
- keeping the recruiters and recruiting staff informed of an applicant's processing progress;
- intervening with the MEPS staff on the applicant's behalf.

Although you will undoubtedly see many individuals at the MEPS from the branch of service in which you are enlisting, only the MEPS liaison is a member of that branch's recruiting staff.

MEPS Processing

MEPS processing is divided into five broad categories. They are (in the order in which you encounter them)

- Aptitude testing
- Physical examination (medical screening)
- Job search
- Background screening
- Oath of enlistment

Applicants taking the ASVAB.

Each step of the MEPS processing is important. These steps ensure that only qualified applicants enlist, and they also determine an applicant's suitability for specific military career fields. The following five processes establish the mental, physical and moral qualifications for enlistment.

APTITUDE TESTING

Aptitude testing includes the Armed Services Vocational Aptitude Battery (ASVAB) (which you may have already taken) as well as other specialty tests that you may be required to take (such as for some electronics specialties or for jobs requiring proficiency in foreign languages).

If you've already taken the ASVAB, you probably won't be taking it again unless you didn't achieve a satisfactory score the first time around. If you are taking it again, you must ensure that enough time has elapsed since the previous test to make you eligible for a retest. Some people think that they can get around the mandatory waiting period for retesting by going to another recruiter. A word of caution: If you've taken the test for another recruiter, even a recruiter for another branch, and you've decided to conceal this fact from your current recruiter, you will get caught and be denied processing. MEPS owns the ASVAB process, not the specific military branches; therefore, if you've ever taken the ASVAB, they'll know about it.

OTHER TESTING

In addition to the ASVAB, there are other tests you may be required to take depending on the branch of service and specific job or career field for which you are applying. If you've taken the ASVAB prior to the day of your MEPS processing, your recruiter may have talked to you about qualifying for a job that requires a specialized test. Or, if you've taken the ASVAB as part of your MEPS processing, the MEPS liaison will probably inform you of your eligibility to take a specialized test. Either way, taking one of the specialized tests can only qualify you for more opportunities and therefore increase the number of your job choices. Some of the specialized (or Special Purpose) tests include

Rest assured that it's been quite a while since this guy has worked at MEPS!

- Army Motor Vehicle Driver Selection Battery (MDB-I)
- Auditory Perception Test (AP)
- Defense Language Aptitude Battery (DLAB)
- Defense Language Proficiency Test (DLPT)
- Electronic Data Processing Test (EDPT)
- English Comprehension Level Test (ECLT)
- Alternate Flight Aptitude Selection Test (AFAST)
- Army Analysis Aptitude Test (AAAT)
- Basic Attribute Test (BAT)

PHYSICAL EXAMINATION

The physical examination you receive at the MEPS will probably be one of the most thorough physicals you've ever received. Because it is important that all individuals enlisting meet the physical fitness standards of the military branches, the MEPS personnel leave no stone unturned in determining whether or not you meet those standards.

Basically, your physical examination will consist of

- Height and weight measurements
- Hearing and vision examinations
- Urine and blood tests
- Drug and alcohol tests
- Muscle group and joint maneuvers
- Complete physical examination and interview
- Specialized tests, if required

Women Applicants

Women applicants will be provided gowns to wear during their physical examination. They will also be examined by the MEPS physician in a private room. A female chaperone will be present during the portion of the exam that requires you to remove your clothing. All female applicants (even if they report that they are not sexually active) receive a pregnancy test.

Disclosure of Your Medical History

As part of the recruiting process, your recruiter should have had you complete an SF-93 (Report of Medical History) form, which includes questions on past and current medical history. I've provided an example of this form in Appendix G. Your recruiter will have used the information provided on this form to determine any potentially disqualifying medical problems. This form will also assist the MEPS medical personnel to better understand your medical history.

Let me reiterate that it is vital for you to be completely honest when completing this form. By honestly answering the questions, you may prevent problems later on. It is not unusual for someone to conceal information that is discovered later during the medical examination, or even worse, during Basic Training.

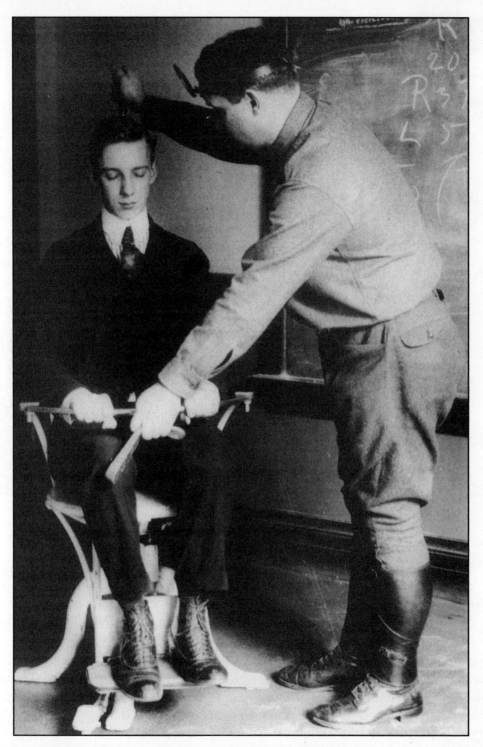

Some things have changed at MEPS since this WWI-era photo was taken.

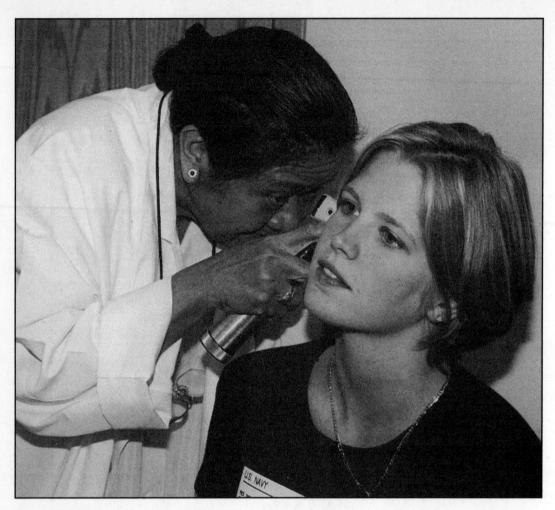

Part of a physical that we can publish.

By signing the SF 93, you are agreeing to the following statement:

I certify that I have reviewed the foregoing information supplied by me and that it is true and complete to the best of my knowledge. I authorize any of the doctors, hospitals, or clinics mentioned above to furnish the Government a complete transcript of my medical record for purposes of processing my application for this employment or service. I understand that falsification of information on Government forms is punishable by fine and/or imprisonment.

While most people probably don't even read this statement before signing the SF 93, it tells it all. Do not lie or conceal information about your medical history. Will you have to pay a fine or go to jail if MEPS personnel discover that you haven't been honest about your medical history? Probably not. However, if you somehow get through the physical and then it's discovered in Basic Training that you weren't 100 percent truthful about your medical history, you may face severe penalties because you'll be an Active Duty service member by then.

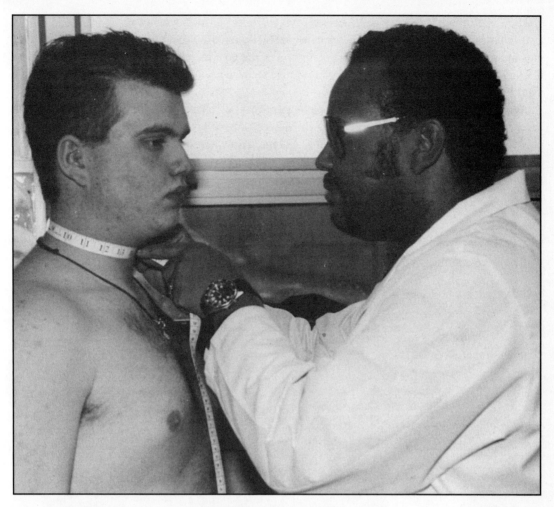

Depending on your weight, you may be required to do a body-fat measurement.

Medical Waivers

Remember that there are certain "disqualifying" medical conditions that can be waived. Only the MEPS medical personnel can determine that on a case-by-case basis. In other words, a history of removal of a tumor, for example, may be waived in one case, but not in another. Certain conditions may never be waived; your recruiter will let you know if that is the case. This is discussed in more detail later in this section.

Completing the SF 93

Before you sign the statement at the bottom of the SF 93, I would like to offer some advice on completing the form.

You are responsible for the answers to each and every question on the form—not your recruiter, not your parents—you! Therefore, no matter what anyone tells you, answer the form truthfully. I can't tell you how many times I've heard applicants say, "My recruiter told me not to say anything about . . ." The truth is that some recruiters may ask applicants to conceal potentially disqualifying information; however, the bottom line is that it is your signature on that form, not your recruiter's. When it comes down to it, it'll be your word against your recruiter's if it is found that you have lied on the SF 93; who do you think they'll believe?

Another problem that occurs when completing this form is "phantom illnesses." These are medical conditions that the applicant never had but was either told he did or were self-diagnosed. A common phantom illness tends to be childhood asthma. Asthma, at any age, is a non-waiverable condition, yet every day applicants claim to have had asthma as a child when, in fact, they never did.

More paperwork?

Quite often, parents tell their children they have asthma when they don't. It could be for one of a number of reasons. Mom doesn't want Johnny to play on the school football team, so she tells him he has asthma, or maybe, it's the infamous "trick" knee or a heart murmur. Chances are that if you've never been treated by a doctor for the illness, you've probably never had it to begin with.

Along the same lines, don't become so afraid of "lying" on the form that you start to self-diagnose and make yourself ineligible for enlistment. My own son almost fell into this trap. When filling out the SF 93, he came to the question about "frequent trouble sleeping." He was about to answer yes when I asked him why. It turns out that for about two weeks prior to that time he was studying for finals, was worried about the upcoming SAT and was anxious about college applications. This caused him some restless nights. This, however, did not warrant a "yes" response to the question about frequent trouble sleeping. Just as being out of breath after running three miles would not justify a yes to the question about "shortness of breath."

A good rule of thumb is that if you are about to answer yes to any question, ask for clarification. Review the sample SF 93 contained in Appendix G with your parents or anyone else who may have knowledge of your medical history. If you can answer yes to any of the questions, ask your recruiter if it would help to provide documentation to explain your illness or injury. Providing documentation often will allow the MEPS medical personnel to clear you on that particular item without the need for further tests.

What to Do if You Are Disqualified

Hopefully, you will be able to get through the MEPS physical without any problems; however, sometimes applicants become medically disqualified. You may be permanently disqualified (PDQ), which, as the name implies, is not a good thing; or you may receive temporary disqualification (TDQ), which, of course is not good, but it is better than being PDQ.

There are several reasons why you may be temporarily disqualified. You may have a particular condition that requires you to wait a period of time to ensure you are completely healed. For example, spontaneous pneumothorax (collapsed lung) is disqualifying for a period of three years following the incident. You may also be temporarily disqualified if more tests or documentation are needed before the MEPS physician can make a final determination. In that case, you may be sent for a consultation by the MEPS, you may be required to return to your own doctor for follow-up or you may have to provide hospital and other medical records. Ultimately, the end result will be either passing the physical or becoming PDQ.

Luckily, even if you are permanently disqualified, there is a chance that you can be granted a medical waiver. Waivers are the military's way of saying, "We know that you are not physically qualified, but in your case, we'll make an exception."

No one will offer you a medical waiver; you must request one. If you are PDQ on the MEPS physical, inform your recruiter that you want to be considered for a medical waiver. Asking for a waiver does not guarantee that you will get one. You may have to undergo more tests (at your own expense) or provide more documentation. Remember that there are certain illnesses and injuries that are not waiverable, no matter what.

Report of Medical Examination (SF 88)

An example of the Report of Medical Examination (SF 88) is contained in Appendix G. The SF 88 is the actual form used as your physical report. I have provided an example so that you can see just how thorough a physical exam you will be receiving. If you have any questions about the physical exam, ask your recruiter or the MEPS physical examination personnel.

BACKGROUND SCREENING

Your background screening actually began with your first meeting with your recruiter. More than likely, she asked you about any criminal offenses, including traffic infractions, that you might have committed. Depending on what you told her, she made a preliminary decision on your acceptability for enlistment. After you decided to move ahead with the enlistment process, your recruiter may have been required to run police checks to determine past and present criminal charges.

As discussed in an earlier chapter, one mistake many people make is not disclosing offenses that occurred when they were juveniles. Most people don't intentionally mean to deceive their recruiters, but, rather they were told by the court that their records would be expunged after a certain period of time and that they would never have to report the offense to anyone. Unfortunately, that's not true.

In all likelihood, expunged offenses will not be recorded in checks reported by local police agencies; however, your background check will go way beyond the local agencies your recruiter contacted. The formal, in-depth, no-holds-barred background screening will begin at the MEPS.

When I was a recruiter, I would brief my applicants that the MEPS personnel would pull no punches when "asking" them about prior law violations. I would rather have dealt with a criminal offense that might have been taken care of with an enlistment waiver than have an applicant not tell me about the incident and then later admit to it at the MEPS. Unfortunately, not all recruiters will push their applicants this hard when asking about law violations. The old adage "ignorance is bliss" does not apply here.

Earlier in this chapter, I advised you to never allow anyone to influence the way you answer questions regarding your health; the same applies to questions regarding law violations. You alone will be held accountable if it is found that you lied about involvement with the law. If a recruiter tells you "Don't worry about mentioning it" or "That's not important enough to list" or makes any similar statement, find another recruiter.

You should be able to go to the MEPS with a clear conscience; you should have nothing to hide. If your recruiter is doing his job properly, you will have any necessary waivers approved (if needed) prior to your MEPS processing. Therefore, you have nothing to worry about during the background-screening portion of your processing.

Your recruiter may not want to push you for answers regarding law violations, but I guarantee you that the MEPS personnel will. You will be threatened with fines and even jail time. They may even try to coerce you into "confessing" with statements like, "Everyone your age has at least one speeding ticket; do you expect me to believe that you don't even have one ticket?"

Don't take this line of questioning personally. Remember the main purpose of the MEPS is to ensure that only qualified applicants are able to enlist in the military. You may be the most honest and law-abiding applicant ever to go through MEPS processing, but the MEPS staff has no way of knowing that. Answer the questions fully and to the best of your ability, and you will have no problems. Remember that if you divulged all information regarding law violations to your recruiter and he determined you weren't morally qualified for enlistment, you wouldn't even be at MEPS.

The "investigation" into your background does not stop at the MEPS. Depending on the branch of service for which you enlist and the job you select, you will receive a more in-depth background check that may include agents actually interviewing friends, relatives and teachers. My own experience with my background check was quite interesting, which you'll see in the next section.

Fingerprinting is required for all applicants.

Drug Involvement

Just as with law violations, your recruiter will have asked you about involvement with illegal drugs (and improper use of prescribed drugs). You should have been briefed on your particular service's policy on drug usage. Whatever that service's policy on past drug use is, one thing is universal among all the services: There is zero tolerance for current drug use by their applicants.

Also as with law violations, the MEPS personnel will push you hard to disclose any drug involvement, past or present. And rest assured that you would not be at the MEPS if you disclosed anything disqualifying concerning drugs to your recruiter.

Once again, if anyone tells you to withhold the truth, don't do it. You alone are responsible for the answers you give. A running joke among recruiters is how some recruiters ask applicants about previous drug usage. Instead of asking "Have you ever, or are you currently now, using any illegal drugs?" they may say, "You haven't ever taken any illegal drugs, have you?" Of course the latter statement would lead an applicant to assume that he'd better say no or be disqualified. In this case, the recruiter hasn't actually told the applicant to lie, but he hasn't asked for the truth either.

You may think that you can outsmart the system by withholding information about prior drug usage. After all, if you've never been arrested on a drug charge, how will they ever know? Think again. Consider the following stories, the first of which is about my own background check that was conducted when I enlisted in the Navy.

The job I was being trained for required a "Top Secret" security clearance, which meant that agents would interview people from my past. One person they decided to interview was a friend of mine. When they asked him if he had ever known me to take any drugs, he thought it would be funny to say yes. One thing you should know about these agents is that they have no sense of humor. Fortunately for me, my friend realized that in a hurry and told them he was only kidding. Had I been involved with drugs in the past, it is quite possible that someone would have told them.

The second story concerns a fellow recruit during Basic Training. Because the military wants to ensure that only qualified individuals become part of their team, you will be asked about your history throughout the enlistment process, and it doesn't stop at the MEPS. Because you are not fully a member of the military until your graduation from Basic Training, the questioning continues there.

If we were asked once, we were asked a thousand times about our usage of drugs. One day a fellow recruit walked into the barracks, and he looked as if someone had shot his dog. I asked him what was wrong, and all he could say was "They found out, somehow they found out." Of course, I had to ask, "They found out what?" "They found out that I once took a puff of a marijuana cigarette at a party."

How could they have possibly found out that information? As it turns out, they hadn't known a thing. They used the "technique" of coercing him by saying, "We know you tried marijuana at least once, everyone has." He packed his belongings, and we never saw him again. Had he told his recruiter about his one time use of marijuana, odds are he would have been marching with the rest of us at graduation.

Drug Testing

You will be subjected to drug testing at the MEPS at initial processing and then again when you leave for Basic Training. Here is a sure-fire way of ensuring that you don't come up positive on the drug test: Don't do drugs! As you are probably aware, the length of time that traces of a drug will stay in your system depends on the drug. Marijuana, for instance, can stay in your system for up to a month. I've heard of people doing all kinds of crazy things because they were told it would beat the drug test, like drinking enough water to fill a fish tank or, my favorite, drinking a bottle of vinegar. A word of advice about tricks to get around drug testing: They don't work!

One more thing about drug tests: Get used to them. All military branches conduct random urinalysis exams to detect drugs. What that means is that at any time during your military career you can be asked to undergo drug testing. Would you want to fly in an airplane if there was a chance that the pilot or the mechanic who works on the plane used drugs?

THE JOB SEARCH

Depending on the branch of service, the purpose of the job search at MEPS may be to choose the actual job for which you will enlist or to choose one or more jobs for which you qualify and will be put on a waiting list. Either way, your service branch MEPS liaison will be the individual who conducts the search. Ultimately, the following criteria will be used to determine which jobs you are qualified for:

- Physical profile
- ASVAB scores

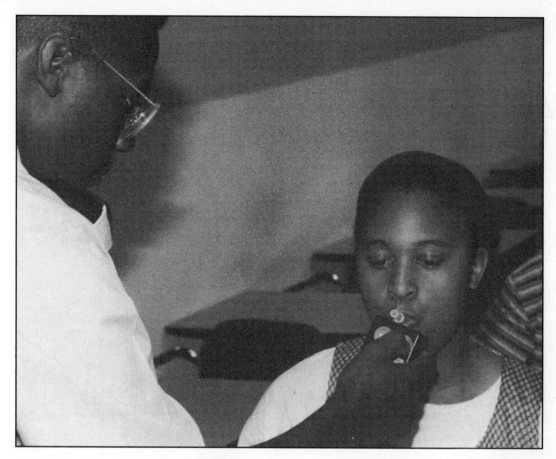

MEPS processing includes alcohol tests for all applicants.

- Record of criminal offenses
- Specialized test scores (if applicable)
- Gender (for certain jobs)
- Citizenship

Perhaps the best of all recruiters, the MEPS liaison will sit down with you to discuss your options. It is his job to match your needs with those of the branch he represents. The key to getting the job you want is flexibility.

Flexibility in the Job Search

The availability of jobs at any particular time is based on several factors. They include

- Current and projected vacancies in the particular career field
- The projected number of openings for classes
- The number of other applicants seeking particular career fields

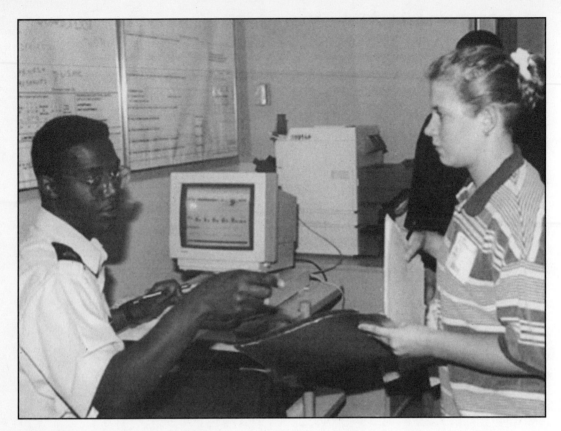

An Army applicant ready for the job search.

The military strives to ensure that all available technical school class seats are full. This makes filling those class seats one of the biggest factors in job availability. Because of this, you can increase the chances of getting the job you want by being flexible in when you are available to leave for Basic Training. For example, by leaving in October instead of November, you may be able to get a particular job because of the availability of a technical school seat. Of course, there may be factors that would prevent you from being flexible in your availability, such as your current school commitments (especially for high school seniors). Because you may remain in the Delayed Entry Program (DEP) for a maximum of 365 days, it may be impossible for you to be flexible in your timing.

Another way you can increase your chances of getting a job you want is to be flexible enough to look for a job category rather than a specific job. In other words, you may be interested in mechanics, administrative work or the medical field. Lots of jobs in the military are closely related to one another. By choosing a job in a particular "field," you will increase your chances of getting something you want.

Appendix A is entirely devoted to explaining the various "occupational fields" in each of the military branches. Spend some time reviewing the section pertaining to the branch for which you are enlisting prior to your MEPS processing. Highlight some of the fields that sound interesting to you even if you've never considered going into (or in some cases never heard of) that field before.

Be open-minded. When I enlisted in the Navy, I chose electronics as my career category. Because I liked to work on cars, I wanted something to do with mechanics; I never even thought of electronics as an option. When I listened to what the MEPS liaison had to say about electronics, it sounded interesting to me and I decided to go for it. The ASVAB showed I had the potential to excel in the electronics field, a career I would never had considered on my own. It's okay to go to the MEPS with a certain job or job category in mind, but also be flexible enough to consider other options.

Advanced Pay Grade

Most people enter the military at the lowest possible pay grade (or rank), E-1. As you'll see in Appendix B, the E-1 is called by different names depending on the service; however, all services utilize the E-1 through E-9 scale to identify (and pay) their enlisted personnel.

Sometimes, however, individuals may enter the military at a higher pay grade (usually E-2 or E-3). Depending on the service, a higher pay grade may be granted based on one of the following:

- College credits earned
- Participation in organizations such as high school JROTC or the sea cadets
- Job selection

Even though you may qualify for a higher pay grade, everyone is treated the same at Basic Training, and there is no rank distinction made. However, you will be paid at the higher pay level even during Basic Training, and you will be able to "sew on" the rank immediately after graduation. If you are entitled to enlist at a higher pay grade, make sure it is in your enlistment contract. (See Appendix B for basic pay scales for each grade.)

It's Okay to Say No

As I stated earlier, it is the MEPS liaison's job to match applicants with available vacancies. Just as a car dealership will push their remaining year-end leftovers, MEPS liaisons will push their "leftovers."

Although you should be pretty certain that the reason you came to the MEPS was to enlist that day, do not be pressured into taking a job choice with which you are not comfortable. Chances are that if you hold your ground you will be offered a job that appeals to you. The MEPS liaison tries to fill the vacancies that have been rejected by other applicants before the vacancies that he knows he will have no problem filling.

Watch for the "impending doom" approach, such as "If you don't leave by a certain date, you will not be able to get a particular job." Although I've told you to remain flexible, don't do anything you are uncomfortable with. Therefore, if you requested to leave in two months and are told that the job you want is available only if you leave in one month, ask if it will be available if you leave in four months instead.

There may be times, however, when the impending doom approach may be legitimate. For instance, an enlistment bonus may be offered for a limited time, and you may have to enlist by a specified date in order to qualify for it. Another example is what occurred in the 1980s: The military changed its method of calculating retirement pay to a less attractive method. At that time, there was a rush to get people enlisted so that they could enlist under the "old" retirement plan.

If all else fails and you are unable to get the job you want (assuming, of course, that you are qualified for that job), there is no shame in going home without enlisting. If this is the case, you may want to check with another service to see if they have a similar job available. Please note that I am not advocating going from branch to branch until you find what you want (you should have already decided which branch will best meet your needs), but in extreme cases, it may be the best solution.

You should, however, keep in close contact with your recruiter in the event that an opening does come up. In most cases, you will find that something will become available (usually at the end of the month).

A Word about Enlistment Bonuses

From time to time, the various services will offer enlistment bonuses for individuals who are willing to enlist in certain career fields. I encountered this a lot when I was a Navy recruiter. An applicant would tell me that the only thing holding him back was the fact that the Army would give him a $5,000 enlistment bonus if he enlisted in "Field Artillery" for four years. While there is nothing wrong with being in Field Artillery, I knew that I could offer certain applicants much more. I would approach those applicants by saying, "Are you willing to do something you really don't want to do for four years for an additional $1,250 per year? $104.17 a month? $3.36 a day? And don't forget the difference in the length of training and college credits by attending the more technical Navy schools." I never lost one applicant to the Army's enlistment bonus!

Are you willing to take a job you don't want for the enlistment bonus? You may, especially if you are joining the military for the experience more than specific training or if you are joining just so you can qualify for the educational benefits.

Negotiation Is Key

Perhaps the most important part of the entire enlistment process, getting the job you want may come down to how well you can negotiate with the MEPS liaison. But by being flexible and by holding your ground, you will be on your way to receiving the best training available!

THE OATH OF ENLISTMENT

After you've met all of the requirements for enlistment and have conducted your job search with the MEPS liaison, it will be time for you to do the one thing you came to the MEPS to do in the first place: enlist!

More than likely, you will enter the Delayed Entry Program (DEP), and therefore this will be the first of two enlistment oaths you will take prior to leaving for Basic Training. The first is an oath to enter the DEP (which puts you in a non-participating reserve status); the second is taken on the day you leave for Basic Training, which officially puts you on active duty.

The oath of enlistment is a solemn ceremony conducted by a military officer. It has a long tradition and should not be entered into lightly. You, as well as other applicants processing for all the different services, will assemble in a room. The officer will stand in front of you, with the United States flag in the background, and ask you to raise your right hand and repeat the following words:

I, [state your name], do solemnly swear (or affirm) that I will support and defend the Constitution of the United States against all enemies, foreign and domestic; that I will bear true faith and allegiance to the same; and that I will obey the orders of the President of the United States and the orders of the officers appointed over me, according to regulations and the Uniform Code of Military Justice. So help me God.

I invite you to read the oath again, and this time think about what its words mean to you. Most times, applicants are not given ample time to read and understand the meaning of the oath before they are asked to recite and sign it. This is understandable considering the amount of paperwork that must be reviewed and signed by an applicant during MEPS processing.

Can you get out of going into the military after taking the oath and "swearing into" the DEP? The answer is, without a doubt, absolutely yes; however, I would urge you not to make a commitment you don't intend to keep. It's sort of like proposing to your girlfriend when you have no intention of ever going through with the wedding. I'll cover this in depth in chapter five.

Taking the oath of enlistment.

Processing for Reserve Components

MEPS processing differs somewhat for applicants enlisting in the reserve components. Depending on the branch of service, applicants may do their job search and oath of enlistment at their reserve unit instead of the MEPS. The following table outlines the procedure for each reserve branch. I must reiterate that policy and processes do change from time to time, so confirm the current procedures with your recruiter.

PROCEDURE PERFORMED AT MEPS?

	Job Search	Oath of Enlistment
Air Force Reserve	No	No
Air National Guard	No	No
Army Reserve	Yes	No
Army National Guard	No	Yes
Coast Guard Reserve	No	Yes
Marine Reserve	No	Yes
Navy Reserve	No	No

Now What?

Once you've completed your oath of enlistment, you should be done for the day. It'll probably be late afternoon by then. You'll be returned to your MEPS liaison, who will ensure that you have all the proper paperwork, and then you will be sent on your way. You will, more than likely, be using the same form of transportation that got you to the MEPS; check with the MEPS liaison just in case there's a change in plans.

If your recruiter is not picking you up at the MEPS, I suggest you phone him the next day if you haven't heard from him. Make sure that the information you were given at the MEPS agrees with the information he was given. This includes

- The job you received
- The length of enlistment
- Ship date (the date you leave for Basic Training)
- Amount of any enlistment bonus
- The pay grade (or rank) you were promised

If for some reason the information does not match, take care of it immediately! Do not put off getting it taken care of, and do not allow your recruiter to put it off. If your recruiter does put it off, contact the MEPS liaison right away (he should have given you his card during your MEPS processing). If it's not on the contract you received from the MEPS, it hasn't been promised to you. So, if you met the qualifications to enter the military as an E-2 and the MEPS liaison told you that you'll receive E-2, but for some reason it was left out of the contract, it needs to be fixed immediately. If your recruiter says, "They'll take care of it when you leave for Basic Training," he's 100 percent mistaken. The same goes for any discrepancies in your contract.

You will be required to keep in regular contact with your recruiter during the time you spend in DEP status (more about this in chapter five).

As I mentioned in the beginning of this chapter, the MEPS is in no way representative of military life. By now you have realized that I like to use a lot of comparisons of the enlistment processing to buying a car, and the MEPS is one case where it is completely opposite. When you walk into a car dealership to purchase a car, you are usually treated very well and everyone is willing to bend over backwards to help you. It isn't until after the sale is made and you have to come back to have your car serviced that you are ignored and treated rudely. If you think of the military applicant as a customer, just the opposite happens at the MEPS. The whole attitude changes once you've taken the oath of enlistment. It is then that you are officially a member of the "team" and will be treated as such. Before then, you are an outsider trying to gain membership and, of course, have to meet the membership requirements.

I don't want to give the impression that the MEPS personnel are all mean-spirited people who have nothing better to do than make your life miserable. However, most applicants have never been through an experience like MEPS processing, and to them their day at the MEPS will be one experience they will most likely never forget.

In addition to reading this chapter on MEPS processing, you should ask your recruiter questions about anything you are not 100 percent clear on, such as

- How am I getting to the MEPS for processing and then home afterward?
- Will I be required to take additional tests at the MEPS?
- What time will the recruiter pick me up, or what time do I need to be at the MEPS?
- Will I be staying at a hotel overnight?
- Do I need to bring any medical records with me?

Of course, there are hundreds of other questions that could be asked, and don't be afraid to do so. In addition, in 1999 MEPS produced a short video entitled A Day at The MEPS. This video, although not very detailed, gives a general overview of MEPS processing. Ask your recruiter to show it to you.

Dos and Don'ts

I would like to close this chapter with a few Dos and Don'ts concerning MEPS processing. Your recruiter, hopefully, should have discussed the following "rules" of the MEPS with you; if he did, then consider this a reminder. In most cases, not complying with these rules will result in the termination of your MEPS processing.

- Bring your Social Security card, birth certificate and driver's license.
- Remove earrings prior to going to the MEPS.
- Profanity and offensive wording or pictures on clothing is not tolerated.
- Hats are not permitted inside the MEPS.
- If you wear either eyeglasses or contacts, bring them along with your prescription and lens case.
- Bathe or shower either the morning of or the night before your processing.
- Wear (clean) underclothes.
- Wear neat, moderate, comfortable clothing.
- Don't bring stereo headphones, watches, jewelry, excessive cash, or any other valuables.
- Conduct yourself in a proper manner, don't use profanity and be polite.
- Report on time.

Chapter Summary

Now that you've made it over the biggest hurdle of the enlistment process, the Military Entrance Processing Station (MEPS), you'll want to make certain that nothing gets in your way before leaving for Basic Training. The next chapter will help prepare you to keep yourself qualified to enter the military.

5 CONGRATULATIONS! YOU'VE ENLISTED: STAYING OUT OF TROUBLE UNTIL YOU'RE OFF TO BASIC TRAINING

Many, if not most, applicants wind up in a Delayed Entry Program (DEP). In this status, the applicant has already sworn in and is awaiting his or her "ship date" to Basic Training. As an enlistee, you can remain in DEP status for up to a year. A lot can happen between the day you swear in and the day you ship. This chapter will discuss things to avoid, keeping in shape and keeping the recruiter informed.

The Delayed Entry Program

Now that you have taken the oath of enlistment, you are no longer an applicant and are now referred to as a DEPer (pronounced **depper**). As a member of the Delayed Entry Program (DEP), you are technically already a member of the military. You have taken an oath of enlistment and are therefore bound to maintain yourself physically, mentally and morally.

Although you have already sworn in once, you will have to swear in one more time on the day you leave for Basic Training. There are, however, many things that may stand in your way of getting to swear in that second time:

- Medical problems that may arise (including injuries)
- Law violations (including traffic violations)
- Weight gain that puts you over the maximum allowable weight (MAW)
- Not graduating from high school (for those who enlisted as high school seniors)
- Becoming pregnant while in the DEP
- Becoming involved in a pending law suit
- Drug usage while in the DEP

While some of these disqualifiers may be out of the DEPer's control, the majority can be avoided.

Medical Problems

Although most medical problems cannot be avoided, some can. For instance, if you've never skydived before, don't wait until you are in the DEP to try it. A broken leg takes time to heal, and if you wind up having pins in your leg, you've just permanently disqualified yourself. On the other hand, having an emergency appendectomy cannot be avoided.

In most cases medical problems that arise while in the DEP are temporarily, rather than permanently, disqualifying. Many times, your "ship date" can be postponed to accommodate the necessary healing period. However, remember that you can only remain in a DEP status for a period of 365 days. Therefore, if the required healing period would put you over the maximum 365 days, you will be discharged from the DEP. If this happens, you will be required to swear in to the DEP again once your condition has healed. More than likely, you will have also lost your job reservation and must go through the job counseling process again, too.

Another situation that may occur is the need for a medical waiver. Just as certain conditions require waiver approval for initial enlistment processing, those same conditions would require a waiver if they occur while you are in the DEP. A waiver may or may not be granted and, depending on the reason for the waiver, may preclude you from certain jobs.

The key to ensuring that you will not encounter problems when it is time to "ship" to Basic Training is keeping your recruiter informed. If you were treated for pneumonia, for instance, don't wait six months—when it is time to leave for Basic Training—to tell your recruiter. Let him know as soon as possible so that he may take the necessary actions. He may require medical records or tests before you are cleared for enlistment. In addition, you may be required to return to the MEPS for further evaluation. If you let your recruiter know early enough, it may not even affect your original "ship" date. If you wait, you may find yourself being delayed by months.

KEEPING YOURSELF HEALTHY

To increase your chances of staying healthy while in the DEP, avoid any activity that may result in serious injury (such as skydiving). Also avoid situations that may expose you to disease. For instance, if your little brother has measles and you've never had them before, you should avoid contact with him. Maintain a healthy diet and exercise regularly; this will keep you in good shape and make you less susceptible to illness. Also, use common sense in your activities, use the appropriate protective gear when playing sports, wear a helmet while bicycling, use your car's seatbelts and, most of all, don't take risks with your personal safety.

Law Violations

Law violations keep many people from being able to ship to Basic Training and are perhaps the most easily avoided ways to get yourself disqualified while in the DEP.

A law violation as simple as a minor traffic ticket can disqualify you from enlistment, especially if you have already been granted an enlistment waiver for previous law violations. Law violations while in the

DEP may also make it necessary for you to be granted a waiver prior to enlistment. The course of action depends on the severity of the violation and on your past history. For instance, if you had no history of previous law violations and were ticketed for running a stop sign, your recruiter would more than likely just have you mention it at the MEPS before you swear into Active Duty. If, however, it was a more serious violation, she may have to initiate the waiver process.

As with medical problems, it is important that you let your recruiter know as soon as possible of any law violations that have occurred while you are in the DEP. If you fail to tell her, you may find yourself leaving the MEPS bound for home instead of Basic Training on ship day.

AVOIDING PROBLEMS

While some law violations occur by accident, such as absentmindedly changing lanes without signaling, most do not. Therefore, drive as if there is always a police car in your rearview mirror.

In addition to traffic violations, avoid committing other crimes as well. Shoplifting, fighting and underage drinking will all get you into trouble. Of course, more serious crimes will also cause problems for you and may permanently disqualify you from military service. Most importantly, if you are under 21, don't consume alcohol. Sadly, many DEPers have been charged with underage drinking while attending their own going away parties.

PAYING FINES

If you find yourself in a situation that requires you to pay a fine, make sure that the fine is paid promptly. Unpaid fines will keep you from going to Basic Training. When I decided to enlist in the military, I had just received a traffic ticket (my first) and determined that I would go to court rather than pay the fine because I knew that I was not guilty. My recruiter put it this way, "Pay the fine, and you can leave for Basic Training; or, you can wait and go to court, where you'll probably be found guilty anyway and have to pay the fine." I paid the fine.

WHAT IF I'M PERMANENTLY DISQUALIFIED?

If you find yourself permanently disqualified from enlisting based on law violations while in the DEP, you may still have a chance of getting into the military, depending on the severity of the violation. Although all the military branches have similar standards, they are not all the same. Therefore, if you find yourself being discharged from the DEP, talk to the recruiters of the other branches and see what they can do for you. You may find that one service may waiver something another service cannot.

Weight Gain

If you gain weight while in the DEP and wind up exceeding the maximum allowable weight (MAW) for your height, you really have only two choices: you can lose the weight or you can grow a few inches. Since you don't have much control over your height, the only real solution is to lose the weight.

Since most people who end up exceeding their MAW while in DEP were close to the maximum weight when they went into the DEP, most recruiters will keep closer tabs on those individuals to ensure they stay within standards. However, it is up to you—not your recruiter—to watch your weight. Maintaining a healthy diet and sticking to a regular exercise program will go a long way toward helping you remain within weight standards. Avoid overeating, and despite what your mother tells you, it's okay to leave some food on your plate.

Check your weight regularly, and use your recruiter's scale when you can. If you find that you have gained weight and are either over or close to the MAW, let your recruiter know. Ideally, you should be seeing your recruiter from time to time while you are in the DEP, and he should be checking your weight on a regular basis. If he doesn't, you need to let him know about your problem. If you arrive at the MEPS to ship and you are overweight, you will find yourself embarrassed and on your way back home instead of on your way to Basic Training.

To get an idea what the maximum (and minimum) allowable weights for your height and gender are, look at the following chart. Although it represents the Air Force standards, all the services are more or less the same when it comes to weight standards.

TYPICAL MILITARY WEIGHT STANDARDS

Height (in inches)	MALE Minimum Weight	MALE Maximum Weight	FEMALE Minimum Weight	FEMALE Maximum Weight
58	98	149	88	132
59	99	151	90	134
60	100	153	92	136
61	102	155	95	138
62	103	158	97	141
63	104	160	100	142
64	105	164	103	146
65	106	169	106	150
66	107	174	108	155
67	111	179	111	159
68	115	184	114	164
69	119	189	117	168
70	123	194	119	173
71	127	199	122	177
72	131	205	125	182
73	135	211	128	188
74	139	218	130	194
75	143	224	133	199
76	147	230	136	205
77	151	236	139	210
78	153	242	141	215
79	157	248	144	221
80	161	254	147	226

NOTE: Fractions of an inch are rounded to the closest inch.

Failure to Graduate from High School

Although some of the branches may take a non-high school graduate (depending on ASVAB scores), I recommend that you complete high school prior to enlisting, even if it means that you must be discharged from the DEP in order to do it. One reason for this recommendation is that non-graduates are usually not qualified to receive the same educational benefits that are afforded high school graduates. If the educational benefits were one of your motivators for enlisting, it becomes a non-issue if you fail to graduate from high school.

A recruiter that pressures you into enlisting without a high school diploma has only one person's best interests in mind, and I can assure you it's not yours!

If you enlisted as a high school senior and then fail to graduate, you may be able to remain in the DEP if you can complete summer school and then graduate. If that is not possible, you'll be discharged from the DEP and may be able to go back into the DEP depending on your chances of graduating the next school year.

AVOIDING PROBLEMS

You can avoid problems by doing your best in school, by not cutting classes and by ensuring that you are taking enough classes to graduate. Get actively involved in your class schedule; do not assume that your guidance counselor will take care of you. If you are having problems in a particular subject, get help. Ask your teacher what you can do to improve your grades, and seek one-on-one tutoring if necessary. Inform your recruiter as soon as possible if there is a chance that you will not graduate so that she can determine the proper course of action.

Pregnancy while in DEP

Becoming pregnant while in DEP (a situation that happens all too often) will, of course, disqualify you for enlistment.

Terminating a pregnancy while in the DEP will require medical documentation and review by the MEPS physicians. Although some women try to conceal the fact that they have terminated a pregnancy, it can be easily detected when you return to the MEPS for shipping to Basic Training. Once again, the key is to keep your recruiter informed. Of course there are ways to prevent this situation from happening in the first place, but it is not the intent of this book to discuss the various methods of preventing unwanted pregnancy.

Although male DEPers do not have to worry about becoming pregnant while in the DEP, there is a chance that they will be named as the father in a paternity case, which will, in fact, make them just as disqualified for enlistment.

Pending Lawsuits

There really is not much that can be said about pending lawsuits other than if you become involved in one, you will become temporarily disqualified for enlistment. This applies to you not only if you have been named in a suit but also if you are bringing the suit against someone else.

All you can do to protect yourself is to ensure that you are able to settle any matters without the need to go to court. If someone threatens to sue you, take him seriously and try to settle things before a lawsuit is filed.

If you are the one who is threatening a lawsuit, consider bringing suit at a later date since there is nothing barring you from initiating a lawsuit as a military member. Just make sure that there is no statute of limitations to deal with.

If you must go to court as a member of the DEP, try to get matters handled as quickly as possible. Ask for an early court date, if possible, and if you are being represented by an attorney, let her know of your situation.

If all else fails, you may need to be discharged from the DEP or have your ship date postponed. Whatever the case, let your recruiter know of a pending lawsuit as soon as possible so that he may determine what needs to be done.

Drug Usage

If you want to be discharged from the DEP and probably barred from enlisting again, then taking illegal drugs is the easiest way to do it. Drug usage of any type is not acceptable in the DEP or on Active Duty, no matter what the circumstances.

Although not probable, it is possible that you may be granted a waiver for drug usage while in the DEP. More than likely, however, you will be discharged from the DEP and permanently disqualified.

Some branches of the service are more lenient than others, so it is possible that if you are discharged from one branch, another branch may be willing to grant you an enlistment waiver. There are no second chances, however, and after being granted a waiver, if there is a "next time," it will be your last.

AVOIDING PROBLEMS

Since there is zero tolerance for drug usage in all the military branches, you will be required to remain drug-free throughout your enlistment. If that is going to be a problem for you, then the military is not the place for you. If, however, you are not a drug user but are tempted by peer pressure to use drugs while in DEP, I have one thing to say: Don't!

You will be required to undergo drug testing prior to leaving for Basic Training, and since certain drugs can remain in your system for quite a while, there is a good chance that they will show up in the drug screening. The bottom line is that you should not use illegal drugs while in DEP, and if you do, you must tell your recruiter.

What if I Keep My Mouth Shut?

Many people think that they can beat the system by withholding information, whether about a medical problem, a law violation or drug usage. The truth is, many of these people do "cheat" the system and become members of the military despite problems they had while in the DEP.

One thing these people can (and should) count on, however, is that these problems have a good chance of catching up with them after they have become military members, whether it is disclosed during a background check, a routine physical examination or a drug screening. The only difference is that if they had disclosed the information while in the DEP, the worst that would have happened would be a discharge from the DEP. As members of the military, they are held accountable under the Uniform Code of Military Justice (UCMJ), which can impose jail time, fines and, of course, discharge under less-than-honorable conditions.

This section has covered many of the potential problems that may occur while in the DEP that might keep a DEPer from going to Basic Training. Of course, not all situations can be addressed; however, a good rule of thumb is that if you have contact with a doctor, a lawyer, a judge, the police or drugs, you should contact your recruiter for guidance.

If your recruiter tells you to forget about it, ask him if it would be okay to reveal the information at the MEPS when you leave for Basic Training. If he says no, tell him that you are uncomfortable with concealing the information.

Getting Yourself Physically Conditioned for Basic Training

Although you may already be in good shape, chances are you could use a little help in preparing yourself physically for Basic Training. If you already maintain a rigorous workout routine, you can skip this section. If, however, you are like most people, you'll want to read this section and put it into practice.

You'll want to get started early on conditioning yourself for Basic Training. Don't wait for the last minute to start exercising. It will be significantly less stressful for you to show up for Basic Training in good shape. You will be able to concentrate on the other aspects of Basic Training rather than worrying about whether or not you'll make the run or be able to do enough push-ups.

When you arrive at Basic Training, there will be minimum physical requirements that you must meet. Most people in reasonable shape are able to meet those requirements. As time goes by, those requirements become more and more difficult.

This is the way you should work your exercise program: start off slow and work your way up to a more stringent and demanding workout. You may have to modify your program depending on your current level of fitness and how much time you have until you leave for Basic Training.

At a minimum you should work on:

- Running
- Push-ups
- Sit-ups
- Pull-ups

RUNNING

Running is one of my least favorite things to do—and it is something you'll do a lot of in Basic Training. If you are not a runner now, you may begin by walking, which can progress into a jog and, finally, running. At first you should strive for distance instead of speed. Although you will have to complete timed runs during Basic Training, it is important for you to build up endurance.

Before you begin to run, you should buy a good pair of well-fitting running shoes. Running in shoes not designed for that purpose is a good way to cause discomfort, pain and even injury.

The best way to start running is to run with a partner, especially if that person regularly runs. Having someone to run with who is able to push you along will help you build up the necessary endurance. If you are in high school or college, join the track team or cross-country team. This is a good way for you to get the practice you need.

You should utilize a track for running, if available. Running in the street poses many dangers, such as being struck by a vehicle, twisting your ankle or falling on uneven pavement and, of course, getting chased by the occasional unfriendly dog. Although a treadmill could be used if the weather doesn't permit running outside, it should not be used as a substitute for running on a track (they are just not the same thing).

You should plan on running about three times a week and gradually work up to the distance and time requirements that are listed in the next chapter for your particular branch of service.

PUSH-UPS

You will, no doubt, hear the following phrase more times than you could ever imagine while at Basic Training: "Get down and give me twenty!" That "twenty," of course, refers to twenty push-ups. Besides a form of exercise, push-ups are used as a form of punishment at Basic Training. And, because of this, you will be required to do a lot of push-ups in your short stay at Basic Training.

If you've never done push-ups before, you should seek the help of someone who has, including gym teachers (if you are in high school), trainers at the health club, your recruiter or friends. The key to doing more push-ups is practice. The more you practice, the more push-ups you will be able to do. It's that simple!

You should consult the next chapter for the minimum number of push-ups that you'll be required to do at Basic Training, and then shoot for doubling that number.

SIT-UPS

Just as with push-ups, you can significantly increase the number of sit-ups you can do by simple repetition. The more you practice, the more sit-ups you'll be able to do.

Do your sit-ups with a partner holding your feet down. Besides keeping you steady, your partner can help motivate you to do more sit-ups. Do as many sit-ups as you can, and then do five more!

Sit-ups have the added benefit of tightening the abdominal muscles. More than likely, you will be sore at first from doing sit-ups; therefore, you should alternate days between sit-ups.

PULL-UPS

Perhaps the most difficult exercise for most people, pull-ups will only become easier with practice.

When I went to Officer Training School (OTS) at age 26, I had not done a single pull-up in at least eight years. To say it was difficult for me to do the required four pull-ups would be an understatement. However, at the end of the twelve weeks of OTS, after many hours of practice, I was doing many more than the minimum amount of pull-ups.

Again, as with push-ups and sit-ups, the key to doing more pull-ups is practice. And, as with sit-ups, the use of a partner to motivate you will help you achieve your desired goal. Besides offering verbal encouragement, you may want your partner to help support your legs while doing the pull-ups. To do this, bend your legs at the knees, and have your partner hold the bottom part of your legs and give you a little support. Do not have your partner do all the work for you, but instead give you an added boost.

You will find that, over time, you will be able to do many more pull-ups than you ever imagined.

Joining a Gym (Health Club)

If you have the resources and the time, you may consider joining a local gym and do your workouts there. Besides having a great deal of exercise equipment available at your disposal, most gyms have trainers available for advice, guidance, encouragement and instruction. If you cannot afford a health club membership, consider the local YMCA/YWCA, or if you are a high school student, consider asking your gym teacher for help and advice.

Wherever you do your workout, make sure that you maintain a routine of three days per week. The sooner you start your exercise program, the more you'll be physically prepared for Basic Training.

DEP Commander's Call

Most recruiters hold a monthly meeting with all of their DEPers (usually referred to as DEP Commander's Call). These meetings have many purposes:

- Exposing the DEPers to marching (known as drill at Basic Training)
- Helping DEPers get into physical shape for Basic Training
- Teaching DEPers military and branch-specific history
- Teaching DEPers about life in the military, including military terminology and rank structure
- Keeping face-to-face contact with DEPers to ensure they are staying out of "trouble"

In the absence of DEP Commander's Calls, your recruiter should be requesting a face-to-face meeting with you at least once a month. If that isn't happening, I suggest that you make it happen! Visit your recruiter every month and let him know what is going on. If you have been close to your MAW, jump on the scale. If you need to make him aware of other things that are happening in your life, it's the perfect opportunity to do so.

Although your recruiter is responsible for making sure that you are ready to go to Basic Training and that you have not disqualified yourself during your time in the DEP, he is not a babysitter. You are ultimately responsible for your own actions.

I Want Out!

What happens if you've enlisted in the DEP, and while waiting to leave for Basic Training you've decided that maybe this wasn't such a good idea after all? The simple answer is that you tell your recruiter and you will be discharged from the DEP.

No one would, or could, hold you to a commitment to enter Active Duty. However, as discussed in Chapter 4, you should have thought long and hard about enlisting in the military, and you should also think long and hard about asking to be let out of your commitment.

Are you just getting "cold feet" (like most people), or is someone pressuring you not to go? Unless you've won the state lottery, landed a six-figure job or been offered a free ride to an ivy league college, I suggest that you review Chapter 2 and reevaluate why you enlisted in the first place.

After you've thought about it, meet with your recruiter and give him the chance to answer any concerns you may have. If your main concern is the military job you received, give him the chance to see if something else can be offered to you.

If you do decide not to enlist, be up front with your recruiter. Don't try to avoid him, and don't just fail to show up on your ship day.

On the other hand, if your recruiter becomes belligerent and tells you that you can't get out of your commitment, don't argue with him—just tell him you want to speak with his supervisor. If that doesn't work, contact the MEPS and ask to speak to the MEPS Commander. I can assure you that this will get your recruiter's attention. The bottom line is this: If you don't want to go, you won't go.

Although being "DEP Discharged" probably will not affect your chances of enlisting in the future, there is a chance that it may. So take your time when deciding whether or not you are doing the right thing.

Chapter Summary

As you now know, getting through the enlistment process does not end at the MEPS. You may have to remain in the Delayed Entry Program (DEP) for up to 365 days. Although there are many obstacles that may prevent you from ever getting the chance to go to Basic Training, I hope that the exposure and guidance offered in this chapter will help you to avoid them altogether or to deal with them effectively should they arise.

By following the physical fitness program presented, you should also be better able to prepare for the rigorous requirements at Basic Training. Hopefully, with the aid of this chapter, you will soon be ready to leave for Basic Training, which will be discussed in the next chapter. Each service's Basic Training is described in detail so that you will have a better under0standing of what goes on there without having to rely on your recruiter for his "version" of what it's all about.

6 BASIC TRAINING AND BEYOND: EARLY TO BED, EARLY TO RISE, MAKES A MAN OR WOMAN HEALTHY, STEALTHY AND SPRY

This chapter will outline the Basic Training in each military branch. Sample training schedules are included as well as some basic advice for getting through the hell that is boot camp.

Though many years ago, some of my most vivid memories of my experiences in the military are of Basic Training, or as we called it back then, "Boot Camp." I learned and experienced things in those eight weeks that I will carry with me for the rest of my life.

No matter what the five military Basic Training mission statements are, the main objective of Basic Training is to transform civilians into well-disciplined military members in a matter of weeks. Performing such a monumental task takes a lot of hard work, both mentally and physically. For most people, Basic Training ends with a parade on graduation day. For some, it ends somewhere short of graduation. It is those "horror stories" that make Basic Training probably the one biggest fear, or anxiety, for those contemplating a military enlistment.

Unlike the boot camp you may have heard about from your Uncle Louie or seen on television, today's Basic Training is void of the verbal and physical abuse of yesterday. All of the military branches are ensuring that all new enlistees are treated fairly and with dignity. I'm not saying that enlistees aren't yelled at (because they are); however, the vulgarity and demeaning verbal attacks that once existed are a thing of the past. There are, from time to time, incidents involving instructors who contradict the military's policies. These violations, however, receive a lot of attention, are thoroughly investigated and usually end up with disciplinary action taken against those involved in the abuses. Just as there are some policemen who abuse their powers, there are Basic Training instructors who do the same. Luckily, however, they are few and far between.

The remainder of this chapter is divided by military branch. If you've already decided on a particular branch of the military, you might want to read just that section. However, I suggest that you at least skim through the other sections for some insight into the other military branches.

If you are still uncertain of which branch you'd like to join, I caution you to not allow what you read in this chapter to be your only deciding factor. If, for example, the Marine Corps meets all your needs and is clearly your first choice, do not select the Air Force because its Basic Training seems easier. Conversely, if the Air Force is clearly your first choice, do not select the Marine Corps because it has the "toughest" Basic Training and you want to prove you are up to the challenge. Basic Training is a means to transform you from civilian life to military life. It happens in a relatively short period of time compared to the entire length of your enlistment. Do not base your choice of which branch to enter based on their Basic Training curriculum.

Some Words on Getting through Basic Training

No matter what you may have heard or read elsewhere, there are no secrets to getting through Basic Training; only common sense and preparation will get you through. Here are some dos and don'ts that should help you survive Basic Training for any of the services.

Although following these guidelines will not ensure your success at Basic Training, your chances for success will be greatly improved by following them.

BEFORE ARRIVING AT BASIC TRAINING

Do:

- Start an exercise program before going to Basic Training
- Maintain a sensible diet
- Stay out of trouble (pay any traffic fines promptly before leaving for Basic Training)
- Ensure that all of your financial obligations are in order
- If you are married, ensure that your spouse has "Power of Attorney"
- Bring the required items listed in the chart later in this chapter
- Give up smoking!

Do not:

- Skip preparing yourself physically because you think that Basic Training will whip you into shape
- Abuse drugs and/or alcohol
- Have a big send-off party and get drunk the night before you leave for Basic Training
- Leave home with open tickets, summonses, warrants, etc.
- Get yourself into heavy debt (such as buying a new car because now you'll be making some serious money
- Bring any prohibited items listed in the chart later in this chapter
- Have your hair cut in a radical manner (This includes having your head shaved. Men will receive a "very close" haircut shortly after arriving to Basic Training.)
- Have any part of your body pierced, tattooed or otherwise altered

I mention open law violations for a particular reason. While some of the don'ts—such as body piercing and high blood alcohol content —can be detected at the MEPS and, in all likelihood, will keep you from ever going to Basic Training, open law violations could take weeks to uncover. There is nothing worse than getting through Basic Training only to be called in right before graduation and told that you have been eliminated from training and will be sent home.

ONCE YOU ARE AT BASIC TRAINING

Do:

- Follow all instructions given to you
- Speak up when called upon to do so
- Maintain a positive attitude (remember: Basic Training won't last forever)
- Keep yourself well groomed
- Be a team player
- Look out for others
- Write home often
- Keep going to religious services (or start going if you haven't been)
- Study course material

Do not:

- Question authority
- Voice your opinion
- Assume you know everything (This is particularly important for those who were in high school Junior ROTC, the sea cadets, etc.)
- Consider yourself better than anyone else (Sure, you may have scored higher on the ASVAB and graduated high school with a 3.9 GPA, but that means nothing here. Doing your best at Basic Training is all that counts.)
- Look for ways to cheat the system
- Lose sight of why you came to Basic Training in the first place

General Information about Basic Training

The information presented in this section pertains to all services' Basic Training. It is information that you may or may not hear about from your recruiter.

LIVING QUARTERS

In the movie Private Benjamin, the main character arrives at Basic Training to find that a terrible mistake has been made. She was sent to the wrong boot camp—she signed up "for the Basic Training with the private condos and the swimming pools." She immediately finds out the truth about living conditions at boot camp. While there may be swimming pools there, they are not used for leisurely swims and sunbathing, and the living quarters are hardly private condos.

Although Basic Training recruits live in open barracks, each of which is composed of one large room, these rooms (or barracks) are—of course—segregated by gender. Each recruit sleeps in a single bed (in some cases, bunk beds are used) and is assigned a locker in which to store his or her belongings. It is the recruits' responsibility to keep their beds made and maintain their lockers. Recruits are taught how to fold their clothes and how to store their belongings, and they are expected to keep their locker exactly as instructed.

Bathroom and shower facilities are communal, very similar to those found at the average high school gym. Recruits are expected to get ready very quickly in the morning and are allowed a very short amount of time to take care of "business" in the bathroom (latrine or head, depending on the branch of service). If you are the type of person who likes to take long showers, you will be cured of that habit in no time! One habit you will pick up, however, (again in no time) is cleaning up after yourself, since recruits are responsible for maintaining the cleanliness of the communal bathroom.

MEALS

When I graduated from high school, I weighed all of 138 pounds. As much as I tried to gain weight, I just couldn't do it. Shortly after graduation, I enlisted in the Navy and was off to boot camp in San Diego, California. In December, I graduated from Basic Training at 160 pounds! Although a lot of people lose weight at Basic Training, some gain weight, partly because of muscle gain and partly because of the three nutritious meals served every day.

Unlike in high school, when I never had time for breakfast, skipped lunch sometimes, and ate dinner on the run, meals at Basic Training were mandatory. At the same time each day, we would march to the chow hall and have our trays filled with food. It certainly wasn't home-style cooking, but it wasn't like fast food either; and it was edible and, at times, even good.

Unfortunately, the military does not offer special meals based on its recruits' dietary needs. Therefore, if you are a vegetarian, for example, you will have to eat everything except the meat—there will be no soy-based meat substitute foods. If you are a Muslim, you have to avoid pork products; and if you must eat only kosher foods, I can offer no suggestions.

One last comment about the meals at Basic Training: You'll be given very little time to eat; meals are more inhaled than eaten. You'll be given approximately 10 minutes for each meal.

OFF-DUTY TIME

Each branch of service allows their recruits some personal time each day. That time, however, is spent at the Basic Training facility. In most cases, you will not be allowed to leave the Basic Training grounds until graduation.

Branch-Specific Information

The next sections are listed alphabetically by service branch. As I have mentioned previously, things change from time-to-time, and every effort is made to keep up with those changes. However, this chapter is just a guide to Basic Training; it should not be used as a substitute for information given to you by your recruiter.

Each of the following sections differs slightly in the detail of information. This is due to the fact that each military branch has provided the information they feel is important for prospective Recruits. In some cases, information was provided from outside sources in order to get the entire picture.

Air Force

BASIC MILITARY TRAINING (BMT)

There is one certainty you can count on if you decide to join the Air Force (including the Air Force Reserve or Air National Guard)—you will spend at least six weeks in beautiful San Antonio, Texas!

The Air Force's only location for Basic Military Training (BMT), Lackland Air Force Base has a long history of training some of the finest men and women ever to wear a military uniform. Each year, approximately 35,000 new enlistees enter through this "Gateway to the Air Force." Because policies and procedures change from time to time, you'll want to check with your recruiter to ensure the currency of the material presented in this section.

Temperatures in San Antonio range from mild to sizzling. Average daytime summer temperatures are in the 90s and mid-70s at night. Winter is a little cooler, with daytime temperatures in the 70s and nights in the 50s.

CURRICULUM OVERVIEW

Upon arrival at BMT, you will be assigned to a Flight. A Flight is the smallest group of trainees; a group of Flights makes up a squadron. Every Flight is overseen by several Military Training Instructors (MTIs) whose sole purpose is to get you through BMT or to ensure that those not suited for service in the Air Force are identified. Your MTI will become your mentor, your friend and, at times, seemingly, your enemy. Remember, though, that one of the "dos" to getting through BMT is to follow all of the instructions given to you. If you follow that one bit of advice, your experiences with your MTI will be a lot more pleasurable.

Following is an overview of what you can expect at BMT; more detail is provided later on in this section.

BASIC MILITARY TRAINING CURRICULUM

Period	Activities
Zero Week	You will arrive to BMT midweek. The first few days will be spent on activities such as getting haircuts, having uniforms and equipment issued and learning the rules of life in the dormitory.
Block 1	Reporting and saluting, medical and dental appointments, GI Bill briefing, ID cards, Dorm Guard class, career guidance, individual drill (as in marching), flight drill, dorm preparation, personal fitness, dorm inspection, personal appearance, military insignia recognition, military citizenship, personal interviews, second clothing issue and haircuts (yes, again)
Block 2	Flight photographs (just try smiling), dorm inspection, human relations class, flight drill, national security training, Air Force career progression, educational support, Honor Flight drill test, formal retreat practice (retreat in this case is a ceremony held at the end of the day to lower the nation's flag), dorm inspection, parade practice and written test

Recruits checking in at military reception at the San Antonio airport.

BASIC MILITARY TRAINING CURRICULUM

Period	Activities
Block 3	Warrior Week, confidence course, physical conditioning, Law of Armed Conflict, field training experience (you're gonna' love this!) and marksmanship training
Block 4	Open ranks inspection, hometown news releases, formal retreat (remember what I told you about retreat?), haircuts (yes, once again), travel arrangements, departing briefing, town pass briefing, orders pickup and graduation parade

In addition to the topics listed above, you will participate in daily physical conditioning, periods of dorm cleanup and individual study time. It all seems like a lot to cram into a six-week period, but don't worry—you'll have plenty of time since your day will start at 5 a.m.!

ARRIVAL AT BMT

The BMT experience will begin with your arrival at the San Antonio International Airport. Once you've collected any luggage that you checked in, you'll report to the Air Force Receiving Station, which is

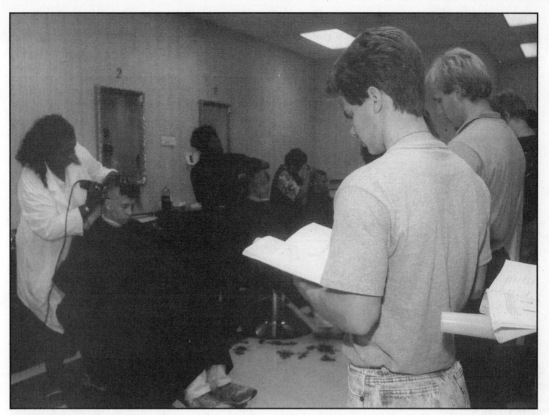

The first of many haircuts!

located in the "A" Terminal. Be sure to have a copy of your orders (which were given to you at the MEPS) ready to turn over to the Military Training Instructor who greets you.

Next, you'll learn one of BMT's most notable sayings, "hurry up and wait," as you are directed to sit and wait for the bus that will take you on the hour-long ride to BMT. Because there will be people arriving from all parts of the country, flight arrival times are varied, and you must wait until everyone is accounted for. Your official in-processing begins upon your arrival at the Shipping and Receiving Center. With the preliminary processing completed, you'll get back on a bus and head for your dormitory.

If they haven't started already, expect the orders to begin at the Shipping and Receiving Center. You will be told where to stand and how to stand, where to sit and how to sit. You will, in all likelihood, be chastised for something you did—or didn't—do. It will be during the time you spend in the Shipping and Receiving Center that you will ask yourself for the first time, "What did I get myself into?" Don't worry—everyone who has come before you and everyone who will come after goes through the same moment of doubt. Just remember the reasons why you joined the Air Force in the first place.

PHYSICAL CONDITIONING

You will receive Physical Conditioning at least six times per week throughout your entire stay at BMT. Physical conditioning consists of running, stretching exercises and circuit training (which includes deltoid lifts, bicep curls, tricep extensions and other exercises).

In addition to your weekly Physical Conditioning schedule, you will be given two Physical Conditioning Assessments. The first of the assessments will be conducted on the weekend after your arrival at BMT. The second is conducted during Block 2 of your training. In order to graduate from BMT, you must be able to pass the second assessment.

All trainees must successfully complete a 2-mile run and meet standards for sit-ups and push-ups. There are different standards for male and female trainees, as shown in the following table.

PHYSICAL FITNESS REQUIREMENTS

	Males	Females
2-Mile Run	18 minutes	21 minutes
Sit-Ups	45 (in 2 minutes)	38 (in 2 minutes)
Push-Ups	30 (in 2 minutes)	14 (in 2 minutes)

Physical conditioning—a way of life at BMT.

DAILY ROUTINE

You will be kept quite busy throughout your six-week stay at BMT. There will be many activities that will take up your time. You will spend most of your time in classroom instruction studying topics such as military customs and courtesies, Air Force history, how to wear the Air Force uniform and identifying military ranks. Some of the special topics that are covered include:

- Sexual Harassment
  The Air Force has a zero-tolerance policy regarding sexual harassment.
- Religious Freedom
  There is zero tolerance of discrimination based on religious beliefs and preference. In fact, you will be encouraged to attend the religious services of your choice while at BMT. The following services are offered:

- Protestant
- Roman Catholic
- Eastern Orthodox
- Jewish
- Other: Muslim, Eckanar, Wicca, Baha'I, NSA Buddhist

DETAILS

Some of you may decide to join the Air Force to escape living at home with your parents and those awful household chores you are forced to do. You may be thinking that you can leave home and let Dad deal with mowing the lawn. Well, there's some good news and some bad news. The good news is that you're right—Dad will have to fend for himself. The bad news is that BMT has its own version of chores, called details. What makes the bad news even worse is the fact that details make mowing your parents' lawn look like a walk in the park by comparison!

You will find yourself scrubbing the latrine (bathroom), cleaning pots and pans in the dining hall and participating in marathon lawn mowing. You will, however, not be alone. Details build team spirit; they bring the trainees together in one common goal. When you are finished, you will experience the satisfaction and pride of a job well done!

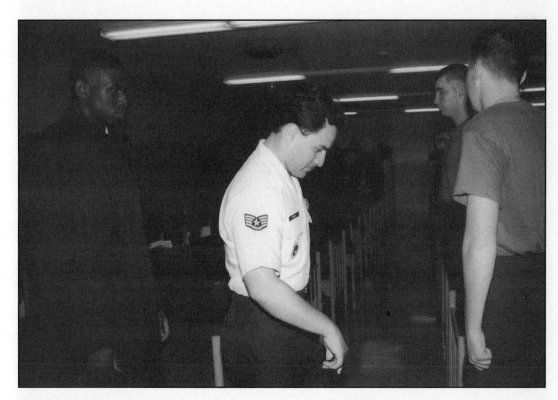

Dormitory inspection.

DRILL

Your primary (well, really your only) mode of transportation at BMT will be marching. You will begin to learn how to march even before you receive your uniform. From then on, you will be expected to know all aspects of drill. If you have had experience in Junior ROTC or similar organizations, you will have a distinct advantage in the beginning. However, in no time at all, everyone will learn how to drill like an expert. By the time graduation day arrives, even those who never marched before arriving at BMT will be marching with precision!

MARKSMANSHIP

One activity at BMT that some view as fun while others dread is Marksmanship Training—or, put in layman's terms, "shooting the guns." During BMT, you will be given the opportunity to fire an M-16 rifle on the firing range, but only after you have received thorough training on the safe handling of the weapon. Although individuals who have had experience dealing with firearms generally do better in this aspect of training, many people do very well on the firing range after a minimum amount of instruction. Even though most Air Force personnel will never handle a firearm in their day-to-day duties, as members of the Armed Forces they must always be prepared to do so.

CONFIDENCE COURSE

Another part of training loved by some and despised by others is the 21-station obstacle course known as the confidence course. This course will test your strength, stamina, willpower and team spirit. Even though it's not dangerous, the confidence course is extremely challenging. And although completing the confidence course is an individual effort, getting through it is a team effort. You will be called upon to support and cheer on your fellow trainees, and they may have to return the favor.

FIELD TRAINING EXPERIENCE

A fairly new addition to the BMT curriculum is the Field Training Experience, referred to as FTX. The purpose of FTX is to prepare trainees for deployment (in other words, being sent overseas to places like Kuwait, Bosnia or Somalia).

The FTX site is located approximately five miles from the regular training facilities. Trainees spend a day and a half at the facility, where they eat, sleep and participate in survival training.

GRADUATION

The graduation ceremony, the end of Basic Military Training, marks the beginning of your future in the Air Force. It is a very proud and emotional time for the graduates and their families. Your friends and family are welcome (and even encouraged) to attend BMT graduation. Because there is no leave granted between BMT and Technical Training, this may be the last chance you get to see them for quite a while.

There's a chance you'll get a little wet on the confidence course.

Because minor things can cause setbacks in training and delay your graduation, I would suggest that anyone planning to fly in for graduation wait as long as possible before locking themselves into nonrefundable airline tickets.

SMOKING POLICY

The use of any type of tobacco product is prohibited during your entire stay at BMT. This includes, but is not limited to, cigarettes, cigars, any type of smokeless tobacco and pipes. If you currently use any tobacco products, I recommend that you stop now instead of going cold turkey when you get to BMT. You will have enough stress adapting to military life; you don't need the added burden of nicotine withdrawal.

OTHER USEFUL INFORMATION

Here's some other information that you'll find useful to know prior to arriving at BMT.

Communication with Friends and Family

Even though your contact with the outside world will be limited during your stay at BMT, you will be able to stay in contact with friends and family members through letters and an occasional telephone call. You will be required to make contact with your family within 72 hours after arrival at BMT. If there is a family emergency, you can be reached at any time.

Personal Effects

As mentioned earlier in this chapter, there are certain items that you should bring with you to BMT and others that you should definitely leave at home. The following table lists those items. And don't worry—you'll be able to purchase any of the items on the "do bring list" once you reach BMT.

WHAT TO BRING—AND NOT TO BRING—TO BMT

Bring These Items:	Do Not Bring These Items:
Toothbrush/Case	Guns
Toothpaste	Knives
Comb/Hairbrush	Any weapons
Deodorant	Pornography
Liquid soap	Tobacco products
Shampoo	Racist literature
Nail clippers	Food/Candy
Extra civilian clothing *	Magazines/Books
Sport bras (white) (Females only!)	Radio/CD player
Razor	

*Although civilian clothes are not worn during BMT, you will get to wear them during technical school and your first assignment. Since you'll be leaving BMT with all of your newly issued Air Force gear, you'll want to limit the amount of civilian clothes you bring to BMT to one suitcase.

You will be issued clothing items two times during Basic Military Training. You will be responsible for purchasing and maintaining all other clothing items thereafter; however, as an enlisted member of the Air Force, you will receive an annual clothing allowance. Although the clothing items you are given at BMT are of good quality, many people choose to replace these "issue" items with items of better quality and fit. You can purchase them at the Clothing Sales store on any Air Force base. The following table lists clothing items that will be issued to you during Basic Military Training.

CLOTHING ITEMS ISSUED AT BMT

Male		Female	
Initial Issue	Final Issue	Initial Issue	Final Issue
1 duffle bag	1 pair low quarter shoes	1 duffle bag	1 pair low quarter shoes
6 briefs	2 ties	6 briefs*	2 neck tabs
4 pair cotton socks	1 pair U.S. insignia	1 pair leather gloves	1 pair U.S. insignia
4 pair wool socks	5 white T-shirts	4 pair cotton socks	2 skirts
5 brown T-shirts	1 garrison cap	4 pair wool socks	1 garrison cap
2 towels	1 belt	5 brown T-shirts	1 belt

	Male		Female	
Initial Issue	Final Issue	Initial Issue	Final Issue
1 belt	1 belt buckle	2 towels	1 belt buckle
1 belt buckle	3 long-sleeve shirts	1 belt	3 long-sleeve shirts
2 PC shorts	3 short-sleeve shirts	1 belt buckle	3 short-sleeve shirts
1 pair sweat pants	4 trousers	2 PC shorts	2 slacks
1 pair running shoes	1 service coat	1 pair sweat pants	1 service coat
4 pair battle dress uniform (BDU) trousers	1 light-weight jacket	1 pair running shoes	1 light-weight jacket
4 BDU tops	1 all-weather coat	4 pair battle dress uniform (BDU) trousers	1 all-weather coat
2 BDU caps		4 BDU tops	1 black handbag
		2 BDU caps	

*Female trainees are given a cash allotment to purchase their own undergarments.

SUMMARY

I would like to close this section by, once again, saying that the information contained here is up-to-date at the time of this writing. Because things change from time to time, you should verify this information with your recruiter before departing for Basic Military Training. Your recruiter is required to have you view a videotape about BMT; in fact, you were probably asked to sign a statement indicating you have seen it. If you were not shown this video, insist on seeing it as soon as possible.

Army

INITIAL ENTRY TRAINING (IET)

Upon enlistment in the Army you will be sent to one of five Initial Entry Training (IET) installations:

- Fort Benning, Georgia
- Fort Jackson, South Carolina
- Fort Knox, Kentucky
- Fort Leonard Wood, Missouri
- Fort Sill, Oklahoma

The Army (by far the largest of all the military branches) is unique in that where you are sent for Basic Training depends on your Military Occupational Specialty (MOS). This allows the Army to train many of its soldiers at one location all the way from Basic Training to Advanced Individual Training (AIT).

The Basic Training portion of Army IET is referred to as Basic Combat Training (BCT), while AIT refers to the job-specific training that soldiers receive after completing BCT. The following table presents the specific BCT locations for each MOS category.

MILITARY OCCUPATIONAL SPECIALTIES

MOS Category	BCT Location
Infantry	Fort Benning, Georgia
Armor	Fort Knox, Kentucky
Combat Engineers	Fort Leonard Wood, Missouri
Field Artillery	Fort Sill, Oklahoma
All Others	Fort Jackson, South Carolina

Of the five BCT locations, women are trained at Fort Jackson, Fort Leonard Wood and Fort Sill.

Just a few words of advice (whether or not you want it): As I mentioned at the beginning of this chapter, it would be foolish for you to make a decision as to which military branch to join based solely on the Basic Training curriculum. It would also be equally foolish to choose an MOS based on the BCT location. Remember, don't make what could amount to be life-changing decisions based on where you receive nine weeks of training. If you decide the Army is the right choice for you, choose your MOS based on your needs and the factors discussed in this book.

According to the Army, IET is "the new soldier's introduction to the Army. The goal of IET is to transform civilians into technically and tactically competent soldiers." This training prepares soldiers for the Army's basic mission—to fight and win in combat. Over 75,000 men and women enter BCT every year!

The training you'll receive at BCT will be tough, challenging and, most of all, rewarding. Not everyone who enters BCT completes the training; those who do, however, will go on to receive some of the finest training available anywhere.

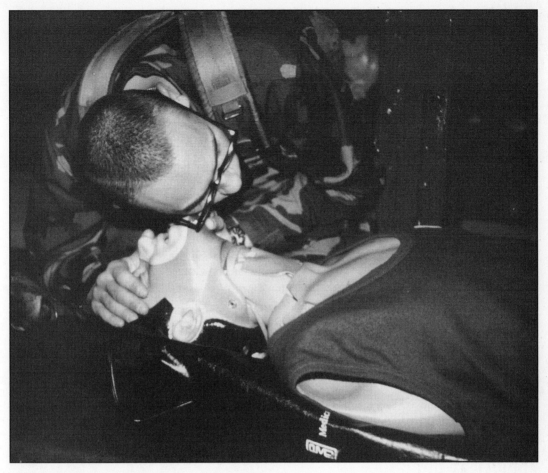

All soldiers learn CPR during Basic Combat Training.

CURRICULUM OVERVIEW

Basic Combat Training is nine weeks long and is divided into three phases. They are referred to as the Red (Patriot), White (Gunfighter) and Blue (Warrior) phases. The following table presents an overview of the aspects of each phase. More detail on most of these items can be found later in this section.

BASIC COMBAT TRAINING CURRICULUM—BY WEEK

Period	Activity
Red Phase (Weeks 1-2)	Begin instilling Army values Participate in physical training Receive communications instruction Negotiate victory tower Learn basic first aid

Period	Activity
White Phase (Weeks 3-5)	Learn map-reading skills
	Practice drill and ceremony
	Learn military justice system
	Test skills and knowledge in phase testing
	Continue Army values training
	Improve fitness through physical training
	Learn, practice and qualify in basic rifle marksmanship
	Learn about U.S. military weapons
Blue Phase (Weeks 6-9)	Learn about chemical warfare and participate in gas chamber exercise
	Participate in bayonet training
	Negotiate obstacle course
	Test skills and knowledge in phase testing
	Continue Army values training
	Participate in physical training
	Learn individual tactical techniques
	Participate in Victory Forge
	Perform foot marches
	Negotiate confidence course
	Execute obstacle course
	Test skills and knowledge in phase testing

ARRIVAL AT BCT

Upon your arrival at Basic Combat Training, your first stop will be the Reception Battalion. While there, you will:

- Complete administrative and logistical processing
- Receive your first (of many) haircuts
- Receive your initial uniform issue
- Complete personnel file screening
- Complete medical screening
- Begin learning Army core values
- Perform physical fitness screening

You can plan on remaining at the Reception Battalion from three to fifteen days. You will not be released for BCT until you have passed a Physical Fitness Assessment comprised of push-ups, sit-ups and a one-mile run. Those not meeting physical fitness standards will be assigned to a Fitness Training Unit (FTU) instead of proceeding directly to BCT.

Climbing a rope bridge on the confidence course.

You may remain in the FTU for up to four weeks. You will be released upon successful completion of the exit criteria if you do so before four weeks are up or, if you were unable to meet the criteria, at the end of the four weeks.

While assigned to the FTU, you will learn basic military skills such as military knowledge, drill and ceremonies and uniform appearance in order to prepare you for BCT.

In order to pass the Physical Fitness Assessment, you must, at a minimum, meet the criteria presented in the following table:

PHYSICAL FITNESS REQUIREMENTS

	Males	Females
Push-ups	13	3
Sit-ups	17	17
1-mile run	8 minutes 30 seconds	10 minutes 30 seconds

Uniform inspection.

DAILY ROUTINE

You will be kept very busy during your nine weeks at BCT. Besides the many hours you will spend involved in physical activities, you will spend countless hours in a classroom environment learning how to be a soldier. Here's an outline of a typical day at BCT.

TYPICAL DAY AT BASIC COMBAT TRAINING

Time	Activity
5:00 a.m.	Wake up
5:30 a.m.	Physical training
6:30 a.m.	Breakfast
8:30 a.m.	Training
12:00 p.m.	Lunch
1:00 p.m.	Training
5:00 p.m.	Dinner
6:00 p.m.	Drill Sergeant time
8:30 p.m.	Personal time
9:30 p.m.	Lights out

Female recruits drill during BCT.

DRILL

If you learn nothing else in BCT, you'll learn to march! Besides getting soldiers from place to place in an orderly fashion, marching (also known as drilling) helps soldiers learn coordination, teamwork and discipline.

Those who've had some drill experience, such as in Junior ROTC, will find this aspect of training somewhat easier. However, with practice, even those with no experience will be marching like experts in no time.

MARKSMANSHIP

One of the many graduation requirements for BCT is qualifying with the M-16A2 rifle. As a soldier, you will be expected to become proficient with this weapon. Therefore, you will receive expert training on the handling, caring and firing of this rifle.

Individuals with previous experience with firearms may find this part of BCT less challenging; however, these people, too, must learn the Army way of handling weapons. Many individuals with no previous experience with firearms do very well after receiving even minimum training.

Reviewing rifle qualification scores.

VICTORY FORGE

Victory Forge is a field training exercise conducted over a four-day period during the Blue Phase. You will apply the basic combat knowledge you acquired earlier in BCT. Here's an outline of Victory Forge activities:

VICTORY FORGE ACTIVITIES

Day	Activity
Day 1	10-kilometer foot march, occupy position and establish defense
Days 2 and 3	Teamwork reaction course, tactical exercise lanes and night tactical exercise
Day 4	Return foot march, ceremony and after-action review, super meal and after-operation maintenance

PERSONAL TIME

Every soldier is granted at least one hour of personal time each day. Although one hour may not seem like a lot of time, the rest of your day will be full of other activities (usually in a group). You will be grateful for any time that you can get on your own.

GRADUATION REQUIREMENTS AND GRADUATION DAY

There are certain minimum requirements that you must meet in order to graduate from Basic Combat Training. The Army will do its best to prepare you to meet and perhaps exceed the requirements that are presented in the following table.

GRADUATION REQUIREMENTS FOR BCT

Qualify with the M-16A2 rifle
Complete 3-, 5-, 8-, 10- and 12-kilometer foot marches
Pass the Army physical fitness test
Participate in buddy team live-fire exercise
Throw two live hand grenades and successfully complete the hand grenade qualification course
Negotiate the infiltration course
Pass all performance-oriented phase tests
Participate in hand-to-hand combat
Negotiate obstacles at Victory Tower
Participate in Victory Forge
Negotiate bayonet assault course and participate in pugil-stick training
Demonstrate understanding of, and a willingness to live by, the Army's seven core values
Negotiate all obstacles on the confidence course
Demonstrate the discipline, motivation and adherence to Army standards of conduct of a soldier
Complete gas chamber exercise to standard

Your friends and family are welcome (and even encouraged) to attend your graduation from BCT. The graduation ceremony marks the beginning of your future in the Army. It is a very proud and emotional time for the graduates as well as their families. The Army will even grant you an off-post pass so that you may spend time with family members after the graduation ceremony. Since you will not be granted any time off between BCT and advanced training, this may be your last opportunity to see your loved ones in quite a while.

Because minor things can cause setbacks in training and delay your graduation, I would suggest that family members planning to fly in for graduation wait as long as possible before locking themselves into nonrefundable airline tickets.

Marching in formation during graduation.

SMOKING POLICY

The use of any type of tobacco products is prohibited during your stay at BCT. This includes, but is not limited to, cigarettes, cigars, any type of smokeless tobacco and pipes. If you currently use any tobacco products, I would suggest that you stop now instead of going cold turkey when you get to BCT. You will have enough stress adapting to military life; you don't need the added burden of nicotine withdrawal.

RELIGIOUS WORSHIP SERVICES

Have you ever heard the expression "There are no atheists in foxholes"? To that end, the Army provides all its trainees the opportunity to attend weekly worship services. These can also be a good morale booster during Basic Combat Training. Although not every religious denomination is represented, you are bound to find a service you will be comfortable attending.

OTHER USEFUL INFORMATION

Here are some other pieces of information that you'll find useful to know prior to arriving at BCT.

Communication with Friends and Family

Even though you will be extremely busy with day-to-day activities at BCT, you will be encouraged to maintain contact with your friends and family. You will be given the opportunity to write on a regular basis and will be allowed to make an occasional telephone call. Take advantage of these opportunities; they will help keep your spirits up and reassure those at home that you are doing well. In the event of a family emergency, the Army will ensure that you are notified as soon as possible.

Personal Effects

As mentioned earlier in this chapter, there are certain items that you should bring to BCT and others that would be best left at home. The following table lists the items that the Army recommends you bring with you. Even though the Army does not provide a list of items that should not be brought to Basic Training, the MEPS does, and that list is provided here.

WHAT TO BRING—AND NOT TO BRING—TO BCT

Bring These Items:	Do Not Bring These Items:
Toothbrush/Case	Guns
Toothpaste	Knives
Comb/Hairbrush	Any weapons
Deodorant	Pornography
Soap/Case	Tobacco products
Shampoo	Racist literature
Dental floss	Food/Candy
Extra civilian clothing *	Magazines/Books
Sport bras (white) (Females only!)	Radio/CD player
1 pair calf-length white athletic socks	
Washcloth	
Towel	
Lock, combination or padlock	
Razor/Shaving cream	

*Although civilian clothes are not worn during BCT, you will get to wear them during technical school and your first assignment. Since you'll be leaving BCT with all of your newly issued Army gear, you'll want to limit the amount of civilian clothes you bring to BCT to one small suitcase.

SUMMARY

I would like to close this section by, once again, saying that the information contained here is up-to-date at the time of this writing. Because things change from time to time, you should verify this information with your recruiter before departing for Basic Combat Training.

Your recruiter has, or can get, a videotape about BCT. Because a picture is worth a thousand words (and a video a million), I suggest that you view this videotape at least once.

Coast Guard

RECRUIT TRAINING

If you've always wanted to visit New Jersey, you'll be happy to know that since the closing of the Recruit Training Center at Alameda, California, in the early 1980s, the Coast Guard's only Basic Training facility is located in Cape May, New Jersey. The center was established on May 31, 1948, when all Coast Guard Recruit Training facilities were moved from Mayport, Florida.

According to the Coast Guard, the mission of Recruit Training Command is

> To graduate motivated entry-level enlisted men and women ready and able to serve with a sense of pride and commitment in the world's premiere maritime service, and to proudly provide quality services to our people and others throughout the Coast Guard.

Furthermore, the stated training objectives of Training Center Cape May are

> to prepare you for shipboard duty and stresses of daily life associated with emergency response situations. Our expert and professional training staff will work with you on Physical Fitness, Water Survival and Swim Qualifications, Wellness and Nutrition, Self Discipline, Military Skill and Military Bearing. Your Vocational Skills and Academics will also be tested. We strive to instill a sense of Pride and Honor in every individual to bring you, along with your company, to a new level of excellence.

CURRICULUM OVERVIEW

Coast Guard Recruit Training consists of many phases of training, each designed to ensure that, once you have graduated, you are ready and capable of joining the men and women serving in the Coast Guard.

- Forming
- Company formation
- Physical training
- Classroom training
- Drill
- Mid-Training
- The Final Phase

Detailed descriptions of each phase are presented in the following sections.

FORMING

You'll arrive at Recruit Training by bus on a trip that more than likely originated from the Philadelphia airport. The Forming process begins immediately upon your arrival.

It is here that you will get your first military haircut, receive a medical screening and get your first uniform issue. In addition, you will also complete a ton of paperwork. It is in the Forming phase that you

Forming up on the first day at recruit training.

will probably question your decision to join the Coast Guard. You are not alone; you'll soon learn that just about everyone goes through the same self-doubt.

COMPANY FORMATION

Approximately three days after arriving at Recruit Training, you and the others you arrived with will be formed into a training unit called a Company. The responsibility of turning a group of civilians into a well-trained Recruit Company lies with your Company Commander (CC). Your CC is a senior enlisted Coast Guardsman who will become your coach, mentor and, at times, surrogate parent.

PHYSICAL TRAINING

An important aspect of Recruit Training, Physical Fitness Training will push you to your limits and beyond. You will participate in physical fitness throughout all phases of training.

In order to graduate from Recruit Training, you will have to meet the requirements presented in the following table:

One of the least-liked aspects of recruit training—immunizations.

PHYSICAL FITNESS REQUIREMENTS

Event	Male	Female
Push-ups	22 (in 1 minute)	20 (in 1 minute)
Sit-ups	32 (in 1 minute)	24 (in 1 minute)
1.5-mile run	12:44 minutes or less	15:00 minutes or less
Complete swim circuit	Jump off 5-foot platform into the pool, swim 100 yards, and tread water for 5 minutes	Jump off 5-foot platform into the pool, swim 100 yards and tread water for 5 minutes

If you aren't currently capable of meeting these requirements, you must start an exercise program well before you leave for Recruit Training. Although you won't be expected to meet all the requirements immediately, showing up for Recruit Training prepared to meet them will tremendously reduce your stress level!

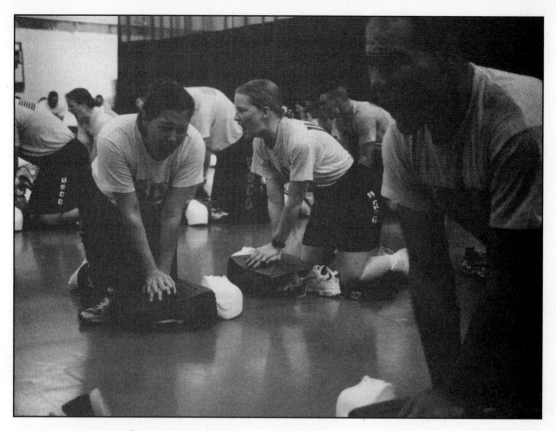

Push-ups are only one part of physical training at recruit training.

CLASSROOM TRAINING

Although much of Recruit Training is physical in nature, you will also spend many hours in a classroom environment. You will learn Coast Guard history, customs and courtesies, nautical terminology, the Coast Guard mission and Coast Guard ranks.

DRILL

Drill is just another way of saying marching. If nothing else, before you graduate from Recruit Training you will have mastered the art of marching. Besides being an efficient way to get a group of people from place to place, drilling also serves as a way to build confidence and to teach discipline and order. Some individuals may have an initial advantage because of prior marching experience (such as in Junior ROTC). However, marching is a team effort, so if one person is out of step, the entire company looks bad. Therefore, everyone works together to ensure that all members of the company become at least minimally competent in marching.

Recruits go through the "drill."

MID-TRAINING

Mid-Training begins with the end of the fourth week of training and the midterm exam. From then on, your training will be more hands-on and practical in nature. Of course, the physical and classroom training will continue; you will also receive instruction in:

- Fire fighting
- Marksmanship
- Line handling
- Seamanship

You may not think that you joined the Coast Guard to become a firefighter, but the truth is that everyone in the Coast Guard may be called at one time or another to fight a fire. That fire may be on your own Coast Guard vessel or you may be called upon to save a burning vessel at sea. When that call comes, you must be ready!

Marksmanship training is one aspect of Recruit Training that excites some and causes dread in others. You will be given expert instruction on the handling, firing and care of firearms. Even those with no experience with firearms have done well in marksmanship training.

Fire fighting training.

During Mid-Training, you will also fill out your Assignment Data Card (ADC). The ADC is a way for the Coast Guard to know where you would like to be assigned after training. The Air Force has a similar form, which is lovingly referred to as a "Dream Sheet." Although every effort will be made to match your desires with available openings, remember that the needs of the Coast Guard come first. You will receive your assignment orders at the end of the fifth week of training.

THE FINAL PHASE

During the Final Phase, you will continue with practical, physical and classroom training. During this time, you will also practice for graduation and make travel arrangements.

GRADUATION

The graduation ceremony, the end of Recruit Training, marks the beginning of your future in the Coast Guard. It is a very proud and emotional time for the graduates as well as their families. Family and friends are welcome to attend the ceremony; your family will be sent a package regarding graduation near the end of your training.

Recruits on the firing range.

If you have excelled during Recruit Training, you may be one of the 3 percent of all graduates who are presented the Honor Graduate Ribbon. Various other awards are presented to individuals who stood out during Recruit Training.

Because minor things can cause setbacks in training and delay your graduation, I would suggest that anyone planning to fly in for graduation wait as long as possible before locking themselves into nonrefundable airline tickets.

SMOKING POLICY

The use of any type of tobacco products is prohibited during your entire stay at Recruit Training. This includes, but is not limited to, cigarettes, cigars, any type of smokeless tobacco and pipes. If you currently use any tobacco products, I recommend that you stop now instead of going cold turkey when you get to Recruit Training. You will have enough stress adapting to military life; you don't need the added burden of nicotine withdrawal.

RELIGIOUS WORSHIP SERVICES

A good source of morale during Recruit Training is attending weekly religious services. The Coast Guard conducts Sunday services for Catholic and Protestant recruits. However, arrangements can be made in the local community to accommodate recruits of other faiths.

OTHER USEFUL INFORMATION

Here are some other pieces of information that you'll find useful to know prior to arriving at Recruit Training.

Communication with Friends and Family

Even though your contact with the outside world will be limited during your stay at Recruit Training, you will be able to stay in contact with friends and family members. Besides the telephone call you will make upon arrival to let everyone know you arrived safely, other telephone privileges will not come until near the end of training. If there is a family emergency, however, you can be reached at any time.

Your primary source of communication will be through cards and letters. You will be given ample opportunity to write home and read letters from family and friends. Besides serving as a means to keep up with news from home, receiving letters serves as a morale booster.

Personal Effects

As mentioned earlier in this chapter, there are certain items that you should bring to Recruit Training, items that you are permitted (but not required) to bring, and other items that would be best left at home.

The following is a list of items that are mandatory for you to bring with you to Recruit Training. In addition, there are items listed that you may bring with you or that you may purchase them at the Recruit Training Center. Although the Coast Guard does not provide a list of items that you should not bring with you to Recruit Training, the MEPS does, and that list is provided here. Check with your recruiter if you have any questions regarding restricted items.

WHAT TO BRING—AND NOT TO BRING—TO RECRUIT TRAINING

All Enlistees Must Bring These Items:	Do Not Bring These Items:
1 pair quality running shoes*	Guns
6 to 10 white V-neck T-shirts	Knives
6 pair black dress socks	Any weapons
6 to 10 pair underpants	Pornography
1 pair pantyhose (women only, skin tone)	Tobacco products
6 sports bras (women only, skin tone)	Racist literature
1 half slip (women only)	Food/Candy
	Magazines/Books
	Radio/CD player

*You should purchase only quality, well-fitting running shoes.

   Although not mandatory, the Coast Guard strongly recommends that you bring $50 to cover the cost of additional items that may need to be purchased.

   In addition to the mandatory items, you are permitted to bring the items listed in the following table. They must be brought to Recruit Training in a collapsible bag (no suitcases are authorized).

WHAT YOU ARE PERMITTED—NOT REQUIRED—TO BRING TO RECRUIT TRAINING

All Enlistees Are Permitted to Bring:	
Address books	
After-shave lotion	Religious medallion (with chain long
All white athletic socks (4 pair)	enough so as not to be seen under
Black eyeglass retaining strap	a V-neck T-shirt)
Black pens/pencils	Shampoo (12 oz)
Cartridge type razor	Soap (2)
Comb/brush	Spray starch
Dental floss	Stationary, envelopes, stamps
Deodorant	Sunblock
Electric razor/clippers	Talcum powder
Long underwear (white only)	Toothbrush
Manicure kit	Wallet
Pen flashlight	Watch
Religious materials	Wedding bands

In Addition, Women Enlistees Are Permitted to Bring:

Birth control pills (if already using them to maintain cycle)
Engagement rings
Feminine hygiene items
Gold ball earrings (1/4 inch, one set worn in lowest hole of ear)
Hair barrettes/bobby pins (hair color only)
Hair dryer
Makeup (moderate amounts)

SUMMARY

I would like to close this section by once again saying that the information contained here is up-to-date at the time of this writing. Because things change from time to time, you should verify this information with your recruiter before departing for Recruit Training.

Your recruiter has, or can get, a videotape that gives a pretty good look at what Recruit Training's all about. Because a picture is worth a thousand words (and a video a million), I suggest that you view this videotape at least once. The Coast Guard also has a publication called **The Helmsman,** which I consider the most thorough publication provided by the military concerning the Basic Training curriculum. Insist on seeing a copy of **The Helmsman** well before you are scheduled to leave for Recruit Training.

Saying goodbye after completing Recruit Training.

Marine Corps

RECRUIT TRAINING

The Marine Corps operates two locations for its Recruit Training. All males enlisting east of the Mississippi and all females nationwide are sent to Parris Island, South Carolina, while males enlisting west of the Mississippi are sent to the Marine Corps Recruit Depot in San Diego, California.

No matter which of the two Recruit Training sites you attend, you can count on twelve weeks of intense training. You will be challenged physically, mentally and emotionally throughout your entire stay at Recruit Training. Although Recruit Training is officially twelve weeks long, that does not count the first week, which includes in-processing and orientation. Therefore, you will spend thirteen weeks in Recruit Training.

CURRICULUM OVERVIEW

Upon arrival at Recruit Training, you will make your first stop at Recruit Receiving. This is where you will spend your first few days in the Marine Corps. You will receive your first of many haircuts and your initial uniform issue, be given a thorough medical and dental screening, meet your senior drill instructor and take your Initial Strength Test. The Strength Test consists of a 1.5-mile run, sit-ups and pull-ups.

From Recruit Receiving, you will move on to the next phase of training, called Forming. In this phase, you will be taken to your training company and you will meet your drill instructor for the first time. During the three to five days that you'll spend in this phase, you'll be taught the basics of marching and how to wear the uniform.

The following table lists the training events by week. Specifics of the various Recruit Training activities will be covered later in this section.

RECRUIT TRAINING CURRICULUM—BY WEEK

Week	Activity
Week 1	1.5-mile formation run
	Introduction to bayonet fighting
	Circuit course
	Close-combat training
	Introduction to M-16A2 Rifle
Week 2	First-aid classes
	Close-combat training
	Weapons-handling classes
	Core values classes
	Academic classes
	Physical training

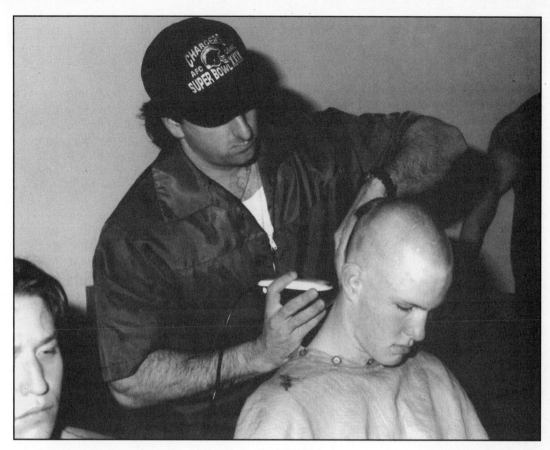

Receiving a "regulation" haircut.

Week	Activity
Week 3	Pugil sticks
	Close-combat training
	Core values classes
	First-aid class
	3-mile march
	Confidence course
	Academic classes
	Physical training
Week 4	Pugil sticks
	Initial drill evaluation
	Core values classes
	Academic classes
	5-mile march
	Physical training

RECRUIT TRAINING CURRICULUM—BY WEEK

Week	Activity
Week 5	Combat survival swimming
	Core values classes
	Inspections
	Physical training
Week 6	6-mile march
	Field skills classes
	Core values classes
	Nuclear, biological and chemical (NBC) instruction
	Rappelling
	Academic testing
	Confidence course
	Physical training
Week 7	Introduction to marksmanship
	Physical fitness test
	Customs and courtesies
	First-aid practical application test
	10-mile march
Week 8	Service-rifle qualification
	Fundamentals of rifle marksmanship
	Field meet
	Physical training
Week 9	Team Week
Week 10	Fundamentals of field firing
	Field training
	Physical training
Week 11	Core values classes
	Company Commander's inspection
	The Crucible
	Eagle, Globe and Anchor Ceremony
	Warrior's Breakfast
Week 12	Heroes of the Corps
	Commandant's Message
	Financial management
	Battalion Commander's inspection
	Core values classes
	Motivation run
	Family Day and recruit liberty
	Graduation

Uniform issue.

DRILL

Some things about Basic Training never change, and Drilling (or marching) is one of them. Besides getting platoons from place to place, drilling is used to instill discipline, team pride and unit cohesion. Although individuals with marching experience will initially have an advantage over those with no experience, most people will become proficient with some practice.

PHYSICAL TRAINING

Physical training (PT) is a way of life at Recruit Training. You will run, exercise and participate in conditioning marches throughout your entire stay at Recruit Training. If you do not want to be challenged physically on an almost daily basis, maybe you should look elsewhere for a career.

Marching in formation.

Recruits participating in a PT run.

ACADEMIC TRAINING

Besides being challenged physically, you will also be challenged mentally. Academic training will consist of subjects such as Marine Corps history, customs and courtesies and basic lifesaving procedures.

CORE VALUES

As you can see in the Recruit Training Curriculum table just presented, quite a bit of time is spent on core values because these values are considered the bedrock of a Marine's character. The core values are

- Honor
- Courage
- Commitment

In addition to these three core values, you will also be taught integrity, discipline, teamwork, duty and esprit de Corps. Furthermore, these values are reinforced throughout the entire time you'll spend in Recruit Training.

Preparing for barracks inspection.

CLOSE COMBAT

Close-combat training teaches fighting techniques that Marines may need to employ in combat. Drill Instructors will teach the use of pugil sticks and the practical application of bayonet fighting. You will also receive instruction on offensive and defensive skills.

Practicing hand-to-hand combat.

CONFIDENCE COURSE

One aspect of Recruit Training that some love—and others love to hate—is the confidence course. As the name implies, its main purpose is to build recruits' confidence; the other purpose is to build upper body strength. You will be given two opportunities to navigate the 11-station course while at Recruit Training.

COMBAT WATER SURVIVAL

What is the exact opposite of skinny-dipping? The answer is combat water survival. All recruits will receive instruction on a variety of water survival and swimming techniques, dressed in full camouflage utility uniform!

Negotiating the confidence course.

After instruction, you are expected to pass a minimum level of proficiency in combat water survival. Recruits exceeding the minimum level may go on to more advanced training, which requires you to train in full combat gear. This includes rifle, helmet, flak jacket and pack. Definitely not your average day at the beach!

BASIC WARRIOR TRAINING

This phase of training serves to introduce you to living in the field. During the three days you spend in this phase, you will learn everything from putting up a tent to field sanitation and camouflage. This is also when you will be introduced to the rappel tower and go through the gas chamber.

MARKSMANSHIP TRAINING

The proper handling, firing and maintaining of the M-16A2 service rifle is essential for every Marine. You will receive two weeks of intense marksmanship training. During the first week of training (called Snap-In Week), you will learn the four shooting positions as well as how to fire and to adjust sites. During the second week, you will fire on a known-distance course, with ranges of 200, 300 and 500 yards. You will be required to qualify with the M-16A2 rifle on Friday of week two.

Individuals with prior firearm experience may start with an advantage over those with no experience. However, after minimum training, beginners may actually out-shoot experienced shooters. This can be

Swim qualifications.

attributed to the fact that experienced shooters may have to unlearn some bad habits while beginners do not have to overcome this obstacle.

FIELD MEET

Designed to promote teamwork and unit cohesion, Field Meet is an opportunity for recruits to have fun while competing against other platoons in physical events such as tug-of-war and relay races.

A-LINE

In Marksmanship Training, you are given the opportunity to fire weapons at single targets while in a stationary position. A-Line provides you with the opportunity to fire weapons in field conditions. You will fire on multiple moving targets in low-light conditions and while wearing a gas mask.

TRANSFORMATION WEEK

It is at the end of this week that you are called a Marine.

THE CRUCIBLE

Described by the Marine Corps as "Recruit Training's Defining Moment," the Crucible is a training event that tests the your strength, endurance, will, team spirit and determination.

For 54 hours, you are subjected to physically and mentally challenging training. You are allowed a total of 8 hours of sleep during the entire 54 hours and are given 2 1/2 MREs (Meals Ready to Eat). As an added note about MREs: These ready-made pre-cooked meals are packaged in foil wrappers that are almost impossible to open; the contents vary from spaghetti to hot dogs and my favorite, "Barbecue Meatballs."

The entire training event is conducted in the field where the little sleep you are allowed is done in a primitive wooden hut. The Crucible is an event that is, at the very minimum, unpleasant, but when you've completed it, you will have a sense of accomplishment second only to the feelings you'll have on graduation day.

It is at this time that the new Marines are presented with the "Eagle, Globe and Anchor," the emblem of the Marine Corps, during a ceremony that can bring tears of pride to even the toughest of recruits.

TRANSITION WEEK

The last week spent at Recruit Training, Transition Week (as the name implies) helps you transition into becoming a Marine. During this week, more responsibility is placed on you, and you begin calling your Drill Instructor by his or her rank rather than sir or ma'am.

FAMILY DAY AND GRADUATION

The last two days at Recruit Training are devoted to Family Day and graduation. New Marines are granted on-base liberty to spend time with their family members. This may be the last chance you get to see them for quite a while. The following day, you graduate in an elaborate and impressive ceremony and parade. The ceremony marks the beginning of your future in the Marine Corps. It is a very proud and emotional time for the graduates as well as their families.

Because minor things can cause setbacks in training and delay your graduation, I would suggest that anyone planning to fly in for graduation wait as long as possible before locking themselves into nonrefundable airline tickets.

SMOKING POLICY

The use of any type of tobacco products is prohibited during your entire stay at Recruit Training. This includes, but is not limited to, cigarettes, cigars, any type of smokeless tobacco and pipes. If you currently use any tobacco products, I would suggest that you stop now instead of going cold turkey when you get to Recruit Training. You will have enough stress adapting to military life; you don't need the added burden of nicotine withdrawal.

Graduation day.

RELIGIOUS WORSHIP SERVICES

Although the Marines do not have chaplains of their own (they utilize Navy chaplains), you will be provided the opportunity to attend the religious services of your choice. Not all denominations are represented at Recruit Training, but you should be able to find services you feel comfortable attending.

OTHER USEFUL INFORMATION

Here are some other pieces of information that you'll find useful to know prior to arriving at Recruit Training.

Communication with Friends and Family

Even though your contact with the outside world will be limited during your stay at Recruit Training, you will be able to stay in contact with friends and family members. You will be given the opportunity and encouraged to write home often. You will also be given at least one opportunity to place a telephone call. If there is a family emergency, you can be reached at any time.

Personal Effects

While the other branches of the military provide a list of things to bring and not to bring to Basic Training, the Marine Corps puts it quite simply: "Don't bring anything except yourself." Certain prescription drugs may be allowable, so check with your recruiter before leaving for Recruit Training.

SUMMARY

I would like to close this section by once again saying that the information contained here is up-to-date at the time of this writing. Because things change from time to time, you should verify this information with your recruiter before departing for Recruit Training.

Your recruiter has, or can get, a videotape about Recruit Training. Because a picture is worth a thousand words (and a video a million), I highly recommend that you view this videotape at least once and ask any questions you may have.

Graduating from recruit training.

Navy

RECRUIT TRAINING

I started my military career in October 1978 by enlisting in the Navy. At the time of my enlistment, I was given the choice of which of the three Navy Recruit Training Centers I'd like to attend: Orlando, Florida; San Diego, California; and Great Lakes, Illinois. It didn't take me long to figure out that I didn't want to be in Illinois in the winter. And since I had never been to the West Coast, I decided to go to San Diego. It was great returning to New York on leave in December with a suntan.

In late 1998, I once again traveled to San Diego, this time for a recruiting meeting. I figured it would be great to visit "Boot Camp" twenty years later. To my surprise, however, I discovered that the Navy no longer trained their recruits in San Diego. In fact, since 1994, Great Lakes, Illinois, had been the only location for Navy Recruit Training! I remember thinking that if I had chosen Great Lakes over San Diego, instead of a suntan, I would have been returning on leave with windburn. (Of course, that wouldn't actually happen— the Navy takes precautions to protect Recruits from the sometimes-harsh Midwestern winters.)

CURRICULUM OVERVIEW

Upon arrival at Recruit Training, you will be dropped off at the Recruit In-Processing Center. This is your home for the next two hours, and it is here that your training begins. You will be instructed where to stand, when to stand, and how to stand. You will fill out more forms than you knew even existed and will be led around like a herd of cattle. In order to let the folks back home know you arrived safely, you will be allowed one phone call (sort of like prison, but hopefully you won't be calling your attorney).

After all the paperwork, you will be issued a Navy sweat suit (your first "official" uniform), and then you'll undergo urinalysis (they don't fool around about drugs). You'll then receive your first instructions on how to make your bed (and you thought your mom was tough) and will receive training on the fire safety requirements. By this point, you will have asked yourself (at least once) what you got yourself into. Don't panic: It's a kind of culture shock, buyer's remorse and cold-feet feeling that everyone goes through, and most people overcome it.

On the first full day of Recruit Training, recruits are separated into "divisions," which are headed up by a Recruit Division Commander (RDC). These RDCs are senior Petty Officers who are responsible for transforming a group of "clueless" civilians into a division of well-trained sailors.

Almost immediately, you will begin an eight-week journey that includes physical training, classroom instruction, hands-on training and water survival courses. The following table outlines the week-by-week schedule of events. Most of these events will be explained in more detail later in this section.

RECRUIT TRAINING CURRICULUM—BY WEEK

Week	Activity	
P-Week	Ditty bag issue	UCMJ/Grievance
	MOT/NAFMET	Standards of conduct
	Medical SCANTRON	Uniforms and grooming
	Medical/Dental Exams	Note-taking skills
	Wellness/OB GYN	Discrimination
	Urinalysis	Chaplain, human values
	Uniform issue	RDC PT (X2)
	DDS enrollment	Listening skills
	Uniform stenciling	
Week 1	Recruit receipts	Rank/Rate recognition
	Initial swim qualification	Rape awareness
	Special physicals	Core values
	Dental	Equal opportunity
	CART drill	Sexual harassment/Fraternization
	CART PI/DMI	RDC PT (X4)
Week 2	Haircuts	Watch standing
	Dress uniform issue	Customs and courtesies
	Stenciling	Test one
	Professionalism One	Confidence course
	Test taking	RDC PT (X3)
	Chain of command	
Week 3	Naval history	Basic seamanship
	TSTA One PI	Line handling lab
	Test two	First aid with lab
	Conduct during armed conflict	SU Navy Ships/aircraft
	Money management	RDC PT (X3)
	Shipboard communications	
Week 4	Classifications	Test three
	Haircuts	Service week indoctrination
	Dress uniform pickup	Marlinespike lab
	Tailor two/photos	RDC PT (X3)
	TSTA One drill	PT test one
Week 5	Service Week	
Week 6	Division photos	Fire fighting team trainer
	TSTA Two PI	RDC PT (X3)
	TSTA Two drill	Confidence course
	Basic damage control	Capt Cup competition
	Fire fighting one/two	Weapons simulator
	CBR/Gas chamber	

RECRUIT TRAINING CURRICULUM—BY WEEK

Week	Activity	
Week 7	TSTA Three drill	CPA/Terrorism
	TSTA Three PI	Goal card review
	Uniform/history/	Fire fighting application
	grooming	Final PT test
	Test four	RDC PT (X2)
	Dependent care	Battle stations
	DAPA	
Week 8	DDS out-brief	Ships officer PI
	Ticket order pickup	Pass-in-Review practice
	Transfer brief	Pass-in-Review
	Transfer	Chaplain, core values
	UCMJ	Core values
	Rank/Rate other services	Personal finance
	Professionalism Two	Goal Card review
	Career path/advancement	RDC PT (X3)

Don't worry if you don't understand all the acronyms in this chart. You'll become a master of acronyms before you leave Recruit Training. I suggest that you ask your recruiter any specific questions you may have concerning this schedule.

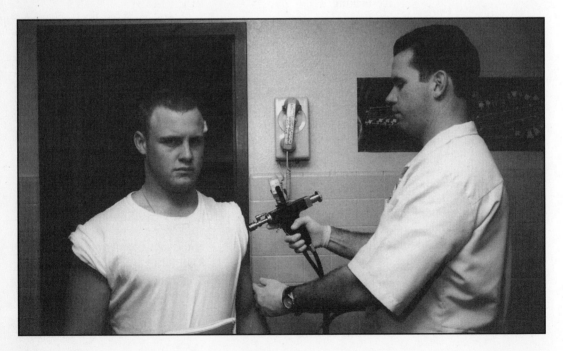

More shots?!!

DAILY ROUTINE

As you can see, you will have a full schedule while attending Recruit Training. You may feel that it will be impossible to get all your daily activities accomplished, but you can put your worries to rest. You'll have plenty of time since you'll start your day at around 4 a.m.!

UNIFORM ISSUE

Perhaps one of the most interesting and memorable parts of Recruit Training is uniform issue. You'll be led through a huge facility whose sole purpose is to issue and fit more than 35 million uniforms every year. For those who enjoy shopping and trying on clothes, this is like no other shopping trip you've ever experienced!

WATER SURVIVAL

Here's a surprise for you: If you join the Navy, chances are that sooner or later you'll be on a ship. Therefore, it's important for all sailors to receive at least a minimum amount of water survival training. You will receive instruction on water safety and survival techniques and then be given a swim test to determine your skill level. If you are unable to meet the minimum swimming requirements, you will be given individual instruction until you are able to do so.

CONFIDENCE COURSE

The Navy's confidence course is unlike those found at Army, Air Force and Marine Corps Basic Training. The Navy has created what it terms a "maritime obstacle course" to build recruit confidence, challenge you physically, familiarize you with shipboard equipment and build team spirit.

Instead of rewarding individual effort, you successfully pass the confidence course only when every member of your team of four recruits completes the course. Some of the challenges of the confidence course are

- Wearing an oxygen-breathing apparatus (usually worn while fighting shipboard fires)
- Carrying sandbags
- Tossing life rings
- Climbing through a scuttle (a small circular door found on ships) with full seabags (known as duffel bags to most other military branches)

When you complete the confidence course, you will experience a sense of pride that can only come from being part of a team.

SERVICE WEEK

Service Week is probably the most dreaded time of Recruit Training and turns out to be the most enjoyable. If you've ever worked in the food industry, you may think that Service Week will be no

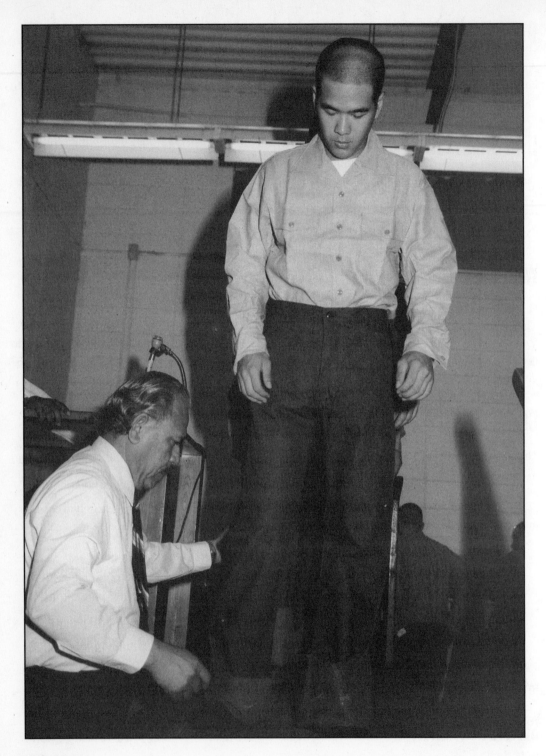

Uniform issue.

different than a week at your local fast-food restaurant. Think again: In one year, the Recruit Training Galley prepares 9.45 million meals, which include:

- 146,000 pounds of ground beef
- 447,000 loaves of bread
- 261,000 gallons of milk
- 223,000 pounds of chicken

In addition, there are the cooked vegetables, salads, soups and so on.

In order to get the 54,000 recruits who pass through Recruit Training each year fed three times a day, every recruit is required to spend a week working in the Galley. You will perform tasks such as washing trays, cleaning pots and pans, preparing vegetables for the salad bar and helping to serve food.

Service Week is long hours of hard work, but it builds team spirit and individual character. It is definitely an experience you won't soon forget.

BATTLE STATIONS

Anyone who has ever watched an old World War II movie (or **Star Trek,** for that matter) knows the meaning of "Battle Stations!" Aboard ship, the call to battle stations means that everyone must come together as a crew to prepare for meeting the enemy. Everyone has his or her job to do, and there is no room for not doing that job to the best of your ability.

The purpose of the Battle Stations event during Recruit Training is to instill in each recruit the confidence, dedication and team spirit necessary for you to become a productive member of a ship's crew. All of the training you receive during your time at Recruit Training culminates in this event.

You'll work as a team to complete physically and mentally challenging tasks that will test your endurance and ability to work as a team. Battle Stations ends with a ceremony that can only be described as a rewarding experience.

DRILL

One aspect of Recruit Training that every military branch has in common is Drill. Drill refers to the art of marching, and if drill is an art, you will become an artist by the time you graduate from Recruit Training.

Although individuals who have had some experience with marching (such as those who belonged to high school Junior ROTC) will have an initial advantage at first, everyone will soon become at least competent at marching.

BARRACKS INSPECTIONS

Recruits are housed in 1,000-bed barracks. It is the responsibility of the recruits to keep their barracks "shipshape." Besides making your own bed and ensuring that your clothes are folded just right, you and your fellow recruits will scrub, wash, wipe and dust every inch of your barracks in preparation for barracks inspection.

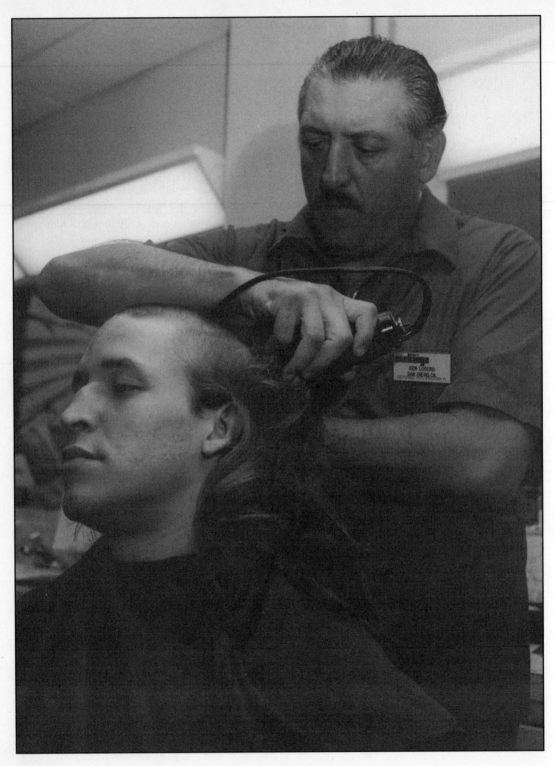

The first of many Navy haircuts.

Besides the obvious reasons for keeping your living quarters clean, working as a team cleaning the barracks and then doing well on an inspection helps build team spirit and pride in a job well done. If you're used to having your mother make your bed and pick up after you, I suggest that you get out of that habit before you get to Recruit Training.

CORE VALUES

You probably noticed that core values were mentioned several times in the Curriculum for Recruit Training earlier in this section. You will find the core values of honor, courage and commitment evident throughout all your training. They are considered the bedrock principles of Naval service.

PHYSICAL TRAINING

A good part of Recruit Training will be devoted to physical conditioning. You are expected to achieve minimum standards in running, push-ups, sit-ups and pull-ups. If you are not currently involved in sports, or do not maintain a regular exercise program, start now, before you arrive at Recruit Training. Although most people, regardless of their level of physical fitness, are able to work up to the minimum standards, life at Recruit Training is a whole lot easier if you show up ready to meet at least the minimum requirements.

CLASSROOM TRAINING

Although a great deal of time is devoted to physical training, marching and hands-on instruction, a lot of time in Recruit Training is spent in the classroom. You'll receive instruction on such topics as Naval history, sexual harassment, proper wear of the uniform and basic seamanship. You will also be required to pass several written tests in order to graduate from Recruit Training.

SMOKING POLICY

The use of any type of tobacco products is prohibited during your entire stay at BMT. This includes, but is not limited to, cigarettes, cigars, any type of smokeless tobacco and pipes. If you currently use any tobacco products, I would suggest that you stop now instead of going cold turkey when you get to Recruit Training. You will have enough stress adapting to military life; you don't need the added burden of nicotine withdrawal.

GRADUATION

Graduation from Recruit Training is known as "Pass-in-Review." An elaborate and emotional ceremony, it marks the end of Recruit Training and the beginning of the future of those individuals who nine weeks earlier were civilians, became Recruits, and can now be called Sailors. Family and friends are welcome and are encouraged to attend graduation ceremonies. This may be the last chance you get to see them for quite a while.

Questions?

Because minor things can cause setbacks in training and delay your graduation, I would suggest that anyone planning to fly in for graduation wait as long as possible before locking themselves into nonrefundable airline tickets.

Graduations are held on Thursday afternoons and Friday mornings. The following table outlines the order of events.

AGENDA FOR GRADUATION DAY

Thursday Afternoon	Friday Morning	Event
2:00 p.m.	7:00 a.m.	Building 1313 (Visitor's Center) opens.
3:15 p.m.	8:15 a.m.	Guests are escorted to review area.
3:45 p.m.	8:45 a.m.	Parents of award winners and honor recruits receive special escort to the review area.
4:00 p.m.	9:10 a.m.	Commence review introductions.
6:00 p.m.	11:00 a.m.	Conclude review ceremony.

The no-tobacco rule applies to everyone at the Recruit Training Center, including guests for graduation. Smoking, even in vehicles, is prohibited.

RELIGIOUS WORSHIP SERVICES

An activity that can help ease the stresses of Recruit Training is attending religious services. You will be given the opportunity to attend the services of your choice throughout Recruit Training. Although not every religious denomination is represented, you are bound to find a service that you are comfortable attending.

OTHER USEFUL INFORMATION

Here are some other pieces of information that you'll find useful to know prior to arriving at Recruit Training.

Communication with Friends and Family

Even though your contact with the outside world will be limited during your stay at Recruit Training, you will be able to stay in contact with friends and family members. Besides the one telephone call you were allowed when you first arrived at Recruit Training, you will get few chances to make any others. If there is a family emergency, however, you can be reached at any time.

Your primary source of communication will be through cards and letters. You will be given ample opportunity to write home and read letters from family and friends. Besides serving as a means to keep up with news from home, receiving letters also serves as a morale booster.

Graduation parade.

SUMMARY

I would like to close this section by once again saying that the information contained here is up-to-date at the time of this writing. Because things change from time to time, you should verify this information with your recruiter before departing for Recruit Training.

Your recruiter has, or can get, a videotape about Recruit Training. Because a picture is worth a thousand words (and a video a million), I highly recommend that you view this videotape at least once and ask any questions you may have. Although videotapes tend to be somewhat dated because of the production costs involved in updating them, it will give you a visual idea of what Recruit Training is all about. If your recruiter doesn't offer to show it to you, insist that he does show it.

Things have changed a little since this recruiting poster was used.

MILITARY OCCUPATIONS

This appendix lists the occupational groups offered by each branch of the armed forces. These are not specific jobs but rather "fields," such as electronics or mechanics.

As you learned in Chapter 4, which dealt with the Military Entrance Processing Station (MEPS), being flexible in your job selection is a good idea. By focusing on a broad field rather than a specific job, your chances of getting a job (and training) in something that interests you and makes you happy are much greater.

I encourage you to read through all the job categories for all the services. As also mentioned in Chapter 4, there may be a career field that you have never heard of that might be of interest to you.

Ultimately, the results of the Armed Forces Aptitude Battery (ASVAB) exam and the physical examination will determine the career fields that you are best suited for. It helps, however, if you also have some interest in that field.

Go through the following tables and highlight (unless you've borrowed this book) all the job categories that interest you. Once you've compiled your list of job categories, ask your recruiter for information about the jobs that are included in those categories.

Also, take your list with you to the MEPS and share it with the MEPS Liaison. And, keeping flexibility in mind, go prepared to discuss two or more job categories. Rank order them, and start by talking about your number one choice.

If you cannot find a job category that interests you from the many in these tables, perhaps you need to look elsewhere for a career.

Air Force Occupations

VEHICLE/MACHINERY MECHANICS

Career field	Duties & responsibilities	Qualifications	Examples of civilian jobs
Aircraft Maintenance	Performs the mechanical functions of maintenance; repair and modification of helicopters, turbo-props, reciprocating engines and jet aircraft.	Considerable mechanical or electrical aptitude and manual dexterity. Physics, hydraulics, electronics, mathematics and mechanics desirable.	Aircraft mechanic and airframe inspector.

VEHICLE/MACHINERY MECHANICS

Career field	Duties & responsibilities	Qualifications	Examples of civilian jobs
Aircraft Systems Maintenance	Performs maintenance on aircraft accessory systems and propulsion systems; fabrication of metal and fabric materials used in aircraft structural repair and inspection and preservation of aircraft parts and materials.	Electrical or mechanical aptitude and manual dexterity. Electronics, mathematics, hydraulics, mechanics, chemistry, metalworking and mechanical drafting desirable.	Aircraft mechanic, aircraft electrician, sheet metal worker, welder and machinist.
Intricate Equipment Maintenance	Overhauls and modifies photographic equipment; works with fine precision tools, testing devices and schematic drawings.	Considerable mechanical ability and manual dexterity; algebra and physics desirable. Must have normal color vision.	Camera repairer, statistical machine and medical equipment service person.
Mechanical/Electrical	Performs installation, operation, maintenance and repairs of base direct support systems and equipment.	Physics, mathematics, blueprint reading and electricity.	Elevator repairer, electrician, lineman, powerhouse repairer, diesel mechanic, pipefitter, steamfitter and heating and ventilation worker.
Vehicle Maintenance	Overhauls and maintains powered ground vehicles and mechanical equipment for transporting personnel and supplies.	Machine shop, mathematics and training in the use of tools and blueprints helpful.	Automobile accessories installer, automobile and truck mechanic.

ELECTRONIC/ELECTRICAL SYSTEMS

Career field	Duties & responsibilities	Qualifications	Examples of civilian jobs
Avionics Systems	Installs, maintains and repairs airborne bomb navigation, fire control, weapons control, automatic flight control systems and radio and navigational equipment and maintains associated test and precision measurement equipment.	Electronic aptitude, manual dexterity and normal vision. Mathematics, physics, chemistry, electronics and trigonometry desirable.	Radar, TV and precision instrument maintenance technician.
Communications-Electronics Systems	Installs, modifies, maintains, repairs and overhauls airborne and ground TV equipment, high-speed general and special purpose data processing equipment, automatic communications and cryptographic machine systems, teletypewriter, teleautographic equipment, telecommunications systems control and associated electronic test equipment.	Basic knowledge of electronic theory. Mathematics and physics desirable. Normal color vision mandatory.	Communications, electronics technician, radio and television repairer, meteorological and teletype equipment repairer.

Career field	Duties & responsibilities	Qualifications	Examples of civilian jobs
Aircrew Operations	Primary duties require frequent and regular flight. In-flight refueling operator performs duties associated with in-flight refueling of aircraft. Defensive aerial gunner is a B-52 integrated crewmember with responsibility for defense of aircraft. Aircraft loadmaster supervises loading of cargo and passengers and operates aircraft equipment. Pararescue/recovery personnel perform aircrew protection skills. Flight engineers ensure mechanical condition of the aircraft and monitor in-flight aircraft systems.	High electrical and mechanical aptitude, manual dexterity, normal vision and good physical condition. Mathematics, physics, general science, English, typing, computer principles and shop work desirable.	Aircraft mechanic, electrician, hydraulic tester, oxygen system tester, cargo handler, dispatcher and shipping clerk, depending on the area in which training and experience is received.
Fuels	Receives, stores, dispenses, tests and inspects propellants, petroleum fuels and products.	Chemistry, math and general science desirable.	Petroleum industry supervisor and bulk plant manager.

LOGISTICS AND SUPPLY

Career field	Duties & responsibilities	Qualifications	Examples of civilian jobs
Munitions and Weapons Maintenance	Maintains and repairs aircraft armament. Assembles, maintains, loads, unloads and stores munitions and nuclear weapons. Disposes of bombs, missiles and rockets and operates detection instruments.	Mechanical or electrical aptitude, manual dexterity, normal color vision and depth perception. Mathematics, mechanics and physics desirable.	Aircraft armament mechanic, armorer, ammunition inspector and munitions handler.
Supply	Designs, analyzes and operates supply data systems. Responsible for operation and management of material facilities.	Accounting and business administration.	Junior accountant, machine recourse section supervisor and receiving, shipping and stock clerk.

PERSONNEL/BASE SUPPORT

Career field	Duties & responsibilities	Qualifications	Examples of civilian jobs
Accounting, Finance and Auditing	Prepares documents required to account for and disburse funds, including budgeting, allocation, disbursing, auditing and preparing cost analysis records.	Dexterity in the operation of business machines. Typing, mathematics, statistics and accounting desirable. High administrative aptitude mandatory.	Public accountant, auditor, bookkeeper, budget clerk and paymaster.
Administration	Prepares correspondence and statistical summaries; arranges priority and distribution systems; maintains files; prepares and consolidates reports, and arranges graphic presentations.	Business, English, typing and mathematics courses desirable.	Clerk typist, file secretary, stenographer and receptionist.

Career field	Duties & responsibilities	Qualifications	Examples of civilian jobs
Band	Plays musical instruments or sings in concert bands and orchestras, repairs and maintains instruments. Performs as drums major, arranges music and maintains music libraries.	Knowledge of elementary theory of music and orchestration desirable.	Orchestrator, music librarian, music teacher and instrumental musician.
Dental	Operates dental facilities and provides paraprofessional dental care and preventive dental services, treats oral tissues and fabricates prosthetic devices.	Knowledge of oral and dental anatomy, biology and chemistry.	Dental hygienist and dental assistant.
Education and Training	Conducts formal classes of instruction, uses training aids, develops material for various courses of instruction, teaches classes in general academic subjects and military matters and administers educational programs.	English composition and speech desirable.	Vocational training instructor, counselor, educational consultant or administrator.
Fire Protection	Operates fire fighting equipment, prevents and extinguishes aircraft and structural fires. Rescues and renders first aid. Maintains fire fighting and fire prevention equipment.	Good physical condition. No allergies to oil and fire extinguishing solution. General science and chemistry desirable.	Fire chief, fire extinguisher service person, firefighter or fire marshal.

Career field	Duties & responsibilities	Qualifications	Examples of civilian jobs
Legal	Takes and transcribes verbal accordings of legal proceedings. Uses a stenomask. Performs office administrative tasks. Processes claims.	Knowledge of stenomask, typing, legal terminology, military processing of claims. English grammar and composition. Ability to speak clearly and distinctly.	Law librarian, court clerk and shorthand reporter.
Medical	Operates medical facilities, works with professional medical staff as they provide care and treatment. May specialize in such medical services as nuclear medicine, cardiopulmonary techniques, physical and occupational therapy and administrative services.	Knowledge of first aid, ability to help professional medical personnel. Anatomy, biology, zoology, high school algebra and chemistry desirable in most specialties and are mandatory requirements for some.	X-ray and medical records technician, medical laboratory and pharmacist assistant, respiratory therapy technician and surgical technologist.
Morale, Welfare and Recreation	Conducts physical conditioning, coaches sports programs, administers recreation, entertainment, sports and club activities.	Good muscular coordination. English, business math and physical education desirable.	Athletic or playground director, physical education instructor and manager of a recreational establishment.
Public Affairs	Interviews people, reports news, composes, proofreads, writes and edits news copy. Provides public affairs advice.	High general aptitude. English grammar and composition, speech, journalism, radio/ television and history.	Reporter, copyreader, historian, public relations representative, editorial assistant, broadcast or program director and announcer.

Career field	Duties & responsibilities	Qualifications	Examples of civilian jobs
Safety	Performs functions related to the conduct of both safety and disaster preparedness programs; conducts safety programs; surveys areas and activities to eliminate hazards; analyzes accident causes and trends; trains personnel to accomplish the primary mission under the handicaps imposed by enemy attack or natural disaster.	Knowledge of industrial hygiene, safety education, safety psychology and blueprint interpretation. Typing, English, public speaking, mathematics and science desirable.	Safety inspector and instructor.
Sanitation	Operates and maintains water and waste processing plant systems and equipment and performs pest and rodent control functions.	Physics, biology, chemistry and blueprint reading desirable.	Purification plant operator, sanitary inspector, exterminator and entomologist.
Security Police	Provides security for classified information and material. Enforces law and order. Controls traffic and protects lives and property. Organizes as local ground defense force.	Good physical condition, vision and hearing. Civics and social sciences desirable.	Guard, police inspector, police officer and superintendent of police.
Transportation	Ensures service and efficiency of transportation of supplies and personnel by aircraft, train, motor vehicle and ship.	Driver training, operation of office machines and business math.	Cargo handler, motor vehicle dispatcher, shipping or traffic rate clerk, trailer truck driver and ticket agent.

PERSONNEL/BASE SUPPORT

Career field	Duties & responsibilities	Qualifications	Examples of civilian jobs
Visual Information	Operates aerial and ground cameras, motion picture and other photographic equipment. Processes photographs and film. Edits motion pictures. Performs photographic instrumentations and operates airborne, field and precision processing laboratories.	Considerable dexterity on small precision equipment. Excellent eyesight. Mathematics, physics, chemistry, public speaking, commercial art, drafting, photography, drama, communicative arts and computer science desirable.	Photographer, darkroom technician, film editor, aerial commercial photograph finisher, sound mixer and motion picture camera operator.

ENGINEERING, SCIENCE AND TECHNICAL

Career field	Duties & responsibilities	Qualifications	Examples of civilian jobs
Aircrew Protection	Performs functions involved in the instruction of aircrew and other designated personnel on the principles, procedures and techniques of global survival. This includes life support equipment, recovery, evasion, captivity, resistance to exploitation and escape.	Good physical condition required. Knowledge of pioneering and woodsman activities helpful. Courses in communication, science and education desirable.	No civilian job covers the scope of the jobs in this career field, but a related job is that of hunting or fishing guide.

Career field	Duties & responsibilities	Qualifications	Examples of civilian jobs
Communications-Computers	Operates radio and wire communications systems, automatic digital switching equipment, cryptographic devices, airborne and ground electronic countermeasures equipment, all kinds of communications equipment and the management of radio frequencies.	Knowledge of telecommunications functions and operations of electronic communications equipment. Typing or keyboard experience and clear speaking voice desirable in many specialties. Business math, algebra and geometry desirable.	Central office operator (telephone and telegraph), cryptographer, radio operator, telephone supervisor and photo-radio operator. Card-type converter or computer operator, data typist, data processing control clerk, high-speed printer operator and programmer.
Control Systems Operations	Operates control towers. Directs aircraft landings with radar landing control equipment. Operates ground radar equipment, aircraft control centers, airborne radar equipment, space tracking and missile warning systems.	Equipment dexterity, clear voice and speech ability and excellent vision. English desirable.	Aircraft log clerk, airport control operator and air traffic controller.
Geodetics	Procures, compiles, computes and uses topographic, photogrammetric and cartographic data in preparing aeronautical charts, topographic maps and target folders.	Ability to use precision instruments required in measuring and drafting. Algebra, geometry, trigonometry and physics necessary.	Cartographer, topographical drafter and mapmaker.

Career field	Duties & responsibilities	Qualifications	Examples of civilian jobs
Intelligence	Collects, produces and disseminates data of strategic, tactical or technical value from an intelligence viewpoint. Maintains information security.	Knowledge of techniques of evaluation, analysis, interpretation and reporting. Foreign languages, English composition, photography, mathematics and typing desirable.	Cryptoanalyst, draftsperson, interpreter, investigator, statistician, radio operator and translator.
Structural/Pavements	Constructs and maintains structural facilities and pavement areas; maintains pavements, railroads and soil bases; performs erosion control; operates heavy equipment; performs site development, general maintenance, cost and real property accounting, work control functions and metal fabricating.	Blueprint reading, mechanical drawing, mathematics, physics and chemistry are desirable.	Plumber, bricklayer, carpenter, stonesman, painter, construction worker, welder and sheet metal worker.
Weather	Collects, records and analyzes meteorological data; makes visual and instrument weather observations; forecasts immediate and long-range weather conditions.	Visual acuity correctable to 20/20. Physics, math and geography desirable.	Meteorologist, weather forecaster and weather observer.

Army Occupations

COMBAT SPECIALTIES

Career field	Duties & responsibilities	Qualifications	Examples of civilian jobs
Air Defense Artillery	Operates and maintains electrical systems. Uses technical diagrams to locate and replace defective parts. Conducts communications with air traffic controllers. Supervises or assists in repairing electronic or radar equipment. Monitors computers and telemetry display systems.	Basic mechanical, electronic, mathematical abilities; emotional stability; and a high degree of observational and reasoning ability.	Systems specialist and radar operator and data processing equipment, electronic instruments and systems, radar, radio equipment and teletype repairer.
Armor	Operates and maintains heavy equipment over rough terrain. Serves as a member of a reconnaissance, security or special operations force. Interprets maps and operational data.	High state of physical fitness and possess a high degree of ability in leadership, communications, mathematics and mechanical maintenance.	Supervisor, heavy equipment operator or repairman, truck mechanic and armament machinist and operator.
Combat Engineering	Constructs, repairs and maintains roads, fixed bridges, port facilities, pipelines, supply tanks and related facilities. Performs as a team leader and supervisor in construction and demolition.	Mathematical reasoning ability, auto mechanics, carpentry, woodworking, mechanical drawing and drafting courses.	Construction worker, supervisor, heavy equipment operator, drafter, rigger, bridge repairer, lumber worker and blaster.

COMBAT SPECIALTIES

Career field	Duties & responsibilities	Qualifications	Examples of civilian jobs
Field Artillery	Serves or supervises in the operation/intelligence, fire support, and target acquisition activities of a highly specialized organization. Operates unique rocket launching computers that assist cannons and rockets in obtaining maximum accuracy. Operates and maintains radar, meteorological and survey equipment.	Mathematical reasoning, abilities in mechanical maintenance, meteorology and communications and a high state of physical fitness.	Supervisor, surveyor, topographical drafter, cartographer, meteorologist and radio operator.
Infantry	Serves in closely coordinated teams organized for highly unified action. As a supervisor, provides effective leadership and management of a highly motivated organization.	Highest state of physical fitness. Organizational maintenance, leadership and communications abilities. Mechanical aptitude.	Supervisor, human relations counselor, physical education instructor, supply clerk, computer operator, dispatcher and security officer.

VEHICLE/MACHINERY MECHANICS

Career field	Duties & responsibilities	Qualifications	Examples of civilian jobs
Aircraft Maintenance	Performs the mechanical functions of maintenance, repair and modification of helicopters and turboprop engine aircraft.	Considerable mechanical or electrical aptitude and manual dexterity. Shop mathematics and physics desirable.	Aircraft mechanic and plane inspector.

VEHICLE/MACHINERY MECHANICS

Career field	Duties & responsibilities	Qualifications	Examples of civilian jobs
Aircraft System Maintenance	Performs maintenance of aircraft accessory systems, propulsion systems, armament systems, fabrication of metal materials used in aircraft structural repair and inspection and preservation.	Electrical and mechanical aptitude. Shop mathematics and shop work desirable.	Aircraft mechanic, aircraft electrician, sheet metal machinist.
Mechanical Maintenance	Services and repairs land and amphibious wheel and track vehicles ranging from cars and light trucks to tanks and self-propelled weapons; installs and repairs refrigeration, bakery and laundry equipment. Automotive mechan-	ics, electricity, blueprint reading, machine shop and physics. Automotive mechanic,	motor analyst, bakery or refrigeration equipment repairer, frames, wheel alignment and tractor mechanic.

ELECTRONIC/ELECTRICAL SYSTEMS

Career field	Duties & responsibilities	Qualifications	Examples of civilian jobs
Air Defense Missile Maintenance	Inspects, tests, maintains and repairs guided missile fire control equipment and related radar installations that guide missiles to the targets.	Mathematics, physics, electricity and electronics.	Radio installation and repair inspector, electronic equipment technician, radio and TV repairer.
Aviation Communications-Electronic Systems Maintenance	Repairs and maintains navigation, flight control and associated communications equipment.	Electrical/electronic theory and repair.	Electronics technician, radar repairer, electrical instrument mechanic/repairer.

ELECTRONIC/ELECTRICAL SYSTEMS

Career field	Duties & responsibilities	Qualifications	Examples of civilian jobs
Aviation Operations	Maintains, installs and repairs aviation communication radar systems used for aircraft navigation and landing; performs air traffic control duties.	Mathematics and shop courses in electricity and electronics useful.	Radio and television or electrical instrument repairer, communications, electrical and electronics engineer and radio engineer.
Ballistic/Land Combat Missile and Light Air Defense Weapons Systems Maintenance	Inspects, tests, maintains and repairs tactical missile systems and related test equipment and trainers.	Mathematics, physics, electricity, electronics (radio and TV) and blueprint reading.	Radio control room technician, radio mechanic, transmitter, radio and TV repairer.
Communications-Electronic Maintenance	Installs and maintains radar and radio receiving, transmitting, carrier and terminal equipment.	Electricity, mathematics, electronics and blueprint reading.	Radio control room technician, radio mechanic, transmitter, radio and TV repairer.
Electronics Warfare Intercept Systems Maintenance	Installs, operates and maintains intercept, electronic measuring and testing equipment.	Physics, mathematics, electricity, electronics (radio and TV) and blueprint reading.	Electrical instrument repairer and electronic equipment inspector.

PERSONNEL/BASE SUPPORT

Career field	Duties & responsibilities	Qualifications	Examples of civilian jobs
Administration	Performs general administrative duties such as typing, stenography, postal functions and specific administrative duties such as personnel, legal, equal opportunity and chapel activities.	Basic clerical and communication abilities, typing, bookkeeping, stenography or office management skills desirable.	Clerk, typist, secretary, employment interviewer, postal clerk, recreation specialist, office manager, personnel clerk, bookkeeper, cashier, payroll clerk and court clerk.

Career field	Duties & responsibilities	Qualifications	Examples of civilian jobs
Audiovisual	Operates radio and television equipment, still/motion picture photography, audiovisual equipment repair and graphic illustration.	Normal color vision, verbal ability, clear speech and attentiveness.	Cameraman, camera repairer, photographer, illustrator and video editor.
Band	Plays brass, woodwind or percussion instruments in marching, concert, dance, stage and show bands, combos or instrumental ensembles. Sings in vocal groups, writes and arranges music.	Vocal audition or instrumental audition with bass, woodwind or percussion instrument.	Bandsman, bandmaster, musician, accompanist, arranger, music director, orchestrator, music teacher, orchestra leader and vocalist.
Finance and Accounting	Maintains pay records for military personnel; prepares vouchers for payment; prepares reports; disburses funds; accounts for funds to include budgeting, allocation, auditing; compiles and analyzes statistical data and prepares cost analysis records.	Dexterity in the operation of business machines. Typing, mathematics, statistics and basic principles of accounting desirable. High administrative aptitude mandatory.	Paymaster, cashier, statistical or audit clerk, accountant, budget clerk and bookkeeper.
Food Service	Plans regular and special diet menus, cooks and bakes food in dining facilities and during field exercises. May serve as aide and cook on personal staff for general officer.	Home economics, work in a restaurant, bake shop or meat market.	Cook, chef, caterer, baker, butcher, kitchen supervisor and cafeteria manager.

Career field	Duties & responsibilities	Qualifications	Examples of civilian jobs
Health Care	Assists or supports physicians, surgeons, nurses, dentists, psychologists, social workers and veterinarians in 32 separate job classifications. Some provide direct patient care in hospitals and clinics, others make and repair eyeglasses, dentures or ortho-medical equipment, or maintain medical records.	Biology, chemistry, hygiene, sociology, general math, algebra, animal care, knowledge of mechanics, electronics and general clerical skills.	Social worker (case aide), practical nurse, nurse's aide, dental assistant, surgeon's assistant, psychological aide, hospital attendant or orderly, veterinary assistant, food quality control, medical or dental laboratory technician, physical therapist assistant and dietetic technician.
Military Police	Enforces military regulations; protects facilities, roads, designated sensitive areas and personnel; controls traffic movement; guards military prisoners and enemy prisoners of war.	Sociology and demonstrated leadership in athletics and other group work helpful.	Police officer, plant guard, detective, investigator, crime detection laboratory assistant and ballistics expert.
Public Affairs	Prepares and disseminates news releases on military activities; prepares scripts and newsletters, announcements and public speaking engagements.	Clerical aptitude, verbal ability, clear speech and attentiveness.	Newspaper editor, editorial assistant, public information specialist and photo-journalist.

Career field	Duties & responsibilities	Qualifications	Examples of civilian jobs
Ammunition	Handles, stores, reconditions and salvages ammunition, explosives and components; locates, removes and destroys or salvages unexploded bombs and missiles.	Mechanical aptitude, attentiveness, good close vision, normal color discrimination, manual dexterity and hand-eye coordination.	Toxic chemical handler, ammunition inspector and acid plant operator.
Petroleum	Receives, stores, preserves and distributes bulk-packaged petroleum products; performs standard physical and chemical tests of petroleum products; storage and distribution of purified water.	Hygiene, biology, physics, chemistry and mathematics.	Biological laboratory assistant, petroleum tester and chemical laboratory assistant.
Supply and Service	Receives, stores and issues individual, organizational and expendable supplies, equipment and spare parts; establishes, posts and maintains stock records; repairs and alters textile, canvas and leather supplies, rigs parachutes, decontaminates materials; performs mortuary and grave registration functions.	Mathematical ability and perceptual speed in scanning and checking supply documents. Verbal ability; courses in bookkeeping, typing and office machine operation.	Inventory clerk, stock control clerk or supervisor, shipping or parts clerk, warehouse manager and parachute rigger.

LOGISTICS AND SUPPLY

Career field	Duties & responsibilities	Qualifications	Examples of civilian jobs
Transportation	Operates and performs preventive maintenance on personnel, light, medium and heavy cargo vehicles; operates and maintains marine harbor craft, performs as air traffic controller.	Mechanical aptitude, manual dexterity, hand-eye coordination, FAA certification for air traffic control, license for vehicle operation.	Truck driver and FAA air traffic controller.

ENGINEERING, SCIENCE AND TECHNICAL

Career field	Duties & responsibilities	Qualifications	Examples of civilian jobs
Automatic Data Processing	Operates a variety of electrical accounting and automatic data processing equipment to produce personnel, supply, fiscal, medical, intelligence and other reports.	Reasoning and verbal ability, clerical aptitude, manual dexterity and hand-eye coordination. Knowledge of typing and office machines.	Coding clerk, keypunch, computer and sorting machine operator and machine records unit supervisor.
Chemical	Provides decontamination service after chemical, biological or radiological attacks, produces smoke for battlefield concealment, repairs chemical equipment and assists in overall planning of chemical, biological or radiological activities.	Biology, chemistry and electricity.	Laboratory assistant (biological, chemical or radiological), pumper and repairer (chemical) and exterminator.
Communications—Cryptologic Operations	Installs and maintains field telephone switchboards and field radio communications equipment.	Mathematics, physics and shop courses in electricity.	Communications engineer assistant, plant electrician and radio electrician or operator.

Career field	Duties & responsibilities	Qualifications	Examples of civilian jobs
Electronic Warfare—Cryptologic Operations	Collects and analyzes electromagnetic warfare duties in fixed or mobile operations.	Verbal and reasoning ability and perceptual speed; hearing and visual acuity.	Radio and telegraph operator, navigator, intelligence research analyst, statistician and signal collection technician.
General Engineering	Provides utilities and engineering services such as electric power production, building and roadway construction and maintenance, salvage activities, airstrip construction, fire fighting and crash rescue operations.	Mechanical aptitude, emotional stability and ability to visualize spatial relationships. Carpentry, woodworking or mechanical drawing.	Carpenter, construction equipment operator, electrician, firefighter, driver, plumber, welder and bricklayer.
Military Intelligence	Gathers, translates, correlates and interprets information, including imagery, associated with military plans and operations.	English composition, typing, foreign languages, mathematics and geography.	Investigator, interpreter, records analyst, research worker and intelligence analyst (government).
Topographic Engineering	Performs land surveys; produces construction drawings and plans, maps, charts, diagrams and illustrates material; constructs scale models of terrain and structures, operates offset duplicators, presses and bindery equipment.	Mechanical drawing and drafting, blueprint reading, commercial art, fine arts, geography and mathematics.	Drafting (structural, mechanical and topographical), cartographic and art layout, model maker, commercial artist and physical.

Coast Guard Occupations

VEHICLE/MACHINERY MECHANICS

Career field	Duties & responsibilities	Qualifications	Examples of civilian jobs
Aviation Maintenance Technician	The AMT inspects, services, maintains, troubleshoots and repairs aircraft power plant, power train and structural systems. The AMT maintains metal, composite and fiberglass materials, fabricates cables, wire harnesses and structural components; and performs aircraft corrosion control, nondestructive testing, basic electrical troubleshooting and record keeping. Also, AMTs hold an aircrew position in specific Coast Guard aircraft.	Automobile or aircraft engine work; algebra and geometry are helpful. High degree of mechanical aptitude. Metal shop, woodworking, algebra, plane geometry, physics and experience in automobile body-work are desirable.	Airport serviceperson, aircraft engine test mechanic, small appliance repairer, mechanic, machinist, flight engineer. Welder, sheet metal repairer, hydraulics technician, aircraft repairer.
Machinery Technician	Operates, maintains and repairs ship's propulsion, auxiliary equipment and outside equipment such as steering, engineer, refrigeration/air conditioning and steam equipment.	Aptitude for mechanical work. Practical or shop mathematics, machine shop, electricity and physics valuable.	Boiler house repairer, engineer maintenance, machinist, marine engineer, turbine operator, engineer repairer, air conditioning and refrigeration repairer.

Career field	Duties & responsibilities	Qualifications	Examples of civilian jobs
Avionics Technician	Inspects, services, maintains, trouble-shoots and repairs aircraft power, communications, navigation, auto flight and sensor systems. AVTs perform minimum performance checks, system alignments, avionics corrosion control and record keeping. Also, AVTs hold an aircrew position in specific Coast Guard aircraft.	Algebra, trigonometry, physics and shop experience in electrical work are desirable. High degree of aptitude for electrical work.	Aircraft electrician, electrician, substation operator, instrument inspector and electrical consultant, radio mechanic, electronics technician, radio repairman/technician, TV repairer.
Electrician's Mate	Tests, maintains and repairs aviation electronics equipment including navigation, identification, detec-tion, reconnaissance, special purpose equipment; operates warfare equipment.	Aptitude for electrical and mechanical work. Electrical, practical and shop mathematics and physics are useful.	Electrician, electric motor and electrical equipment repairer, armature winder and radio/TV repairer.
Electronics Technician	Maintains all elec-tronic equipment used for communications, detection ranging, recognition and countermeasures, worldwide naviga-tional systems, computers and sonars.	Aptitude for detailed mechanical work. Radio, electricity, physics, algebra, trigonometry and shop valuable.	Electronics technician, radar and radio repairer, instrument and electronics mechanic, telephone repairman.

ELECTRONIC/ELECTRICAL SYSTEMS

Career field	Duties & responsibilities	Qualifications	Examples of civilian jobs
Telephone Technician	Installs and maintains telecommunications equipment ranging from towers, antennas, pole lines and underground cables to computer-based data communications and processing systems, telephone and data switching systems and networks, and public address, security and remote control systems.	An interest in electrical equipment and an above average ability to solve math problems. School courses in algebra, physics, trigonometry, electricity and communications useful. Experience with electronics, electrical or communications equipment is helpful.	Electronics technician, telephone installer, telephone lineman, data/computer equipment technician, telephone repair.

LOGISTICS AND SUPPLY

Career field	Duties & responsibilities	Qualifications	Examples of civilian jobs
Aviation Survival Technician	The Aviation Survival Technician inspects, services, maintains, troubleshoots and repairs aircraft and aircrew survival equipment and rescue devices. Also, ASTs perform the duties of a rescue swimmer and provide aircrew survival training to all aviators.	Must perform extremely careful and accurate work. General shop, math and sewing desirable. Experience in use and repair of sewing machines.	Parachute packer, inspector, repairer and tester, sailmaker, ammunition foreman and rescue gear specialist.
Boatswain's Mate	Operates small boats, stores cargo, handles ropes and lines and directs work of deck force.	Must be physically strong. Practical math desirable. Algebra, geometry and physics.	Motorboat operator, pier superintendent, able seaman, rigger, cargo wincher, longshoreman, marina operator and heavy equipment operator.

LOGISTICS AND SUPPLY

Career field	Duties & responsibilities	Qualifications	Examples of civilian jobs
Storekeeper	Orders, receives, stores, inventories and issues clothing, food, mechanical equipment and other items; serves as a payroll clerk.	Typing, bookkeeping, accounting and commercial math, general business and English are helpful.	Sales or shipping clerk, warehouse worker, buyer, invoice control clerk, purchasing agent, accountant.

PERSONNEL/BASE SUPPORT

Career field	Duties & responsibilities	Qualifications	Examples of civilian jobs
Food Service Specialist	Cooks and bakes; prepares menus; keeps cost accounts; assists in ordering provisions; inspects food.	Experience or course in food preparation, dietetics and record keeping are helpful.	Cook, steward, butcher, chef and restaurant manager.
Health Services Technician	Administers medicine; applies first aid; assists in operating room; nurses patients; assists dental officers.	Hygiene, biology, first aid, physiology, chemistry, typing and public speaking are helpful.	Practical nurse, medical, dental or X-ray technician.
Public Affairs Specialist	Reports and edits news; publishes information about service members and activities through newspapers, magazines, radio and television; shoots and develops film and photographs.	High degree of clerical aptitude. English, journalism, typing and writing experience are helpful.	News editor, copy-reader, script writer, reporter, free-lance writer, rewrite or art layout person, producer, public relations advertising specialist and photographer.
Yeoman	Performs typing and filing duties; operates office equipment; prepares and routes correspondence and reports; maintains personnel records and publications.	Same qualifications required of secretaries and typists in private industry. English, business, stenography and typing are helpful.	Office manager, secretary, general office clerk, administrative assistant, legal clerk, personnel manager and court reporter.

Career field	Duties & responsibilities	Qualifications	Examples of civilian jobs
Damage Controlman	Fabricates, installs and repairs shipboard structures, plumbing and piping systems; uses damage control in fire fighting; operates nuclear, biological, chemical and radiological defense equipment; construction work.	High mechanical aptitude. Sheet metal foundry, pipefitting, carpentry, mathematics, geometry and chemistry are valuable.	Firefighter, welder, plumber, shipfitter, blacksmith, metallurgical technician and carpenter.
Fire Control Technician	Operates, tests, maintains and repairs weapons control systems and telemetering equipment used to compute accuracy of naval guns and missiles.	Ability to perform fine, detailed work. Extensive training in mathematics, electronics, electricity and mechanics are useful.	Radar or electronics technician, test range tracker, instrument repairer and electrician.
Gunner's Mate	Operates and performs maintenance on guided missile launching systems, rocket launchers, guns and gun mounts; inspects/repairs electrical, electronic, pneumatic, mechanical and hydraulic systems.	Prolonged attention and mental alertness, ability to perform detailed work. High aptitude for electrical and mechanical work. Arithmetic, shop math, electricity, electronics, physics, machine shop and welding are helpful.	Gunsmith, locksmith, machinist, instrument repairer, hydraulics, pneumatic or mechanical technician, small appliance or test equipment repairer.
Marine Science Technician	Makes visual/instrumental weather and oceanographic observations; conducts chemical analysis; enters data on appropriate logs, charts and forms; analyzes/interprets weather and sea conditions.	Ability to use numbers in practical problems. Algebra, geometry, trigonometry, physics, physiology, chemistry, typing, meteorology, astronomy and oceanography are helpful.	Oceanographic technician, weather observer, meteorologist, chart maker, statistical clerk and inspector of weather and oceanographic instruments.

Career field	Duties & responsibilities	Qualifications	Examples of civilian jobs
Quartermaster	Performs navigation of ship's steering; lookout supervision, ship control, bridge watch duties, visual communication and maintenance of navigational aids.	Good vision and hearing and ability to express oneself clearly in writing and speaking. Public speaking, grammar, geometry and physics are helpful.	Barge, motorboat or yacht captain, quartermaster, harbor pilot aboard merchant ships, navigator and chart maker.
Radarman	Operates surveillance and search radar, electronic recognition and identification equipment, controlled approach devices and electronic aids to navigation; serves as plotter and status board keeper.	Prolonged attention and mental alertness. Physics, mathematics and shop courses in radio and electricity are helpful. Experience in radio repair is valuable.	Radio operator (aircraft, ship, government service, radio broadcasting), radar equipment supervisor.
Telecommunications Specialist	Operates communication equipment; transmits, receives and processes all forms of military record and voice communications.	Good hearing and manual dexterity. Mathematics, physics and electricity desirable. Experience as amateur radio operator is helpful.	Telegrapher, radio dispatcher, radio/ telephone operator and computer operator.

Marine Corps Occupations

COMBAT SPECIALTIES

Career field	Duties & responsibilities	Qualifications	Examples of civilian jobs
Field Artillery	Maintains 155mm, 8-inch and 105mm howitzers; and self-propelled 8-inch and 105mm howitzers.	Mathematical reasoning, mechanical aptitude, good vision and stamina; mechanics, electricity and meteorology.	Surveyor, meteorologist, radio operator, recording engineer and ordnance inspector.
Infantry	Performs as rifleman, machine gunner or grenadier, infantry unit leader; supervises training and operations of infantry units.	Verbal and mathematical reasoning, good vision and stamina; general mathematics, mechanical drafting, geography and mechanical drawing.	Firearms assembler, gunsmith, policeman, immigration inspector and plant security policeman.
Tank and Amphibian Tractor	Performs as driver, gunner and loader in tanks, armored amphibious tractors.	Mechanical ability and stamina; auto mechanics, machine shop, electricity and mechanical drawing.	Automotive mechanic, bulldozer operator or repairman, armament machinist-mechanic and gunsmith assistant.

VEHICLE/MACHINERY MECHANICS

Career field	Duties & responsibilities	Qualifications	Examples of civilian jobs
Aircraft Maintenance	Performs the mechanical functions of maintenance, repair and modification of Marine air and ground support equipment.	Mechanical or electrical aptitude with manual dexterity; shot mathematics desirable.	Aircraft mechanic, electrician or hydraulics specialist, aviation machinist, sheet metal worker and aircraft instrument maker or repairer.
Motor Transport	Performs auto mechanics and body repair, motor vehicle and amphibian truck operations.	Automotive mechanics, machine shop, electricity and blueprint reading useful.	Automobile mechanic, electrical systems repairer, truck driver, motor vehicle dispatcher and motor transport.

Career field	Duties & responsibilities	Qualifications	Examples of civilian jobs
Avionics	Installs and repairs aircraft electrical, communications/ navigation and fire control equipment and air-launched guided missiles; serves as electrician and instrument repairman.	Mathematics and shop course in electricity, hydraulics and electronics useful.	Radio and TV or electrical instrument repairer, communications, electrical or electronics engineer and radio operator.
Data/Communications Maintenance	Installs, inspects and repairs telephone, teletype and crypto-graphic equipment and cables, calibrates precision electronic, mechanical, dimen-sional and optical test instruments.	Mathematics, electric-ity and blueprint reading courses helpful.	Telephone installer and trouble shooter
Electronics Mainte-nance	Installs, tests and repairs air search radar, radio, radio relay, missile fire control and guidance systems.	Electronics, mathemat-ics, electricity and blueprint reading useful.	Radio and TV repair, radio engineer, electrical instrument repairer, recording communications and electrical engineer.
Training and Audiovi-sual Support	Operates still, motion picture and aerial cameras; develops film and prints; repairs cameras; edits motion picture films; and performs as illustrator or draftsman.	Mathematics, chemis-try and shop courses in electricity; normal color perception desirable.	Commercial illustra-tor, photographer, cinematographer, copy camera operator, motion picture film editor, camera and instrument repairer.

Career field	Duties & responsibilities	Qualifications	Examples of civilian jobs
Airfield Services	Maintains aircraft log books, publications and flight operations records, prepares reports and schedules; installs and repairs aircraft launching and recovery equipment.	Typing, geography and mechanical drawing useful.	Airplane dispatch clerk, flight dispatcher, timekeeper and airport crash truck driver.
Auditing, Finance and Accounting	Prepares and audits personnel pay records, processes public vouchers and administers and audits unit fiscal accounts.	Computational work and attention to detail; typing, bookkeeping, office machine and mathematics useful.	Payroll or cost clerk, bookkeeper, cashier, bank teller, accounting and audit clerk and accountant.
Food Service	Performs as cook, baker or meat cutter.	Hygiene, biology, chemistry, home economics and bookkeeping courses useful.	Cook, chef, baker, meat cutter or butcher, caterer, executive chef, dietician and restaurant manager.
Legal Services	Prepares legal documents, operates stenotype machines.	Manual dexterity, English.	Law clerk, court reporter, chief clerk and stenotype operator.
Marines Corps Exchange	Keeps and audits books and financial records, performs sales and merchandise stock control duties.	Typing, bookkeeping, business, arithmetic, office machine operations and accounting useful.	Salesman, stock control supervisor, buyer, bookkeeper, accounting clerk, accountant and auditor.
Military Police and Corrections	Enforces military orders, guards military and war prisoners and controls traffic.	Sociology and athletic ability helpful.	Policeman, ballistics expert and investigator.
Musician	Performs in Marine Corps Band, unit bands and Drum and Bugle Corps; repairs musical instruments.	Music experience as a member of a high school band or orchestra.	Musician, music librarian, music teacher, bandmaster, orchestra or music director and musical instrument repairer.

Career field	Duties & responsibilities	Qualifications	Examples of civilian jobs
Personnel and Admin-istration	Performs as personnel classification clerk, administrative specialist and postal clerk.	Reasoning, verbal ability and clerical aptitude. English composition, typing shorthand and social studies helpful.	Secretary, typist, vocational advisor, employment inter-viewer, manager, officer manager, job analyst and postal clerk.
Printing and Repro-duction	Performs letterpress and lithographic offset printing; sets type; operates linotype machines, presses, process cameras and bookbinding equip-ment.	General mathematics, printing and other graphic arts useful.	Printing, compositor, linotype operator, photo lithographer, press operator, printing bookbinder, printing plant makeup worker and proof-reader.
Public Affairs	Liaison between the Marine Corps and the public and media. Gathers material for and writes and edits news stories and historical reports; gathers material for, prepares and edits radio and television broadcast scripts. Conducts community relations projects. Assists in operations of Armed Forces Radio and Television Service detachments worldwide.	English grammar and composition, typing aptitude required, speech, journalism and photography helpful.	Public relations, TV news reporter/anchor, radio DJ, news reporter correspon-dent, columnist, copyreader, copy or news editor, radio television announcer and script writer. TV/radio station program-mer/traffic director, video editor and producer, TV news cameraman and print journalism photogra-pher.

Career field	Duties & responsibilities	Qualifications	Examples of civilian jobs
Ammunition and Explosive Ordnance Disposal	Inspects, issues and supervises storage of ammunition and explosives; locates, disarms, detonates or salvages unexploded bombs.	Mechanics, general science and chemistry useful.	Firearms and ammunition proof director, ordnance technician (government), powder and explosives inspector.
Logistics	Performs administrative duties involving the supply, quartering, movement and transport of Marine units by land, sea and air.	Clerical aptitude, knowledge of verbal and math reasoning; ability to operate office machines and read maps useful.	Inventory or shipping clerk, pier superintendent, stock control clerk or supervisor and warehouse manager.
Supply Administration and Operations	Administration procurement, subsistence, packaging and warehousing; requisitions, purchases, receipts, accounts; classifies, stores, issues, sells, packages, preserves and inspects new scrap, salvage, waste material, supplies and equipment.	Typing, bookkeeping, office machine operation and commercial subjects helpful.	Shipping, receiving, stock and inventory clerk, stock control supervisor, warehouse manager and parts and purchasing agent.
Transportation	Handles cargo and transacts business of freight shipping and receiving and passenger transportation.	Typing, bookkeeping, business, arithmetic, office machine operation and commercial subjects beneficial.	Shipping clerk, cargo handler, freight traffic clerk, passenger and railroad station agent.

ENGINEERING, SCIENCE AND TECHNICAL

Career field	Duties & responsibilities	Qualifications	Examples of civilian jobs
Air Traffic Control and Enlisted Flight Crew/Air Support/ Anti-warfare	Operates airfield control tower and radio-radar air traffic control systems; serves as navigator, radio and radar operator, and intercept controller anti-air warfare missile batteryman.	Clear speaking voice, good hearing and better-than-average eyesight; speech, mathematics and electricity and experience as a ham radio operator helpful.	Airport control tower or flight radio operator, navigator, instrument-landing truck operator and radio or television studio engineer.
Aviation Ordnance	Maintains and repairs aircraft armament systems, gun pods, machine guns, bomb racks and rocket/ missile launcher equipment.	Electricity, hydraulics and mechanics shop courses useful.	Firearms assembler, gunsmith, armament mechanic and aircraft accessories repairer.
Construction Equipment and Shore Party	Performs metalworking operation and maintenance of fuel storage, heavy engineering equipment, construction and repair of military facilities.	Automotive mechanics, sheet metal working, machine shop, carpentry and mechanical drafting useful.	Sheet metal worker, engineering equipment mechanic, carpenter, road machinery operator, rigger and construction superintendent.
Data systems	Operates and programs data processing equipment.	Clerical aptitude, manual dexterity and hand-eye coordination, mathematics, accounting and English useful.	Computer operator or programmer and data, control coordinator.
Drafting, Surveying and Mapping	Makes architectural and mechanical drawings, prepares military maps, creates or copies articles of illustrative materials.	Mathematics, mechanical drawing and drafting, geography and commercial art helpful.	Architectural or mechanical drafting, surveyor or cartographer, illustrator and commercial artist.

Career field	Duties & responsibilities	Qualifications	Examples of civilian jobs
Intelligence	Records and interprets information, makes study of aerial photographs, conducts interrogations in foreign languages, translates written material and interprets conversations.	Geography, history, government, economics, English, foreign languages, typing, mechanical drafting and mathematics useful.	Investigator, research worker, intelligence analyst (government), map drafter, cartographic aide and records analyst.
Nuclear, Biological and Chemical	Performs routine duties to apply detection, emergency and decontamination measures to gassed or radioactive areas. Inspects and performs preventive maintenance on chemical warfare protection equipment.	Must not have any known hypersensitivity to the wearing of protective clothing; be emotionally stable; biology and chemistry background useful.	Laboratory assistant (nuclear, biological or chemical), exterminator and decontaminator.
Operational Communications	Lays communication wire; installs and operates radio, radio telegraph and radio relay equipment; encodes and decodes messages.	Mathematics, typing, courses in electricity and electronics useful.	Radio operator, telephone lineperson, radio broadcaster, traffic manager and communications engineer.
Ordnance	Inspects, maintains and repairs infantry, artillery and anti-aircraft weapons; fire control optical instruments; operates machine tools or modifies metal parts.	Mathematics, mechanics, machine shop and blueprint reading, welding and heat treatment or metal electricity.	Armament mechanic, gunsmith, time-recording equipment service person, electrician, optical instrument inspector and electrical engineer.

Career field	Duties & responsibilities	Qualifications	Examples of civilian jobs
Signals Intelligence/ Ground Electronic Warfare	Performs routine duties for collecting, translating, recording and disseminating information associated with military plans and operations.	English composition, geography and mathematics useful.	Radio intelligence operator, intelligence analyst, investigator and records analyst.
Utilities	Installs, operates and maintains electrical, water supply, heating, plumbing, sewage, refrigeration, hygiene and air-conditioning equipment.	Mechanical aptitude and manual dexterity important; vocational school shop course in industrial arts and crafts beneficial.	Electrician, plumber, steam fitter, refrigeration mechanic, electric motor repairer and stationary engineer.
Weather Service	Collects, records and analyzes meteorological data; makes visual and instrumental observations.	Visual acuity correctable to 20/20, normal color perception; mathematics desirable, meteorology and astronomy helpful.	Meteorologist and weather forecaster/ observer.

Navy Occupations

COMBAT SPECIALTIES

Career field	Duties & responsibilities	Qualifications	Examples of civilian jobs
Aviation Anti-Submarine Warfare	Operator Performs general flight crew duties; operates ASW sensor systems; performs diagnostic functions to effect fault isolation and optimize system performance.	High degree of electrical and mechanical aptitude. Must pass flight physical and be able to swim. Courses in algebra, trigonometry, physics, electricity.	Radar technician and oil well sounding device operator.
Electronic Warfare Technician	Operates and maintains electronic equipment used for detection, analysis and identification of emissions in electro-magnetic spectrums as well as deception and jamming of enemy electronic sensors.	Good arithmetic and record keeping ability. Competence with tools, equipment and machines.	Electronics intelligence operations specialist and electronics mechanic.
Fire Control Technician	Operates, tests, maintains and repairs weapons control systems and telemetering equipment used to compute and resolve factors that influence accuracy of torpedoes and missiles.	Perform fine, detailed work. Extensive training in mathematics, electronics, electricity and mechanics.	Radar or electronics technician, test range tracker, instrument repairer and electrician.

COMBAT SPECIALTIES

Career field	Duties & responsibilities	Qualifications	Examples of civilian jobs
Gas Turbine Systems Technician	Operates, repairs and maintains gas turbine engines, main propulsion machinery including gears, shafts, controllable pitch propellers, related electric and electronic equipment and propulsion.	Mechanical ability. Experience in electricity/electronics repair, blueprint reading, math and physics.	Electronics technician and power plant operator.
Gunner's Mate	Operates and performs maintenance on guided missile launching systems, rocket launchers, guns, gun mounts; inspects/repairs electrical, electronic, pneumatic, mechanical and hydraulic systems.	Prolonged attention and mental alertness, ability to perform detailed work. High aptitude for electrical and mechanical work. Arithmetic, shop math, electricity, electronics, physics, machine shop and shop work.	Electronics mechanic, missile facilities repairer, gunsmith, rocket engine component mechanic and marksmanship instructor.
Sonar Technician	Operates underwater detection and attack apparatus; obtains and interprets information for tactical purposes; maintains and repairs electronic underwater sound detection equipment.	Normal hearing and clear speaking voice. Algebra, geometry, physics, electricity and shop work desirable. Aptitude for electrical and mechanical work.	Oil well sound device operator, radio operator, inspector of electronic assemblies; electronic technician, electrical repairer and fire control mechanic.

VEHICLE/MACHINERY MECHANICS

Career field	Duties & responsibilities	Qualifications	Examples of civilian jobs
Aviation Structural Mechanic	Maintains and repairs aircraft, airframe, structural components, hydraulic controls, utility systems and egress systems.	High degree of mechanical aptitude. Metal shop, algebra, plane geometry, physics; experience in automobile bodywork.	Welder, sheet metal repairer, hydraulics technician, radiographer and aircraft plumbing systems mechanic.
Aviation Support Equipment Technician	Services, tests and repairs gasoline and diesel engines, gas turbine compressors, power generating equipment, liquid and gaseous oxygen and nitrogen servicing equipment, electrical systems and air conditioning systems.	High mechanical aptitude, physical strength, manual dexterity and ability to work well with others.	Automobile mechanic for diesel and gasoline engines, air conditioning systems, ignition systems, hydraulic systems and electrical systems for aviation support equipment.
Construction Mechanic	Maintains, repairs and overhauls automotive and heavy construction equipment.	High mechanical aptitude. Electrical or machine shop, shop mathematics and physics helpful.	Machinist or auto mechanic work. Automotive or diesel engine mechanic, construction equipment mechanic, automotive electrician, automobile body repairer.
Engineman	Operates, services and repairs internal combustion engines, ship propulsion machinery, refrigeration and air conditioning systems, air compressors and related electro-hydraulic equipment.	Clear speech, physical stamina and manual dexterity. Knowledge of arithmetic and internal combustion engines is desirable.	Diesel plant engine operator, diesel mechanic, automobile engine mechanic, marine engine machinist, stationary engineer, fuel system maintenance worker and power plant operator.

VEHICLE/MACHINERY MECHANICS

Career field	Duties & responsibilities	Qualifications	Examples of civilian jobs
Instrumentman	Installs, services, adjusts, calibrates and repairs a wide variety of small instruments. Responsible for the repair and calibration of precision measuring devices, which include pressure and vacuum gauges, thermometers, micrometers, tachometers, pressure/flow regulating devices and watches and clocks.	Manual dexterity, ability to do detailed work and repetitive tasks, good memory, competence in math.	Office machine repairer, electrical instrument repairer, watch repairer and instrument mechanic.
Machinery Repairer	Makes replacement parts and repairs or overhauls ship's engine auxiliary.	Experience in practical or shop mathematics, machine shop, electricity, mechanical drawing and foundry desirable.	Engine lathe operator, machinist tool clerk, bench machinist, turret and milling machine operator and tool-maker.
Machinist's Mate	Operates, maintains and repairs steam turbines used for ship's propulsion and auxiliary equipment such as turbo generators, pumps, refrigeration/air conditioning and laundry equipment.	Aptitude for mechanical work. Practical or shop mathematics, machine shop, electricity and physics valuable. Physical stamina and ability to work well with others.	Power plant operator, oxygen plant operator, marine mechanic, diesel mechanic, stationary engineer/mechanic and refrigeration mechanic.

Career field	Duties & responsibilities	Qualifications	Examples of civilian jobs
Aviation Electronics Technician	Tests, maintains, repairs aviation electronics equipment including navigation, identification, detection, reconnaissance, weapons systems, weapon-control radar, computers, computer sights, gyroscopes, guided missiles equipment and anti-submarine warfare equipment. Source rating for aircrew as in-flight technician; debriefs flight crews.	High degree of electronic, electrical, mechanical and mathematical aptitude. Ability to do detailed work, a good memory, resourcefulness and curiosity.	Aircraft electrician, radio mechanic, electrical repairer, instrument repairer, electronics technician, radar computer repairer and TV repairer.
Construction Electrician	Installs, operates, maintains and repairs electrical generating and distribution systems, transformers, switchboards, motors and controllers.	Interest in mechanical and electrical work. Electricity, shop mathematics and physics helpful; ability to work aloft.	Powerhouse or construction electrician, electrical and telephone repairer, power plant operator and diesel plant operator.
Electrician's Mate	Maintains power and lighting equipment, generators, motors, power distribution systems, other electrical equipment; rebuilds electrical equipment.	Aptitude for electrical and mechanical work. Electrical and shop mathematics and physics are also valuable.	Electrician, electric motor and electrical equipment repairer and power reactor operator.
Electronics Technician	Maintains all electronic equipment used for communications, detection, navigation, ranging, recognition and countermeasures.	Aptitude for detailed electrical and mechanical work. Radio, electricity, physics, algebra, trigonometry and shop are valuable.	Computer-peripheral equipment operator or electronics mechanic.

Career field	Duties & responsibilities	Qualifications	Examples of civilian jobs
Dental Technician	Assists dental officers, administers dental hygiene, makes dental X-rays and performs administrative duties. Some qualify dental prosthetical lab techniques and maintenance and repair of dental equipment.	Scientific background or interests, normal color vision; competence with tools; good communication skills; ability to perform repetitive tasks without losing interest.	Dental assistant, dental records clerk, dental laboratory technician, dental X-ray technician, dental hygienist, dental equipment and repairman/technical representative.
Disbursing Clerk	Maintains military pay records; prepares payrolls and maintains related fiscal records and reports.	Typing, bookkeeping, accounting, business math and office practices.	Paymaster, cashier, statistical or audit clerk, bookkeeper, bookkeeping machine operator and cost accountant.
Hospital Corpsman	Assists in the prevention and treatment of disease and injuries. May function within over 40 specialties, technician health care or special operational fields. May specialize as a health care provider who performs independent of a physician in the air, ashore or at sea, aboard surface ships or submarines. May attain additional specialty training for assignment with Navy SEALS, USMC reconnaissance or deep sea diving.	Scientific background or interest in providing health care is extremely important. Good communication skills, writing and arithmetic abilities are necessary.	Technician fields of pharmacy, nuclear medicine, laboratory specialties, surgery/operating room, emergency medicine, medical photography, industrial health and safety, radiology/X-ray, EEG, orthopedics/cast room, cardiopulmonary, respiratory therapy, optician/ocular, physical/occupational therapy.

Career field	Duties & responsibilities	Qualifications	Examples of civilian jobs
Illustrator Draftsman	Designs, sketches, does layouts, makes signs, charts and training aids; operates visual presentation equipment; uses art media, computer reproduction systems and graphic arts equipment.	Previous experience as draftsman, tracer or surveyor valuable. Art, mechanical drawing and blueprint reading valuable. Creativity, manual dexterity and competence in math.	Structural draftsman, technical illustrator, specification writer, electrical draftsman and graphic artist.
Lithographer	Operates print shops, which produce Navy publications, such as newspapers, forms, manuals, magazines and training materials.	Work with machinery and chemicals. Printing, physics, chemistry, English and shop mathematics valuable.	Lithographic and plate press operator, bookbinder, engraver, camera operator, photolithographer, printer and composing room machinist.
Mess Management Specialist	Orders, prepares and serves food. Prepares menus; maintains records for food supplies and financial budgets. Manages personnel living quarters.	Ability in arithmetic, records keeping and detail work; interest in nutrition and culinary arts valuable.	Baker, cook, butcher, nightclub manager, cake decorator, chef and restaurant manager.
Musician	Provides music for military ceremonies, religious services, concerts, parades, various recreational activities; plays one or more musical instruments.	Proficiency on standard band or orchestral instruments.	Music teacher, instrument musician, orchestra leader, music arranger, instrument repairer and music librarian.

Career field	Duties & responsibilities	Qualifications	Examples of civilian jobs
Photographer's Mate	Operates and maintains various types of cameras for a variety of uses; performs duties as member of flight crew; develops motion picture film and microfilm prints; takes news photographs; operates laboratory and darkroom equipment for film processing.	Ability to relate to people, speaking and writing skills; ability to do detailed work and keep records; good color vision; ability to work as part of a team; manual dexterity; physical strength; a knowledge of math.	Photographer, camera repairer, screen writer, camera operator, photojournalist, film editor, photofinisher and sound mixer.
Photojournalist	Gathers facts and writes articles for publication in civilian and Navy communities; prepares stories for hometown news outlets, gathers facts, photos, writes, edits and proofreads news for radio and TV outlets; prepares layouts for base papers.	Writing and speaking skills, creativity, typing, an interest in people, maturity and manual dexterity.	News editor, screenwriter, reporter, producer, announcer, production manager and photographer.
Postal Clerk	Processes mail, sells stamps and money orders, maintains mail directories and handles correspondence concerning postal operations.	Bookkeeping, accounting, business math, typing and office practices.	Parcel post or mail clerk, mail room manager, stock clerk and cashier.

PERSONNEL/BASE SUPPORT

Career field	Duties & responsibilities	Qualifications	Examples of civilian jobs
Religious Program	Supports chaplains of all faiths and religious activities of the command; assists in management and development of the command's religious programs and determinations of resources; maintains records of various funds; ecclesiastical documents and references.	Typing, ability to express ideas, do detailed work and keep accurate records; good moral character, interest in people, initiative, writing skills.	Church business administrator, religious facilities manager and administrative assistant.

LOGISTICS AND SUPPLY

Career field	Duties & responsibilities	Qualifications	Examples of civilian jobs
Aircrews Survival Equipmentman	Maintains and packs parachutes, survival equipment, flight and protective clothing, life jackets; tests and services pressure suits.	Must perform extremely careful and accurate work. General shop and sewing desirable. Experience in use and repair of sewing machines.	Parachute packer, inspector, repairer and tester; sailmaker.
Boatswain's Mate	Performs seamanship tasks, operates small boats, stores cargo, handles ropes and lines, directs work of deck force personnel.	Must be physically strong. Practical math desirable; algebra, geometry and physics.	Motorboat operator, pier superintendent, able seaman, canvas worker, rigger, cargo wincher, mate, longshore worker and quartermaster.
Storekeeper	Orders, receives, stores, inventories and issues clothing, foodstuffs, mechanical equipment and general supplies.	Typing, bookkeeping, accounting, commercial math, general business studies and English.	Sales or shipping clerk, warehouse worker, buyer, invoice control clerk, purchasing agent, travel clerk, accounting clerk, bookkeeper and stock control clerk.

Career field	Duties & responsibilities	Qualifications	Examples of civilian jobs
Aerographer's Mate	Collects, records and analyzes meteorological and oceanographic data; enters information on appropriate charts; forecasts from visual and instrumental weather observations; operates and maintains computers.	Skills in mathematics, speaking, writing, record keeping and ability to perform repetitive work.	Weather observer, meteorologist, chart maker, oceanographer's assistant and computer programmer.
Air Traffic Controller	Controls air traffic, operates radar air traffic control ashore and afloat; uses radio and light signals; directs aircraft under visual flight and instrument flight conditions; assists in preparation of flight plans.	High degree of accuracy, precision, self-reliance and calmness under stress. Experience in radio broadcasting and good vision.	Air traffic controller, control tower operator, radio telephone operator, flight operations specialist and aircraft log clerk.
Boiler Technician	Operates equipment that produces steam for propulsion engines and steam-driven electric power generator; tests and inventories supplies for fuel and water, maintains boilers, pumps and associated machinery.	Should know how to work with common hand and power tools. Strong interest in mechanical work. Shop courses and practical mathematics are valuable.	Marine firefighter, boiler inspector, boiler maker, stationary engineer, boiler or heating plant technician and fuel system maintenance worker.
Builder	Constructs, maintains and repairs wood, concrete and masonry structures; erects and repairs waterfront structures.	High mechanical aptitude. Carpentry and shop mathematics desirable. Experience with hand and power tools valuable.	Plasterer, roofer, mason, painter, construction worker, carpenter, estimator.

Career field	Duties & responsibilities	Qualifications	Examples of civilian jobs
Cryptologic Technician	Operates and maintains sophisticated electronic equipment in a high-tech environment. Consists of six separate career fields: administration, maintenance, linguistics, communications and collection (manual and electronic).	Individual and immediate family must be U.S. citizens of excellent character. Individual must be motivated, speak and write clearly and work well with others.	Admin/security specialist, electromechanical technician, interpreter/translator, computer programmer and radio-telegraphic operator.
Damage Controlman	Operates, maintains and repairs fire fighting equipment, damage control equipment and chemical, biological and radiological defense equipment.	Good vision and color perception, manual dexterity, a good memory and resourcefulness.	Firefighter, plumber, welder, shipfitter, blacksmith and sheet metal worker.
Data Processing Technician	Operates data processing equipment including sorters, collators, reproducers, tabulating printers and computers.	High clerical aptitude. Typing, bookkeeping and operating business machines desirable. Experience in mechanical work.	Keypunch operator, systems analyst, verifier and tabulating machine operator.
Equipment Operator	Operates automotive and heavy construction equipment.	Good physical strength and normal color perception. Experience in construction work, auto or electrical shop.	Bulldozer operator, power shovel or motor grader operator, excavation foreman, truck driver, asphalt paving machine operator and blaster.
Hull Maintenance Technician	Fabricates, installs, repairs shipboard structures, plumbing and piping systems. Conducts nondestructive tests of metals.	High mechanical aptitude. Sheet metal foundry, pipefitting, carpentry, mathematics, geometry and chemistry useful.	High pressure and nuclear welder, plumber, shipfitter, blacksmith and metallurgical technician.

Career field	Duties & responsibilities	Qualifications	Examples of civilian jobs
Intelligence Specialist	Assembles and analyzes multi-source operations intelligence; prepares maps, graphics, mosaics, charts; extracts information from aerial photos; prepares intelligence reports.	Individual and immediate family must be U.S. citizens of excellent character. Ability to write and speak clearly and work well with others. Math, geography and photography skills valuable.	Aerial photographer, intelligence clerk and intelligence specialist.
Mineman	Tests, maintains and repairs mines, components and mine laying equipment.	Manual dexterity, mechanical inclination and ability to work as a team member.	Electromechanical technician, ammunition inspector and electronics mechanic.
Operations Specialist	Operates surveillance and search radar, electronic recognition and identification equipment, controlled approach devices and electronic aids to navigation; serves as plotter and status board keeper; coordinates aircraft operations at sea.	Prolonged attention and mental alertness. Physics, math and courses in radio and electricity helpful. Experience in radio repair helpful.	Radio operator (aircraft, ship, government service, radio broadcasting), radar equipment supervisor, control tower operator, air traffic controller and computer equipment operator.
Opticalman	Maintains scientifically accurate optical tools used for visual aids and required for navigation and weapons systems. Manufactures optical parts such as lens cells.	Orientation toward fine tools and precision equipment and machinery. Manual dexterity and resourcefulness. Physics, shop math and machine shop/tools helpful.	Precision instrument technician, toolmaker, locksmith, instrument mechanic, optical instrument assembler and camera repairer.

Career field	Duties & responsibilities	Qualifications	Examples of civilian jobs
Quartermaster	Performs navigation of ships, steering, lookout supervision, ship control, bridge watch duties, visual communication and maintenance of navigational aids.	Good vision and hearing and ability to express oneself clearly in writing and speaking. Geometry and physics helpful.	Barge, motorboat, yacht captain, quartermaster and harbor pilot aboard merchant ships.
Radioman	Operates communication, transmission, reception and terminal equipment; transmits, receives and processes all forms of military record and voice communications.	Good hearing and manual dexterity. Mathematics, physics and electricity desirable. Experience as amateur radio operator and personal computer utilization helpful.	Telegrapher, radio dispatcher, radio/ telephone operator and news copy writer.
Utilitiesman	Installs, maintains and repairs plumbing, heating, steam, compressed air systems; fuel storage, collection and disposal facilities and water purification units.	High mechanical aptitude. Apprentice training in plumbing and related fields, mathematics helpful.	Stationary engineer, plumber, pipe fitter, water plant or boiler operator; boiler house supervisor, furnace installer, welder and refrigeration mechanic.

B PAY & BENEFITS

Military pay has never been considered great. Few people, if any, have ever said, "I want to get rich, so I'd better join the military!" However, military pay has increased significantly over the years. I remember stories from veterans who used to be paid $50 a month, and I vividly remember my first military paychecks were $201 every two weeks.

Besides the "basic" military pay, there are lots of other benefits that add up to a very attractive compensation package. This appendix will outline those benefits as well as the various forms of military pay and allowances.

It is not the intention of this appendix to list and explain every military benefit. The reasons for this are that benefits change from time to time, and certain benefits apply to only a select few. If you have any questions about pay and benefits, you should ask your recruiter for the latest information. Another resource for pay information is the Defense Finance and Accounting Service (DFAS). You can get up-to-date pay information on its Web site, www.dfas.mil.

Basic Pay

As the name implies, basic military pay is the base pay you'll receive without any of the allowances you may be entitled to. The amount of basic pay is based on your rank (when it relates to pay, it is referred to as "pay grade") and the amount of time you've been in the military (longevity). Unlike most civilian jobs, where pay raises are sporadic and often based on the mood of management, military pay raises will occur

- upon promotion to the next higher pay grade;
- at regular intervals based on longevity;
- when granted by Congress (usually on January 1 of each year).

Most new military members start out at the lowest level of the military pay scale. However, as mentioned earlier in this book, there may be ways in which you can enter the military at a higher pay grade. The following pay charts are current at the time of this writing; however, keep in mind that there is usually an increase in basic pay every year.

Longevity (years of service) is presented from top to bottom in ascending order starting with less than two years (<2) and going up to twenty-six years. The pay grades are presented left to right in descending order from the highest enlisted grade, E-9, to the lowest grade, E-1. To determine the base pay for a particular grade and length of service, just find the intersection of the years-of-service row and the pay-grade column. If you have put in four years of active-duty service, for example, and your rank is E-3, your base pay would be $1,335.90 per month.

Monthly Basic Pay Chart - Effective July 1, 2000

Years of Service	Pay Grade								
	E-9	E-8	E-7	E-6	E-5	E-4	E-3	E-2	E-1
<2	0.00	0.00	1765.80	1518.90	1332.60	1242.90	1171.50	1127.40	1005.60
2	0.00	0.00	1927.80	1678.20	1494.00	1373.10	1260.60	1127.40	1005.60
3	0.00	0.00	2001.00	1752.60	1566.00	1447.20	1334.10	1127.40	1005.60
4	0.00	0.00	2073.00	1824.30	1640.40	1520.10	1335.90	1127.40	1005.60
6	0.00	0.00	2147.70	1899.30	1714.50	1593.90	1335.90	1127.40	1005.60
8	0.00	2528.40	2220.90	1973.10	1789.50	1593.90	1335.90	1127.40	1005.60
10	3015.30	2601.60	2294.10	2047.20	1861.50	1593.90	1335.90	1127.40	1005.60
12	3083.40	2669.70	2367.30	2118.60	1936.20	1593.90	1335.90	1127.40	1005.60
14	3169.80	2751.60	2439.30	2191.50	1936.20	1593.90	1335.90	1127.40	1005.60
16	3271.50	2840.10	2514.00	2244.60	1936.20	1593.90	1335.90	1127.40	1005.60
18	3373.20	2932.50	2588.10	2283.30	1936.20	1593.90	1335.90	1127.40	1005.60
20	3473.40	3026.10	2660.40	2283.30	1936.20	1593.90	1335.90	1127.40	1005.60
22	3609.30	3161.10	2787.60	2285.70	1936.20	1593.90	1335.90	1127.40	1005.60
24	3744.00	3295.50	2926.20	2285.70	1936.20	1593.90	1335.90	1127.40	1005.60
26	3915.90	3483.60	3134.40	2285.70	1936.20	1593.90	1335.90	1127.40	1005.60

NOTE: E-1 with less than 4 months' service = 930.30

Housing Allowance

Whether or not you will receive a housing allowance depends on two things: your marital status (married couples, as well as single members with minor dependents, are usually authorized housing allowance) and the availability of government-owned quarters (for service members either not married or without dependents).

Most single people will find themselves living in government-owned quarters and, therefore, not entitled to housing allowance. During Basic Training and technical school, however, all personnel are housed in government-owned quarters.

The amount of the housing allowance is based on three things: pay grade, whether or not the service member has any dependents and location of the base.

Housing allowances are generally larger in areas with a higher cost of living. The location used for determining the housing allowance is the zip code of the base at which the service member is stationed, not the location of his or her dependents. Therefore, if a member is stationed in North Carolina in an area with a relatively low cost of living and his dependents are living in New York in an area with a high cost of living, the member's housing allowance will be based on the North Carolina rate.

Consult the DFAS Web site for up-to-date housing allowances. You can search the site using zip codes to find the rates for any area of the United States.

Reflects Pay for One Drill Weekend

Years of Service	Pay Grade								
	E-9	E-8	E-7	E-6	E-5	E-4	E-3	E-2	E-1
<2	0.00	0.00	235.44	202.52	177.68	165.72	156.20	150.32	134.08
2	0.00	0.00	257.04	223.76	199.20	183.08	168.08	150.32	134.08
3	0.00	0.00	266.80	233.68	208.80	192.96	177.88	150.32	134.08
4	0.00	0.00	276.40	243.24	218.72	202.68	178.12	150.32	134.08
6	0.00	0.00	286.36	253.24	228.60	212.52	178.12	150.32	134.08
8	0.00	337.12	296.12	263.08	238.60	212.52	178.12	150.32	134.08
10	402.04	346.88	305.88	272.96	248.20	212.52	178.12	150.32	134.08
12	411.12	355.96	315.64	282.48	258.16	212.52	178.12	150.32	134.08
14	422.64	366.88	325.24	292.20	258.16	212.52	178.12	150.32	134.08
16	436.20	378.68	335.20	299.28	258.16	212.52	178.12	150.32	134.08
18	449.76	391.00	345.08	304.44	258.16	212.52	178.12	150.32	134.08
20	463.12	403.48	354.72	304.44	258.16	212.52	178.12	150.32	134.08
22	481.24	421.48	371.68	304.76	258.16	212.52	178.12	150.32	134.08
24	499.20	439.40	390.16	304.76	258.16	212.52	178.12	150.32	134.08
26	522.12	464.48	417.92	304.76	258.16	212.52	178.12	150.32	134.08

NOTE: E-1 with less than 4 months' service = 124.04

MILITARY HOUSING

Another alternative for members with dependents is military family housing. Military family housing, or "base housing," is exactly what the name implies. It is housing units owned by the government and occupied by service members and their families. In order to live in base housing, military members forfeit their housing allowance; however, there are a few advantages to living in base housing:

- No utility bills
- A secure environment (entrance to most bases is usually restricted to military members and other authorized personnel)
- All maintenance done by the government
- Expenses often less than those incurred living off base (especially in high cost of living areas)

Along with benefits, there are also some disadvantages to living in on-base housing:

- Weekly yard inspections—There is no putting off getting the lawn mowed or raking the leaves; you are required to maintain the outside of your base house. Of course, this can also be looked at as positive since you do not have to deal with neighbors who never take care of their lawns (every neighborhood has them).

- On-base houses typically are smaller than those available off-base—Since housing is assigned based on rank and number of dependents, you will usually receive a house that "fits" your family. Generally this means no spare rooms (although this does not apply to married couples with no children).
- Waiting list—Sometimes based on a higher demand for on-base housing than the number of available houses, you may be required to go on a waiting list. If this is the case, you will probably have to rent a house or apartment off base until military housing becomes available.

ON-BASE SINGLE QUARTERS

Single enlisted members (in what are called the "junior pay grades") will, in most cases, be required to live in barracks (or dormitories).

Tremendous improvements have been made in single enlisted quarters over the years. When I first entered Active Duty, we were housed in what were called "open bay" barracks. These facilities housed everyone in one very large room with one communal bathroom. Eventually, our facilities were upgraded to dormitory-style rooms with three people to a room and with each room having one bathroom.

Today, most facilities are at least at the dormitory-style room level, and others are at a much higher standard, with private rooms and private bathrooms. Most rooms are equipped with a dorm-sized refrigerator. Military members can often install their own stereo systems and televisions.

Navy and coastguardsmen assigned to shipboard duty, however, will experience very different living conditions. They will, more than likely, live onboard ship in what are known as berthing compartments. The quality and comfort of these berthing compartments will depend on the type and age of the ship.

Basic Allowance for Subsistence

In addition to Basic Pay and Housing Allowance, most military members who are authorized to live off base also receive what is known as Basic Allowance for Subsistence (BAS). This allowance provides enlisted members from $210 to $339 per month to offset the cost of food.

Single enlisted personnel who live on base generally are provided a "meal card" that enables them to eat in government-run dining facilities free of charge. These personnel may also be entitled to Partial BAS, in the amount of $25.50 per month.

Partial BAS was started because the value of being able to eat free of charge at on-base dining facilities is often less than the Full BAS rate. Therefore, Partial BAS makes up the difference.

Clothing Allowance

All enlisted personnel receive an annual clothing allowance to cover the cost of purchasing and maintaining uniforms. The amount of the annual clothing allowance depends on the branch of service and the member's gender. Members are paid at a lower rate for their first three years of service. Currently the allowances range from $205.20 to $324. After three years of service, the allowance ranges from $291.60 to $464.40.

Enlisted members of the Guard and Reserve do not receive an annual clothing allowance. They are, however, entitled to free replacement of worn or damaged uniforms on an as-needed basis.

Other Pay and Allowances

There are many other types of special pay and allowances that military members may receive in addition to those already mentioned. These include:

- **Cost of Living Allowance (COLA)**—This is paid to members living in high cost of living areas as well as to military members stationed overseas.
- **Dislocation Allowance**—This is designed to offset some of the extra expenses associated with moving.
- **Per Diem**—Literally translated, this means "per day." This allowance is paid to military members when serving on temporary duty and is used to offset the cost of lodging and food.
- **Diving Pay**—This is paid monthly to all military members performing diving duties.
- **Flight Pay**—This is paid monthly to military aircrew members.
- **Foreign Language Proficiency Pay**—This is paid monthly to members who have qualified in and remain proficient in a language considered critical to the military; these members may be called upon to act as interpreters or translators.
- **Hazardous Duty Pay**—As the name implies, this is paid to members serving in certain "dangerous" jobs.
- **Sea Pay**—This monthly pay is intended to offset the hardship of having to serve at sea.
- **Special Duty Pay**—Certain enlisted members may receive Special Duty Pay (SDP). For example, recruiters receive a monthly SDP of $375.
- **Submarine Pay**—Sailors serving on board submarines receive "Sub Pay" in addition to their Sea Pay.

As a general rule, any benefit designated as "pay" is taxable, whereas those benefits designated as "allowances" are not. Depending on the amount of your total allowances, your tax savings may add up to be quite considerable.

On-Base Facilities

One of the greatest benefits to military members is the various on-base facilities. While many of these facilities are provided free of charge to military personnel and their families, some are provided at a nominal cost. As you'll see from the following list, military bases are literally their own self-contained towns. Facilities available include:

- **Fitness Centers**—These are the on-base equivalent to health clubs. They feature modern fitness equipment and basketball courts. Some have indoor pools, tracks, racquetball courts and saunas. There is no charge for using the Fitness Centers.
- **Swimming Pools**—Most bases have at least one swimming pool that is open (weather permitting) to all military personnel and their dependents. There is no cost for use of the pools.

- Golf Courses—Just about every base has its own golf course. And just like private golf clubs, you may pay for a membership or you may choose to pay on a per use basis. Courses have driving ranges, pro shops and restaurants (or snack bars). Golf courses are open to military personnel, their families and guests.
- Bowling Alleys—Most bases have a bowling center. These facilities usually (in my experience) provide the best option for lunch on the base. Besides the snack bar, base bowling alleys usually contain state-of-the-art equipment. There are usually adult and children's bowling leagues on most bases.
- Other Sports—Most bases have many other facilities for various sports (both for adults and for children), such as soccer, baseball, softball, track, tennis, football, basketball and volleyball. Quite often there are adult and children's leagues in many of these sports (depending on the season).
- Auto Hobby Shops—If you like working on your own car, the auto hobby shop is where you'll find the facilities to accommodate you. Whether it's something as simple as an oil change or as complex as a complete engine rebuild, you'll find what you need there. Auto hobby shops have lifts, hand tools, specialty tools and almost anything you'll need when working on your car. The auto hobby shops charge by the hour.
- Youth Centers—These facilities provide a safe environment for minor dependents to enjoy themselves. Most youth centers have game rooms, video games and basketball courts. They also sponsor events such as dances.
- Recreation Centers—More commonly called "Rec Centers," these are basically the adult versions of the Youth Centers.
- Aero Clubs—Most Air Force Bases have an Aero Club where you can learn to fly and rent small airplanes.
- Camping—Many bases offer on-base camping as well as an RV park. These facilities often offer boating and fishing activities. Some bases also have their own private beaches available for use by military members and their families.
- Rental Centers—Here you can rent anything from camping equipment to small boats as well as lawn mowers, log splitters, bicycles, sporting equipment and many other items.
- Arts and Crafts—Various arts and crafts activities are available at these centers. These include woodworking, ceramics, picture framing and others. Arts and crafts lessons are usually available, as are necessary supplies.
- On-Base Lodging—Intended to house visiting military members who are on official business, these motel-like accommodations may be used on a space available basis for vacationing service members. In some locations, the military also runs on-base lodging facilities whose sole purpose is for the recreation of military members and their families.
- Libraries—On-base libraries are no different than any other public library.
- Nightclubs—Military clubs are similar to nightclubs that you would find in the civilian community. The main difference is that they also usually offer a wide array of dining facilities. In addition, "membership" in the club usually provides you with discounts on meals.
- Department Stores—The name of the store depends on the branch of service (Base Exchange for the Air Force, Post Exchange for the Army and Navy Exchange and Marine Exchange). These stores offer discounts on items from clothing to garden supplies, household products to computers, shampoo to CDs and everything in between. The main benefit of these "department stores" is that there is no sales tax charged.

- Grocery Stores—Called commissaries, these stores offer substantial savings over grocery stores located in the civilian community. No tax is charged at military commissaries, although there is a surcharge of four percent on all purchases.
- Ticket Offices—Tickets for theme parks and other recreational activities are available at discount rates to military members.
- Movie Theaters—Although you won't find any multi-screen theaters on military bases, base movie theaters do show current features at discount prices.
- Fast Food—Most military bases have at least one nationally known fast food restaurant. In addition, most also have several snack bars and other eating establishments.
- Service Stations—These not only sell gasoline but also offer car repair, auto parts and tires. Besides selling at lower prices, there is no sales tax charged on your purchases.
- Chapels—If you choose to attend religious services, base chapels usually accommodate most religions.
- Horse Stables—Many bases have facilities for military members who own horses.
- Day-care Centers—Facilities are available for all-day care to hourly care. Rates are set according to family income.
- Schools—Most bases run their own schools through the elementary grades.

Health-care Benefits

Active Duty members receive free medical treatment provided by military as well as civilian health-care professionals. Unlike their civilian counterparts, there are no such things as "sick days" in the military. If, for instance, you have a cold and must miss work for a few days, you may be put on "quarters," which means you are excused from work until you are well enough to be cleared to go back.

The good part about this is that you do not have to worry about using up your sick days; however, you can't call in sick because you wake up and decide it would be a good day to go to the beach.

Another advantage is that if you become temporarily disabled, you do not have to worry about losing wages or your job. You will continue to receive full pay and allowances while you are recuperating.

As an Active Duty member, your health-care benefits cover 100 percent of all charges relating to your care, including prescription drugs and dental care.

DEPENDENT CARE

Until recently, military dependents were treated in exactly the same way as their military "sponsors" (with the exception of dental care). That was until the introduction of a system called TRICARE.

TRICARE has been the military's attempt to privatize military dependent health care. Military members may choose the "TRICARE Option" that best meets their needs. There are three TRICARE options to choose from:

- TRICARE Extra—A Preferred Provider Organization (PPO), TRICARE EXTRA contracts with health-care providers to offer its beneficiaries discounted fees. Although there are no fees for enrollment in TRICARE EXTRA, there are standard deductibles that must be met before insurance benefits are paid. These deductibles are based on the military sponsor's rank.

- TRICARE Prime—The military's version of a health maintenance organization (HMO), TRICARE PRIME requires its members to enroll with a Primary Care Manager (PCM), who in effect "manages" the care of the beneficiaries. All care must be pre-approved and referrals issued before patients can be seen by either on-base or approved off-base health-care providers. There are no deductibles; however, small co-pays may be required.
- TRICARE Standard—Based loosely on the traditional "Fee for Service" concept, TRICARE Standard offers patients more of a choice in choosing their health-care providers. Providers are paid a set fee based on a fee schedule. Patients are required to meet a standard deductible, pay co-pays, and in some instances, receive authorization prior to treatment.

Dependent Dental Care

Although military members are entitled to free dental care, their dependents are not. However, there is a low cost dental insurance plan available to offset some of the expenses associated with dependent dental care. The cost of the plan is taken directly out of the military member's pay.

Vacation

Every military member receives 30 days of vacation (known as leave) each year. Leave is accrued at a rate of 2.5 days per month. At times, advance leave may be granted depending on the circumstances.

The main difference between military leave and "ordinary vacation" is that weekends and holidays are usually counted as leave if they fall during the leave period. For example, say that you wanted to take leave the week of Thanksgiving and also the entire next week—even though you would have had Thanksgiving off as a holiday, it would count as leave, as would the weekend following the holiday.

Moving

Periodic moves are a fact of life in the military. Although moving can be stressful, one aspect of moving you will never have to worry about is the cost. The government pays for all the costs associated with official moves. The amount of household goods you are authorized to move at government expense is determined by your rank.

Moves are performed by contracted companies who will not only move your possessions, but will pack, and upon your arrival at your new home, will unpack them and get rid of the packing material. If you prefer to move your own household goods, you may choose to do what is called a Do it Yourself (or DITY) move. Military members are offered a cash incentive to perform their own moves. If you would like, you may also do a Partial DITY move, where the bulk of your household goods are moved by professional movers and the military members move a portion of the household goods.

In addition to the actual moving of household goods, military members are entitled to various other payments made to offset the cost of moving. These include payment for mileage (or air travel), lodging and meal expenses and payments to cover temporary lodging costs (while you are getting settled in).

Military Retirement

One of the greatest benefits of military service is the retirement benefit after just twenty years of service. Although twenty years may seem like a long time, consider that if you enlisted in the military at age 18, you would be eligible for retirement pay at age 38. You would then be starting on a second career (while collecting retirement pay) at an age when many people are struggling with a first career and are likely almost thirty years from retirement.

The way military retirement pay is calculated has changed a great deal over the years. When I entered the military, retirement pay was calculated as 50 percent of base pay after twenty years of service, with increases in the percentage based on years served beyond twenty. The maximum amount of retirement pay allowable is 75 percent.

At present, retirement pay is calculated as follows: The base pay of the highest thirty-six months (usually the last three years on Active Duty) is averaged. That average is then multiplied by 2.5 percent for each year of Active Duty.

For example, suppose that you retired with exactly twenty years of service and you earned $2,000 a month your last year on Active Duty, $1,800 the year prior to retirement, and $1,700 the year prior to that. The three-year average would therefore be approximately $1,833. That number would then be multiplied by 2.5 percent (.025) to give you $45.83, which is then multiplied by 20 to give you a monthly retirement pay of $916.60.

In addition to retirement pay, military retirees also enjoy most of the same privileges as they did on Active Duty, such as use of on-base facilities, health-care benefits and life insurance.

Other Benefits

Some of the other benefits of military service include:

- Service Group Life Insurance—SGLI of up to $200,000 is offered to all military members at a very low rate. The cost of the premium is deducted directly from the military member's pay.
- VA Home Loans—Military members are eligible to receive Veterans' Administration guaranteed home loans. By guaranteeing the loans, the VA makes it easier for military members to secure a mortgage.
- Military Discounts—Many establishments (especially in areas surrounding a military installation) will offer small discounts to military members.
- Burial Expenses—Although not one of the benefits that drove me to join the military nor one that I'm rushing to use, military members (and veterans) are entitled to a burial plot in a national cemetery as well as a headstone.

Summary

As you have seen, there are many benefits of military service in addition to the pay. When you consider the pay and other benefits, it all adds up to a very attractive compensation package.

One very important category of benefits that was not covered in this appendix, however, is the many educational benefits available to military members. Because of their importance, they are covered in a separate appendix.

C OPPORTUNITIES IN THE GUARD AND THE RESERVE

Besides Active Duty, a great way to serve your country, get some excellent training, receive educational benefits and get paid doing it is as a member of the Guard or Reserve. For the sake of simplicity, I'll refer to all Guard and Reserve members as "Reservists."

Each branch of the service (Air Force, Army, Coast Guard, Marines and the Navy) has its own Reserve component. In addition, the Army National Guard and the Air National Guard play a unique role in our nation's defense.

The purpose of this appendix is to familiarize you with the Reserve components and their many benefits. An entire book could be written describing the roles, capabilities and history of the Reserve components, so therefore it is not the intent of this appendix to make you an expert. If you would like more detailed and up-to-date information, I suggest that you use the contact information provided in this book to obtain it.

The Purpose of the Reserve

Although each Reserve component has its own "mission statement," its basic purpose is no different than that of the Active Duty components: "to support and defend the constitution of the United States against all enemies, foreign or domestic." The main difference is not how it does it, but rather, when it does it.

Where Most Reservists Come From

If you are reading this book, you probably have never served in any branch of the military. You are therefore classified as an NPS (Non-prior Service) applicant.

Although the number of NPS applicants joining the Reserve is increasing each year, the majority of Reserve members have had some prior military experience. While some join the Reserve to protect their retirement pay and to continue receiving the many military benefits they enjoyed on Active Duty, others continue to serve because they like the camaraderie of the military and want to continue to serve their country.

Although Prior Service applicants can bring a wealth of knowledge to the Reserve, NPS applicants provide the "new blood" necessary to sustain the Reserve.

Why the Reserve?

If you have decided to join the military, why would you join the Reserve instead of Active Duty? There are many reasons people make that decision; they include

- searching for a good part-time job;
- the desire to stay in the local area;
- attending college (and wanting to stay at that particular school);
- having a good job but wanting to learn new skills;
- family commitments that require you to remain in the local area;
- the desire to serve your country without drastically changing your current lifestyle.

The reasons some people choose the Reserve over Active Duty are many, just as for others Active Duty is a better choice than the Reserve. The decision may be easier for you if you have utilized the "needs analysis" portion of this book.

What Makes the Reserve Components Different from Active Duty?

The basic difference between Active Duty military members and Reserve component members is that being on Active Duty is a full-time job, while Reserve members usually perform their duties one weekend a month and during one two-week period a year.

That being said, however, there are usually opportunities for Reserve members to work additional time to support their Reserve unit. In addition, Reserve component members may be called upon at any time to support worldwide operations. This is what happened during Operation Desert Storm when tens of thousands of Guard and Reserve members were "activated." An unfortunate phenomenon developed, however, when many Guard and Reserve members refused to go to the Middle East—they thought that they had joined for training and education, not to fight wars.

For many of these reservists, it was a case of not wanting to fulfill their obligation; for others, it was due to a misrepresentation on the part of a recruiter. These individuals more than likely did not belong in any branch of the military; they probably would not have joined if they were told that there was a chance they would be called to "deploy." Unfortunately, they were more than likely told by their recruiters that there was little or no chance of them ever deploying, when, in reality, there is always a chance of being "called up."

The one thing to remember is that if you become part of any Reserve component (including a Guard component), you are a member of the United States Armed Forces and as such may be called upon at any time for activation to support the Active Duty military.

In addition, as a member of the Army National Guard or the Air National Guard, you may be activated by the Governor of your state to help during states of emergencies, such as floods, hurricanes and tornadoes.

Military Benefits

As a Reservist, you are entitled to many of the same benefits available to Active Duty members. This section represents a sampling of some of the many benefits available. Because entitlements and regulations change from time to time, it would be impossible to provide detailed information that is up-to-date. Therefore, I encourage you to get the details about benefits and entitlements from your recruiter. Ask specific questions about those benefits and entitlements you are interested in, and if your recruiter is unsure of the answers to your questions, ask him to research the answers for you.

BASE FACILITIES

As a Reservist you are authorized to utilize most of the same on-base facilities as your Active Duty counterparts (see Appendix B for detailed information). There may, however, be some exceptions and restrictions. For instance, your visits to the Commissary are limited to a certain amount each year.

PAY AND ALLOWANCES

Because being a Reservist is a part-time job, you are paid only for the time you are actually "on-duty," which is usually one weekend per month and one two-week period of Active Duty per year. Refer to the pay chart in Appendix B for details about Reserve Pay.

During Drill Weekends, Reservists are paid the equivalent of two days of Base Pay for every day served. During the two-week Annual Active Duty period, Reservists are paid full pay as well as allowances that include housing allowance, Basic Allowance for Subsistence and any other special-duty pay authorized.

MEDICAL AND LIFE INSURANCE

As a Reservist, you are entitled to the same life insurance benefit as your Active Duty counterparts; however, the rules for medical and dental insurance are quite different. Reserve members are covered by military "medical benefits" only while engaged in Active Duty, and family members are not covered unless the member is on what is considered Extended Active Duty. Until recently, Reserve members and their families were not covered under the military dental plan. As of this writing, there have been changes in the plan to allow Reservists and their families to participate (at a minimum cost to the Reservist).

ON-BASE HOUSING

Reserve members are not entitled to on-base housing and only receive housing allowance while serving on periods of Active Duty. However, housing is provided for the Reservist when he or she is performing weekend drills and Active Duty. Facilities range from tents to dormitory rooms to off-base hotel accommodations, depending on the situation.

BASIC TRAINING

With few exceptions, all NPS applicants are required to attend the same Basic Training (Boot Camp) as their Active Duty counterparts. At the time of this writing, the only exception is the Navy Reserve's program, which allows individuals with certain skills to join the Navy Reserve at a higher pay grade and skip Basic Training.

TECHNICAL TRAINING

Most Reservists attend the same technical schools as their Active Duty counterparts. Some of these schools are quite lengthy and, combined with Basic Training, will require you to be on Active Duty status for some time. Therefore, you should consider how this would impact your civilian employment and/or college schedule.

You should use the "needs analysis" portion of this book to determine whether or not the technical training you have chosen fits your needs.

An added benefit (and perhaps the most important benefit to some) of technical training is that it may help to improve your skills in your civilian job or it can open doors for new job opportunities in the civilian workforce.

ADVANCEMENT

Just as on Active Duty, you will have the opportunity for advancement as a Reservist. Although most NPS applicants enter the Reserve as E-1s, there are opportunities for enlistment at advanced pay grades based on college credits and participation in high school Junior ROTC programs (just like Active Duty).

It is imperative that you ask your recruiter if you qualify for advanced pay grade and then ensure that it is entered in your enlistment contract.

EDUCATIONAL BENEFITS

Reservists are entitled to many of the same educational benefits as their Active Duty counterparts. In some cases, the benefits for Reservists are even better!

Some of these benefits can include

- Montgomery G.I. Bill
- Tuition Assistance
- College Level Examination Program (CLEP) exams
- Participation in branch-specific programs, such as the Community College of the Air Force

Also, some states offer members of the National Guard free tuition to state schools. However, be sure to find out all the facts, such as the amount of funding available, whether the funding is guaranteed and what the restrictions are (if any).

RETIREMENT

As with Active Duty, Reservists may retire with as few as 20 years of service. There are two major differences, however, between an Active Duty retirement and a Reserve retirement.

- Instead of calculating retirement pay based on the number of years of service, pay is based on points that are awarded for each day of reserve duty. The higher the number of points, the higher the amount of retirement pay.
- Unlike Active Duty retirement pay, which starts immediately after retirement, the Reservist must wait until he or she turns 60 years old before collecting retirement pay. Retired Reservists, called "Gray Area Retirees," do not receive any health care until they are eligible for retirement pay.

Although not as lucrative as an Active Duty retirement, the Reservist with a retirement plan in his or her civilian job is, in fact, "contributing" to two retirement plans at one time!

TRAVEL AND RECREATION

With few exceptions, Reservists are afforded the same opportunity for travel and recreation as Active Duty members. Many of the same discounts offered to Active Duty members and their families are extended to Reservists and their families. Most military recreation facilities and equipment are open to use by Reservists.

ENLISTMENT BONUSES

Depending on the branch of service you are entering and the specific job you choose, you may be entitled to an enlistment bonus. Usually these bonuses are paid to entice people into hard-to-fill "critical" jobs. Besides cash bonuses, some services are offering increased educational benefits for people enlisting in certain jobs. All of this needs to be considered before enlisting. As stated earlier in this book, however, don't give a high priority to enlistment bonuses unless you are enlisting only for the money.

Before you enlist, make sure that you understand all the terms of the enlistment bonus. For example, ensure that you find out when you will receive the bonus and whether it is paid in one lump sum or is paid out in increments over a certain amount of time. As with everything that is "promised" to you, ensure that the enlistment bonus is part of your enlistment contract. If it is not listed, plain and simple, you haven't been promised it, no matter what has been verbally promised.

Conclusion

Now more than ever, the lines that distinguish the Active Duty Military from their Reserve counterparts are blurred, the major difference lying in not what they do, but rather when they do it. Gone are the days of the "weekend warriors" who were considered by many on Active Duty as second-class citizens. Today, Reservists fill a vital role in the defense of our nation.

Appendix E contains contacts for more information about joining the Reserve or Guard.

D EDUCATIONAL BENEFITS

Many people join the military for the educational benefits—there's nothing wrong with that—and end up staying in the military for the other benefits. The number of educational opportunities offered by the military are growing as it becomes harder and harder to entice young people to join.

Because of the many changes occurring on such a frequent basis, it would be impossible to list all the programs that are available. This appendix covers the programs that are in place at the time of this writing and describes their features. Check with your recruiter to get an up-to-date list of all the educational benefits for which you qualify.

If you qualify for one of the special enlistment educational programs such as the Army's Loan Repayment Program, make sure it's on your enlistment contract. Remember that if it's not listed in your contract, no matter who verbally promised it to you, it is not guaranteed.

Some educational programs, such as Tuition Assistance, are programs that a military member can utilize while on Active Duty. These types of programs are ongoing and are not listed on your enlistment contract. Your point of contact for these programs is your Base (or Post) Education Office.

Education Offices

These offices are, in essence, your on-base guidance office to help you plan your education. They will assist you in determining your goals and help you decide on a course of action to achieve those goals.

How Educational Benefits Differ Among Branches

There are basically two types of educational benefits offered by the military. The first type represents programs that are common to all the branches (such as the Montgomery GI Bill), and the second type is branch-specific (such as the Army College Fund).

Although each branch has its own specific "programs," you'll find that overall they are pretty much the same. Some may have certain features that appeal to you over others, but the bottom line is that it becomes a matter of who can offer the best educational program for your particular needs.

Common Programs

The programs that are common to all military branches are the Montgomery GI Bill, the Tuition Assistance Program, the Defense Activity For Non-Traditional Support (DANTES) testing program and credit for military school. Each of these programs has a very specific and entirely different function.

MONTGOMERY GI BILL

The Montgomery GI Bill allows service members to contribute $1,200 ($100 per month for the first twelve months of service) and receive more than $19,000 in educational benefits.

Active Duty personnel are automatically enrolled in the program upon enlistment and may opt out of the program at that time. If the military member does decide to opt out, he may not enroll at a later date.

Reserve members have their own version of the Montgomery GI Bill; however, there is no contribution required by the service member.

In certain cases the service member may receive more than $19,000 in benefits. If a member agrees to enlist in certain "critical" career fields (these are jobs that are either hard to fill or are undermanned for one reason or another), she may qualify for additional GI Bill funds. The amount of additional funds depends on the branch of service and the job selected.

For Active Duty Members, the Montgomery GI Bill is designed to be used after the service member's term of enlistment; for Reserve members, however, the GI Bill may be used during the enlistment.

For additional information about the Montgomery GI Bill, visit www.gibill.va.gov/education/benefits.htm

TUITION ASSISTANCE PROGRAM

One of the best educational benefits available to military members, the Tuition Assistance Program is also one of the most underutilized. At present, the Tuition Assistance Program pays 75 percent of the service members' college tuition, although most services do have an annual limit. While the Montgomery GI Bill is designed for service members to use after their term of enlistment, Tuition Assistance (TA) is available to Active Duty members (and some Reserve members) for use during their enlistment.

The only possible drawback to the Tuition Assistance Program is that the service member is limited to colleges in his or her local area. However, most military installations contract with several colleges to provide courses to their military members. This is how I was able to earn my master's degree from Troy State University (in Alabama) while stationed at a base in the United Kingdom.

As good as the Tuition Assistance Program is, however, many (actually most) military members do not take advantage of it for one reason or another. For some it may be a lack of initiative or the lack of desire to attend college; for others, however, it may be because the time demands of their jobs don't allow them to use TA. For this reason, it is important to consider your goals when selecting a job or even the branch of service you join. If you wish to pursue your degree in earnest while serving on Active Duty, you must consider whether or not you will have the time to do so.

I was very fortunate. Although I enlisted in the Navy, I was stationed on a ship that very rarely left port. I spent four years in Charleston, South Carolina, and, by coincidence, a local college (Baptist College at Charleston, now Charleston Southern University) had an excellent evening degree program. Because of this, I was able to complete my undergraduate degree while stationed in Charleston utilizing TA. Things would have been quite different, however, if I had been stationed on a submarine or a ship that went to sea more frequently.

Of course, if you are not motivated to attend college, you will find any excuse not to take advantage of TA, no matter how much "free" time you have.

DEFENSE ACTIVITY FOR NON-TRADITIONAL SUPPORT (DANTES)

DANTES testing, another fabulous educational benefit, is a great way to build college credits in a hurry and free of charge.

By utilizing College Level Examination Program (CLEP) tests, you may receive college credits for subject matter that you may have already mastered without taking a college course. These tests are very similar to high school Advanced Placement (AP) tests, which allow you to basically demonstrate your knowledge in exchange for college credit. The main difference, however, is that CLEP exams are offered free to military members.

CLEP exams cover basic courses such as English, basic math and science, but they are also available in other subjects such as calculus, marketing and accounting.

Ultimately, it is up to the school you are attending as to whether or not they will accept CLEP exams for credit. Therefore, it is a good idea to check with them first before wasting your time taking an exam that will count for nothing.

CREDIT FOR MILITARY SCHOOLS

Although not officially an "educational program," most military schools that you attend are eligible for college credit. Again, such as the case with CLEP exams, it will be up to the specific school as to whether or not they will award college credit and, if so, how much.

Depending on the military schools you have attended, the credits you receive may give your college journey a major "jump start." In my own case, I was trained in electronics as well as hydraulic theory (which, believe it or not, counted toward credits for physics). Counting Basic Training, I attended military schools for almost the first two years of my enlistment. The credits I received for my military education, coupled with the basic CLEP exams I managed to pass, amounted to over 30 credit hours toward my bachelor's degree! I was well on my way to earning the required 126 hours necessary to graduate.

Branch-Specific Educational Programs

As stated earlier, each branch has its own specific educational benefits in addition to the common programs offered by all the services.

Although each branch offers its own unique programs, the bottom line is that, with few exceptions, they are basically all the same. You'll probably find the biggest difference in the programs for which you may qualify.

For example, maybe you'll be eligible (based on test scores or job selection) for more educational funding from the Army than from the Navy. Although they might have similar benefits, you may find yourself not qualifying for the benefits of one branch but qualifying for the benefits of another.

Remember, however, to take all factors into consideration before making the decision to join a specific branch of the military for the educational benefits. For instance, I may not have received the same level of training that earned me all those college credits if I had joined another branch of the military. In other words, how much money were those 30-plus college credits worth?

In business management, we call those costs "opportunity costs"—the cost of doing one thing over another. You must look at all the opportunities and compare them to each other.

Branch-Specific Educational Benefits

This section covers the branch-specific educational benefits offered by each of the services. As I stated earlier, things are changing at such a high speed that the specifics of the benefits listed here probably changed before I even typed the words on my computer. Nevertheless, this will give you a good idea of the types of programs offered. I strongly encourage you to get the most current information from your recruiter.

Some of the military branches offer "Loan Repayment Programs" that essentially will pay off, or at least reduce, student loans already incurred. In addition, the Army has just introduced (at the time of this writing) a program that allows you to enlist and then put off entering the Army for two years while you attend college. Because some of these programs have just been introduced (and complete details are not yet available), I have not included them in the text that follows; however, they are important enough to warrant mention and for you to investigate further on your own.

AIR FORCE

Community College of the Air Force (CCAF)

The Community College of the Air Force (CCAF) is the only accredited institution belonging to any of the Armed Forces. The CCAF awards associate degrees in areas of study that relate to the service member's career field.

College credits are granted for military schools, CLEP exams and courses completed through civilian colleges. Enrollment in CCAF is free, and many Air Force members use their CCAF degrees as a springboard to earning their bachelor's degrees. Enrollment in CCAF is also open to Reserve members.

Airman Education and Commissioning Program (AECP)

The Airman Education and Commissioning Program (AECP) is designed to allow outstanding enlisted personnel to complete the requirements for a bachelor's degree (by attending college on a full-time basis) and then apply for commissioning as an Air Force officer.

The AECP program requirements include the following:

- The airman must have completed at least one year of Active Duty.
- The airman must possess at least 45 college credits.
- The airman must be able to be commissioned by his or her 30th birthday.

Other Programs Leading to a Commission

In addition to AECP, there are two other programs that allow Air Force enlisted members to attend college full-time and then earn a commission:

- **Leaders Encouraging Airmen Development**—This allows deserving airmen (with less than six years of service) to attend the Air Force Academy.
- **Scholarships for Outstanding Airmen to ROTC**—this provides for two- and four-year Reserve Officer Corps scholarships for deserving enlisted members with less than six years of service.

Both of these programs offer an excellent opportunity for Air Force members to further their education.

ARMY

The Army College Fund

Depending on the job you select and your qualifications, you may be eligible to receive additional funds in conjunction with the Montgomery GI Bill totaling $50,000 for a four-year enlistment, $33,000 for a three-year enlistment and $26,500 for a two-year enlistment to pursue higher education through the Army College Fund.

Besides enlisting in one of the qualifying career specialties, you must score at least a 50 on the Armed Forces Qualification Test (AFQT) and be a high school diploma graduate.

Loan Repayment

Certain types of federal student loans are eligible for this program. If you qualify, the Army will repay your loans at the rate of one-third of the loan for each year of Active Duty served. A four-year enlistment could qualify you for up to $65,000 in loan repayments.

Concurrent Admissions Program (ConAP)

The Concurrent Admissions Program (ConAP) allows soldiers to enroll in one of 1,200 participating schools. These schools guarantee on-campus enrollment after the soldier's initial term of enlistment. Also, all college credits earned while serving on Active Duty may be transferred.

Green to Gold

The Green to Gold program allows deserving soldiers to apply for two-, three- and four-year college scholarships that will ultimately lead to a commission as an Army officer.

COAST GUARD

Coast Guard Institute

This program is similar in nature to the Community College of the Air Force (CCAF) in that an official transcript is put together from military schools, CLEP exams and civilian schools. However, the Coast Guard Institute does not have the accreditation necessary to issue diplomas.

Pre-commissioning Program for Enlisted Personnel

This program is designed to give an opportunity to deserving enlisted members to complete their college education and then attend Officer Candidate School (OCS) in order to earn a commission as a Coast Guard Officer.

The program requirements and features include the following:

- The coastguardsman must be at least an E-4 (Petty Officer Third Class).
- The coastguardsman must be at least 21 years old but not older than 29 years old.
- The coastguardsman must be able to complete requirements for a four-year degree within twenty-four months.
- The coastguardsman remains eligible for promotion while participating in the program.
- The coastguardsman continues to receive full pay and allowances while participating in the program.

MARINE CORPS

Servicemembers Opportunity Colleges Degree Programs for the Marine Corps (SOCMAR)

SOCMAR is a worldwide network of colleges that are located on Marine Corps bases as well as aboard Navy ships. The two programs, SOCMAR-2 and SOCMAR-4, lead to either an associate degree or bachelor's degree, respectively.

SOCMAR allows Marines to earn their degree as follows:

- The Marine chooses a "home college" to begin the process.
- College credits are awarded for military schools and CLEP exams.
- Transfer of college credit is guaranteed as long as you attend any of the SOCMAR associated colleges.
- Degrees are awarded by the "home college."
- SOCMAR has the advantages of the Community College of the Air Force (CCAF) in that it allows for a generous acceptance of college credits, but also has two additional benefits:
- It may also be used to earn a four-year bachelor's degree.
- It is also available to members of the service member's immediate family.

Marine Corps College Fund

Combined with the Montgomery GI Bill, the Marine Corps College Fund can equal up to $30,000 toward funding your college education. Besides meeting certain qualifications, you must enlist for at least four years to be eligible for the Marine Corps College Fund. Eligible Marines may begin using their benefits after completing two years of enlistment.

Other Programs Leading to a Four-Year Degree and Commission

There are several programs available to enlisted Marines that lead to earning a bachelor's degree and a commission as a Marine Corps officer. They include:

- Broadened Opportunity for Officer Selection and Training Program (BOOST)—This program is designed to help Marines who come from educationally deprived or culturally differentiated backgrounds. Those selected will attend a one-year "prep" school that will get them ready for attendance at the Naval Academy or acceptance to a Naval ROTC program. This program is available to Marines in the rank of Lance Corporal (E-3) or above.
- Naval Reserve Officers Training Corps (NROTC)—NROTC scholarships are available for deserving enlisted Marines to attend one of sixty colleges nationwide that host NROTC units. Besides paying for tuition and books, NROTC scholarship recipients also receive a monthly stipend of $200.
- Naval Academy Prep School—Those selected for the Naval Academy Prep School will attend the school for one year in order to get them prepared for admission to the Naval Academy.

NAVY

Servicemembers Opportunity Colleges (SOC)

Essentially, this is the same program as the Marine Corps' SOCMAR, with a worldwide network of more than 1,250 SOC-associated schools. As in the SOCMAR program, sailors start off by choosing a "home school" and then transfer all their credits back to that school in order to earn their degrees.

Program for Afloat College Education (PACE)

PACE is truly a mobile program, offering college courses on board Navy ships. PACE courses are free and are fully integrated into the SOC and SOCMAR programs.

The Navy College Fund

Available to those enlisting in certain critical and hard-to-fill positions, the Navy College Fund (in combination with the Montgomery GI Bill) can provide up to $50,000 for college.

Navy College Assistance/Student Headstart (Navy CASH) Program

The Navy CASH program allows applicants to enter Active Duty and receive pay and allowances for up to 12 months while attending college. To qualify, applicants must enlist in either the nuclear or submarine electronic/computer field or as a missile technician.

National Apprenticeship Program

If your goal is to receive technical training and apprenticeship certification, then this program may be right for you. The National Apprenticeship Program exists under an agreement between the Navy and the U.S. Department of Labor and allows sailors to earn certification in one of twenty occupations.

The Navy College Program

Similar to the Coast Guard Institute, the Navy College Program allows you to put all of your college credits (no matter where they were earned) into one transcript.

Other Programs Leading to a Four-Year Degree and Commission

Besides the three programs (BOOST, NROTC, Naval Academy Prep School) listed in the Marine Corps section, up to 85 outstanding Naval enlisted personnel are selected each year for direct appointment to the Naval Academy.

NATIONAL GUARD AND RESERVE

Many of the programs listed in this appendix are also offered in one form or another by the National Guard and Reserve components. In addition, some states offer free tuition to state schools for members of their National Guard units.

Although many states offer "free" tuition, it must be noted that many restrictions do apply and are limited to budgetary constraints in some cases. Make sure you get all the facts before assuming that you will get a "free ride" to a state school.

SERVICE ACADEMIES AND RESERVE OFFICER TRAINING CORPS OPPORTUNITIES

Although this book was written for those interested in enlisting in the military, I thought that it would be appropriate to mention the service academies and ROTC programs.

Many young people contact recruiters for information about the service academies and ROTC and wind up enlisting instead. Because the competition and requirements for entrance into the service academies and for ROTC scholarships are so stringent, many people enlist in the military hoping to earn a commission after earning a degree while serving on Active Duty.

As I've mentioned previously in this book, if your sole goal is to attend college and you have the means to do so, then an enlistment in the military is probably not the right decision for you.

Service Academies

The Service Academies include

- The Air Force Academy, Colorado Springs, Colorado
- The U.S. Military Academy (Army), West Point, New York
- The Coast Guard Academy, New London, Connecticut
- Annapolis (The Naval Academy), Annapolis, Maryland
- Merchant Marine Academy, Kings Point, New York

The purpose of the service academies is to provide an education and leadership training to future military officers. With the exception of the Merchant Marine Academy, all graduates of the four-year service academies serve as Active Duty officers upon graduation. Merchant Marine Academy Graduates enter the Naval Reserve upon graduation, although many choose to enter Active Duty. Naval Academy graduates may choose to enter the Marine Corps after graduation since the Marines do not have a separate academy.

The cost of attending a service academy is minimal; in fact, students are actually paid a stipend to attend. This, coupled with the quality of the education received, makes acceptance to a service academy very difficult. Some of the basic requirements include

- a minimum SAT score of 1,000, or the ACT equivalent (although few people with a 1,000 SAT are chosen);
- a nomination from your state senator or local congressman (this is not a requirement for the Coast Guard Academy);
- participation in high school team sports/clubs;
- U.S. citizenship;
- being single with no dependents;
- meeting minimum physical requirements (see Chapter 1 for disqualifying factors);
- passing a physical fitness test;
- having an outstanding high school academic record.

Each academy has its own application process, which is long and tedious. Appendix E contains points of contact for more information about the service academies.

Reserve Officer Training Corps (ROTC)

The Air Force, Army, Navy and Marine Corps (through Naval ROTC) offer programs that allow students to attend civilian colleges and, upon graduation, receive a commission as an officer. Each year ROTC graduates account for the highest percentage of officers entering Active Duty. ROTC units may be found in colleges and universities nationwide.

ROTC offers two-, three-, and four-year scholarships, although students do not have to be scholarship recipients to attend ROTC. Scholarships cover tuition (although there is usually a cap), fees and textbook costs. Scholarship recipients also receive a $200-per-month stipend during the school year.

Requirements for an ROTC scholarship are similar to those of the service academies, with the exception of the congressional nominations and the dependency requirements. As with Service Academy applications, you should start the application process as early as possible. Ensure that you meet all deadlines and don't leave anything to chance. You will find points of contact for information about ROTC scholarships in Appendix E.

A Word about Taking the SAT/ACT

When applying for a service academy or ROTC scholarship, the more times you take the SAT or ACT the better. Because only your highest scores will be used, you have nothing to lose and everything to gain by taking the exams multiple times.

One Last Reminder

I think it is important to remind you one last time that the information contained in this appendix is only as current as the data that is available at the time of this writing. Military benefits, especially ones relating to education, change constantly, and it is important to check with your recruiter for new programs and changes to the ones listed here.

Above all, make sure that if you qualify for any special educational benefits you get your guarantee in writing. Do not accept a verbal promise; make sure you understand how much you will receive, how you will receive payment, and when you will receive payment or be able to start using the benefit.

E CONTACT INFORMATION

To aid you in your research for more information on joining the military, this appendix provides you with contact points for information about each of the military branches. You'll also find contact information for Department of Defense Web sites as well as commercial Web sites that deal with military careers.

As with any literature that is provided by the military services, "Recruiting" Web sites are designed as vehicles for advertising. Just as you would expect an automobile manufacturer's Web site to "push" their product, military recruiting Web sites exist for the same reason. Take in the information you find, digest it, and apply the skills you have learned from reading this book.

Official Recruiting Web Sites and Telephone Numbers

ACTIVE DUTY

Air Force
www.airforce.com
(800) 423-8723

Marine Corps
www.marines.com
(800) 627-4637

Army
www.goarmy.com
(800) 872-2769

Navy
www.navyjobs.com
(800) 872-6289

Coast Guard
www.uscg.mil/jobs
(877) 669-8724

RESERVE COMPONENTS

Air Force Reserve
www.afreserve.com
(800) 257-1212

Coast Guard Reserve
www.uscg.mil/hq/reserve/reshmpq.html
(800) 438-8724

Air National Guard
www.goang.af.mil
(800) 864-6264

Marine Corps Reserve
www.mfr.usmc.mil
(800) 872-8767

Army National Guard
www.1800goguard.com
(800) 464-8273

Navy
www.navy-reserve-jobs.com
(800) 552-8762

Army Reserve
www.goarmyreserve.com
(800) 872-2769

EDUCATIONAL OPPORTUNITIES

Broadened Opportunity for Officer Selection
www.cnet.navy.mil/newport/boostindex.htm

Coast Guard Institute
www.uscg.mil

Coast Guard Pre-commissioning Program for Enlisted Personnel
www.uscg.mil/hq/mcpocg/1trng/ppepadp.html

Community College of the Air Force
www.au.af.mil/au/ccaf

Defense Activity for Non-Traditional Educational Support
www.voled.doded.mil

Department of Defense Education Activity
www.odedodea.edu

Green to Gold
http://147.248.153.211/scholarships/green

Montgomery GI Bill
www.va.gov/benefits.htm

National Apprenticeship Program

http://nnaps.cnet.navy.mil/nnaps/nnap.htm

Navy College

www.navycollege.navy.mil

Navy Enlisted Commissioning Program

www.cnet.navy.mil/nrotc/ecp.htm

(Navy) Program for Afloat College Education

www.navycollege.navy.mil/ncp/pace.html

Scholarships for Outstanding Airmen to ROTC

www.afoats.af.mil

Servicemembers Opportunity Colleges

www.soc.aascu.org

(800) 368-5622

SERVICE ACADEMIES

Air Force Academy

www.usafa.edu

(800) 443-9266

U.S. Military Academy
   (Army)

www.usma.edu

(914) 938-5760

Coast Guard Academy

www.cga.edu

(800) 883-8724

Merchant Marine Academy

www.usmma.edu

(516) 773-5391

Naval Academy

www.usna.edu

(410) 293-4361

ROTC

Air Force
www.afoats.af.mil
(800) 522-0033

Navy/Marines
www.cnet.navy.mil
(800) 628-7682

Army
www.rotc.monroe.army.mil/information/site2/index.html
(800) 872-7682

Department of Defense/Government Sponsored Web Sites

The Web sites listed below are either Department of Defense (DoD) or other U.S. government-owned and -operated sites. Some of the sites are specifically focused on recruiting (such as militarycareers.com), while others (such as dfas.mil) are designed to provide information to those already serving in the military.

Remember that when visiting any recruiting Web site, regardless if it is for a specific branch of the military or a DoD site, the information contained on the site is designed in such a way to "sell" the military. Again, get the information from the Web site, and use it to make an informed decision.

- **Air Force Historical Research Agency**—Official repository for Air Force historical documents. **www.maxwell.af.mil/au/afhra**
- **AFCrossroads.com**—Operated by the Air Force, this Web site, designed with the service member in mind, contains information and news about all of the military branches, including information about military bases and military benefits. There are also many helpful links to other Web sites. **www.afcrossroads.com**
- **Coast Guard History**—History, images and information pertaining to the Coast Guard. **www.uscg.mil/general.html**
- **Defense Finance and Accounting Service**—Information for all money matters. Contains up-to-date and proposed pay charts. **www.dfas.mil**
- **DefenseLink**—Official Web site of the Department of Defense (DoD). Includes information about DoD and the military branches as well as up-to-date news and articles pertaining to military matters. **www.defenselink.mil**
- **House Committee on Armed Forces**—News, information, press releases, hearing schedules, transcripts, etc. **www.house.gov/hasc**
- **Joint Chiefs of Staff**—Official Web site of the JCS, includes up-to-date information pertaining to the military. **www.dtic.mil/jcs**

- Militarycareers.com—An informative joint-service recruiting Web site. Provides excellent information on military careers, almost makes you think that it is an unbiased site. Do not be misled—this is a recruiting Web site. **www.militarycareers.com**
- Myfuture.Com—Joint-service recruiting Web site that is somewhat disguised as a "career/college planner" but is in reality a site for military recruiting. **www.myfuture.com**
- National Security Council—Web site of the President's "forum" for deciding national security and foreign policy. **www.whitehouse.gov/WH/EOP/NSC/html/nschome.html**
- Naval Historical Center—Web site of the Navy's official history program. **www.history.navy.mil**
- Today's Military.Com—Specifically designed for individuals who may be able to influence young men and women of enlistment age. This includes parents, guidance counselors and youth group leaders. Includes a tremendous amount of information about "today's military" opportunities. **www.todaysmilitary.com**
- U.S. Army Center of Military History—Web site of the Army's official history program. **www.army.mil/cmh-pg**
- U.S. Senate Committee on Armed Services—News, information, press releases, hearing schedules, transcripts, etc. **www.senate.gov/~armed_services**
- The White House—Everything you've ever wanted to know about the White House, the President, the Vice President and history. Also has a virtual library. **www.whitehouse.gov**

Commercial Web Sites

If you have browsed the Internet for information about the military, you have undoubtedly come across at least a few commercial (non-government sponsored) Web sites. The unfortunate thing about a lot of these sites is that their sole purpose is to give a biased negative view of the military.

Frequently these Web sites are set up by groups or individuals who have some kind of grudge against the military. Oftentimes, they are set up by people who have had a bad experience (in their minds) with the military. Please keep this in mind if you come across any of these negative Web sites. Do not allow them to cloud your judgment when deciding whether or not the military is right for you.

The Web sites included in this section, although from commercial sources, are positive in nature.

- Army and Air Force Exchange Service—The official Web site of the Army and Air Force "department store." This site will not give you any information about the military, although you will get a look into some of the shopping privileges available to military members. **www.aafes.com** (A related site is the Navy Exchange System: **www.nex.com**)
- The U.S. Constitution—Okay, maybe this isn't a military Web site, but I thought we could all refresh our minds on the reasons why we serve in the military. **wwwsecure.law.cornell.edu/constitution/constitution.overview.html**
- Maingate.com—An outstanding Web site for information about the military, including news and up-to-date information on what's going on in the military. After you have registered, you can even create your own Web site free of charge. **www.maingate.com**
- MilitaryCity.com—The official Web site of Army Times Publishing. Military news as well as some excellent image and audio downloads are available. **www.militarycity.com**

One Last Link

I invite everyone reading this book to visit my Web site and leave a message in my guest book. I want to know what you think of this book and any suggestions you may have to improve its contents. Also, I'd like to hear from those of you with a "recruiter story" (good or bad) that I might be able to use in the next edition of this book. Please do not, however, ask me specific questions about enlistment opportunities (they are better answered by your recruiter).

www.geocities.com/Pentagon/Bunker/9812 (This address is case sensitive.)

Last Words about These Links

The links provided in this appendix are up-to-date as of this writing; however, they may have changed by the time you read this book. In addition, I cannot control the contents of any of the Web sites listed here. I have visited all of these sites and found them to be acceptable. Of course, your view of the contents may be different from mine, and therefore you should use your own judgment when viewing each site.

Although the links provided in this appendix could keep you occupied for a while, I suggest that you do some surfing on your own to find others. If, by chance, you stumble across one you find helpful that is not listed in this book, please visit my Web site and leave the address for me.

OTHER USEFUL INFORMATION

This appendix contains some other useful information that will help you get a head start on Basic Training. The more you know before arriving at Basic Training, the less you'll have to learn when you get there. While others are struggling to memorize information, you'll already be ahead of the game.

Military Time

Have you ever watched a war movie and wondered what the heck they were talking about when they said, "We'll rendezvous at zero six thirty"? Well, I'm about to unravel the mystery for you, and it really isn't that difficult to learn!

Civilian time is based on a 12-hour clock, with the two halves of the day divided into a.m. and p.m. Military time is based on a 24-hour clock, which starts counting at midnight. The following table shows how to translate military time into civilian time, hour by hour. It also indicates how to pronounce military time. Civilian a.m. times are pronounced "oh" followed by the time in hundreds. For example, 1 a.m. is pronounced "oh one hundred." Civilian p.m. times are pronounced as hundreds, such as "sixteen hundred" for 4 p.m.

TIME CONVERSION AND PRONUNCIATION

Military	Civilian	Pronunciation
0000	12 a.m.	zero-zero-zero-zero
0100	1 a.m.	oh one hundred
0200	2 a.m.	oh two hundred
0300	3 a.m.	oh three hundred
0400	4 a.m.	oh four hundred
0500	5 a.m.	oh five hundred
0600	6 a.m.	oh six hundred
0700	7 a.m.	oh seven hundred
0800	8 a.m.	oh eight hundred
0900	9 a.m.	oh nine hundred
1000	10 a.m.	ten hundred
1100	11 a.m.	eleven hundred
1200	12 p.m.	twelve hundred
1300	1 p.m.	thirteen hundred
1400	2 p.m.	fourteen hundred
1500	3 p.m.	fifteen hundred
1600	4 p.m.	sixteen hundred
1700	5 p.m.	seventeen hundred

Military	Civilian	Pronunciation
1800	6 p.m.	eighteen hundred
1900	7 p.m.	nineteen hundred
2000	8 p.m.	twenty hundred
2100	9 p.m.	twenty-one hundred
2200	10 p.m.	twenty-two hundred
2300	11 p.m.	twenty-three hundred

For exact times, it's as simple as adding the number of minutes to the hour. For example, if it's 2:15 p.m. civilian time, you start with the 1400 and add 15, which makes it 1415 or "fourteen fifteen" military time. Notice that it isn't "fourteen hundred fifteen," as you might think it would be. That's because when expressing a more exact "PM" time, the hundred is dropped from the pronunciation.

Here are a few more pronunciation tips:

- For any time between 1 and 9 minutes past the hour, you add "zero" to the minutes: 0905 is "oh nine zero five," and 1607 is "sixteen zero seven."
- You can also say "zero" instead of "oh" at the beginning of a time, as in "zero nine hundred" for 0900.
- The time 0005 is pronounced "zero zero zero five" and 0030 is pronounced "zero zero thirty."

An easy way to convert from civilian to military time (for p.m.) is to add 12 to the civilian time (hour). For example, 2:15 plus 12 equals 1415. To convert from military to civilian (for p.m.), subtract 12 from the first two digits (1415 minus 12 equals 2:15).

Phonetic Alphabet

Just as there is a specific way to express the time, there is a specific way to express each letter of the alphabet. Have you ever had to spell your name for someone who has responded, "Is that 'B' as in 'boy'?" Someone else may ask, "Is that 'B' as in 'ball'?"

The military has an established set of words that are used to express each letter. Study the chart below, and you'll memorize them in no time.

Letter	Name	Letter	Name	Letter	Name	Letter	Name
A	ALFA	H	HOTEL	O	OSCAR	U	UNIFORM
B	BRAVO	I	INDIA	P	PAPA	V	VICTOR
C	CHARLIE	J	JULIETT	Q	QUEBEC	W	WHISKEY
D	DELTA	K	KILO	R	ROMEO	X	X-RAY
E	ECHO	L	LIMA	S	SIERRA	Y	YANKEE
F	FOXTROT	M	MIKE	T	TANGO	Z	ZULU
G	GOLF	N	NOVEMBER				

Military Terminology and Acronyms

A complete dictionary of military terminology and acronyms would take up this entire book and, for the most part, would be overkill. Fortunately, there is a complete dictionary available on line for your use. The official *DoD Dictionary of Military Terms* can be found at www.dtic.mil/doctrine/jel/doddict

G FORMS

This appendix contains examples of three important forms that are filled out during the enlistment process:

- DD Form 1966, which is the Record of Military Processing - Armed Forces of the United States (your application for enlistment)
- Form SF 93, which is the Record of Medical History
- Form SF 88, which is the Report of Medical Examination

Note that although the actual forms may have been revised by the time you read this book, they are not likely to be substantially different.

RECORD OF MILITARY PROCESSING - ARMED FORCES OF THE UNITED STATES

(Read Privacy Act Statement and Instructions on back before completing this form.)

Form Approved
OMB No. 0704-0173
Expires Jul 31, 2000

The public reporting burden for this collection of information is estimated to average 20 minutes per response, including the time for reviewing instructions, searching existing data sources, gathering and maintaining the data needed, and completing and reviewing the collection of information. Send comments regarding this burden estimate or any other aspect of this collection of information, including suggestions for reducing the burden, to Department of Defense, Washington Headquarters Services, Directorate for Information Operations and Reports (0704-0173), 1215 Jefferson Davis Highway, Suite 1204, Arlington, VA 22202-4302. Respondents should be aware that notwithstanding any other provision of law, no person shall be subject to any penalty for failing to comply with a collection of information if it does not display a currently valid OMB control number. **PLEASE DO NOT RETURN YOUR FORM TO THE ABOVE ADDRESS.**

A. SERVICE PROCESSING FOR	B. PRIOR SERVICE: YES ☐ NO ☐ NUMBER OF DAYS:	C. (1) DIEUS (YYYYMMDD) / (2) DIERC (YYYYMMDD)	D. SELECTIVE SERVICE CLASSIFICATION	E. SELECTIVE SERVICE REGISTRATION NO.

SECTION I - PERSONAL DATA

1. SOCIAL SECURITY NUMBER

2. NAME *(Last, First, Middle Name (and Maiden, if any), Jr., Sr., etc.)*

3. CURRENT ADDRESS *(Street, City, County, State, Country, ZIP Code)*

4. HOME OF RECORD ADDRESS *(Street, City, County, State, Country, ZIP Code)*

5. CITIZENSHIP *(X one)*
- a. U.S. AT BIRTH *(If this box is marked, also X (1) or (2))*
  - (1) NATIVE BORN
  - (2) BORN ABROAD OF U.S. PARENT(S)
- b. U.S. NATURALIZED
- c U.S. NON-CITIZEN NATIONAL
- d. IMMIGRANT ALIEN *(Specify)*
- e. NON-IMMIGRANT FOREIGN NATIONAL *(Specify)*

6. SEX *(X one)*
- a. MALE
- b. FEMALE

7.a. RACIAL CATEGORY
- (1) AMERICAN INDIAN/ALASKAN NATIVE
- (2) BLACK
- (3) ASIAN/PACIFIC ISLANDER
- (4) WHITE

7.b. ETHNIC CATEGORY
- (1) HISPANIC
- (2) SPECIFY ETHNIC GROUP

8. MARITAL STATUS *(Specify)*

9. NUMBER OF DEPENDENTS

10. DATE OF BIRTH *(YYYYMMDD)*

11. RELIGIOUS PREFERENCE *(Optional)*

12. EDUCATION *(Yrs/Highest Ed Gr Completed)*

13. PROFICIENT IN FOREIGN LANGUAGE *(If Yes, specify. If No, enter NONE.)* 1st 2nd

14. VALID DRIVER'S LICENSE *(X one)* YES ☐ NO ☐
(If Yes, list State, number, and expiration date)

15. PLACE OF BIRTH *(City, State and Country)*

SECTION II - EXAMINATION AND ENTRANCE DATA PROCESSING CODES
(FOR OFFICE USE ONLY - DO NOT WRITE IN THIS SECTION - Go on to Page 2, Question 20.)

16. APTITUDE TEST RESULTS

a. TEST ID	b. TEST SCORES	AFQT PERCENTILE	GS	AR	WK	PC	NO	CS	AS	MK	MC	EI	VE

17. DEP ENLISTMENT DATA

a. DATE OF DEP ENLISTMENT (YYYYMMDD)	b. PROJ ACTIVE DUTY DATE (YYYYMMDD)	c. ES	d. RECRUITER IDENTIFICATION	e. PROGRAM ENLISTED FOR

f. T-E MOS/AFS	g. WAIVER (1)	(2)	(3)	(4)	(5)	(6)	h. PAY GRADE

18. ACCESSION DATA

a. ENLISTMENT DATE (YYYYMMDD)	b. ACTIVE DUTY SERVICE DATE (YYYYMMDD)	c. PAY ENTRY DATE (YYYYMMDD)	d. TOE

e. WAIVER (1)	(2)	(3)	(4)	(5)	(6)	f. PAY GRADE	g. DATE OF GRADE (YYYYMMDD)	h. ES	i. YRS./HIGHEST ED GR COMPL

j. RECRUITER IDENTIFICATION	k. PROGRAM ENLISTED FOR	l. T-E MOS/AFS	m. PMOS/AFS	n. YOUTH	o. OA	p. TRANSFER TO (UIC)

19. SERVICE REQUIRED CODES

1	2	3	4	5	6	7	8	9	10	11	12	13	14	15	16	17	18	19	20	21	22	23	24	25
26	27	28	29	30	31	32	33	34	35	36	37	38	39	40	41	42	43	44	45	46	47	48	49	50
51	52	53	54	55	56	57	58	59	60	61	62	63	64	65	66	67	68	69	70	71	72	73	74	75	76	77	78	79	80
81	82	83	84	85	86	87	88	89	90	91	92	93	94	95	96	97	98	99	100	101	102	103	104	105	106	107	108	109	110
111	112	113	114	115	116	117	118	119	120	121	122	123	124	125	126	127	128	129	130	131	132	133	134	135	136	137	138	139	140

19a. DEP/ACCESSION RECORD (TO BE COMPLETED BY MEPS PERSONNEL)

WRK AND STATUS CODE	DATE OF ACTION	Q/C	WRK AND STATUS CODE	DATE OF ACTION	Q/C

DD FORM 1966/1 (ADP), JUL 1999   PREVIOUS EDITIONS ARE OBSOLETE.

PRIVACY ACT STATEMENT

AUTHORITY: Title 10 USC Sections 504, 505, 508, 12102, 520a; Title 14 USC Sections 351 and 632; Title 50 USC Appendix 451; and EO 9397.

PRINCIPAL PURPOSE(S): DD Form 1966 is the basic form used by all the Military Services and the Coast Guard for obtaining data used in determining eligibility of applicants and for establishing recores for those applicants who are accepted.

ROUTINE USE(S): None.

DISCLOSURE: Voluntary; however, failure to answer all questions on this form, except questions labeled as "Optional," may result in denial of your enlistment application.

WARNING

Information provided by you on this form is FOR OFFICIAL USE ONLY and will be maintained and used in strict compliance with Federal laws and regulations. The information provided by you becomes the property of the United States Government, and it may be consulted throughout your military service career, particularly whenever either favorable or adverse administrative or disciplinary actions related to you are involved.

YOU CAN BE PUNISHED BY FINE, IMPRISONMENT OR BOTH IF YOU ARE FOUND GUILTY OF MAKING A KNOWING AND WILLFUL FALSE STATEMENT ON THIS DOCUMENT.

INSTRUCTIONS

(Read carefully BEFORE filling out this form.)

1. Read Privacy Act Statement above before completing form.

2. Type or print LEGIBLY all answers. If the answer is "None" or "Not Applicable," so state. "Optional" questions may be left blank.

3. Unless otherwise specified, write all dates as 8 digits (with no spaces or marks) in YYYYMMDD fashion. June 1, 1997 is written 19970601.

DD FORM 1966/1, JUL 1999   Back of Page 1

20. NAME (Last, First, Middle Initial)	21. SOCIAL SECURITY NUMBER

SECTION III - OTHER PERSONAL DATA

22. EDUCATION

a. List all high schools and colleges attended. *(List dates in YYYYMM format.)*

(1) FROM	(2) TO	(3) NAME OF SCHOOL	(4) LOCATION	(5) GRADUATE YES	NO
				YES	NO
b. Have you ever been enrolled in ROTC, Junior ROTC, Sea Cadet Program or Civil Air Patrol?					

23. MARITAL/DEPENDENCY STATUS AND FAMILY DATA *(If "Yes," explain in Section VI, "Remarks.")*

a. Is anyone dependent upon you for support?		
b. Is there any court order or judgment in effect that directs you to provide alimony or support for children?		
c. Do you have an <u>immediate relative</u> (father, mother, brother, or sister) who: (1) is now a prisoner of war or is missing in action (MIA); or (2) died or became 100% permanently disabled while serving in the Armed Services?		
d. Are you the only living child in your immediate family?		

24. PREVIOUS MILITARY SERVICE OR EMPLOYMENT WITH THE U.S. GOVERNMENT *(If "Yes," explain in Section VI, "Remarks.")*

a. Are you now or have you ever been in any regular or reserve branch of the Armed Forces or in the Army National Guard or Air National Guard?		
b. Have you ever been rejected for enlistment, reenlistment, or induction by any branch of the Armed Forces of the United States?		
c. Are you now or have you ever been a deserter from any branch of the Armed Forces of the United States?		
d. Have you ever been employed by the United States Government?		
e. Are you now drawing, or do you have an application pending, or approval for: retired pay, disability allowance, severance pay, or a pension from any agency of the government of the United States?		

25. ABILITY TO PERFORM MILITARY DUTIES *(If "Yes," explain in Section VI, "Remarks.")*

a. Are you now or have you ever been a conscientious objector? (That is, do you have, or have you ever had, a firm, fixed, and sincere objection to participation in war in any form or to the bearing of arms because of religious belief or training?)		
b. Have you ever been discharged by any branch of the Armed Forces of the United States for reasons pertaining to being a conscientious objector?		
c. Is there anything which would preclude you from performing military duties or participating in military activities whenever necessary (i.e., do you have any personal restrictions or religious practices which would restrict your availability)?		

26. DRUG USE AND ABUSE *(If "Yes," explain in Section VI, "Remarks.")*
Have you ever tried or used or possessed any narcotic (to include heroin or cocaine), depressant (to include quaaludes), stimulant, hallucinogen (to include LSD or PCP), or cannabis (to include marijuana or hashish), or any mind-altering substance (to include glue or paint), or anabolic steroid, except as prescribed by a licenced physician?

SECTION IV - CERTIFICATION

27. CERTIFICATION OF APPLICANT *(Your signature in this block must be witnessed by your recruiter.)*

a. I certify that the information given by me in this document is true, complete, and correct to the best of my knowledge and belief. I understand that I am being accepted for enlistment based on the information provided by me in this document; that if any of the information is knowingly false or incorrect, I could be tried in a civilian or military court and could receive a less than honorable discharge which could affect my future employment opportunities.

b. TYPED OR PRINTED NAME (Last, First, Middle Initial)	c. SIGNATURE	d. DATE SIGNED (YYYYMMDD)

28. DATA VERIFICATION BY RECRUITER *(Enter description of the actual documents used to verify the following items.)*

a. NAME (X one)	b. AGE (X one)	c. CITIZENSHIP (X one)
(1) BIRTH CERTIFICATE	(1) BIRTH CERTIFICATE	(1) BIRTH CERTIFICATE
(2) OTHER (Explain)	(2) OTHER (Explain)	(2) OTHER (Explain)
d. SOCIAL SECURITY NUMBER (SSN) (X one)	e. EDUCATION (X one)	f. OTHER DOCUMENTS USED
(1) SSN CARD	(1) DIPLOMA	
(2) OTHER (Explain)	(2) OTHER (Explain)	

DD FORM 1966/2, JUL 1999

Page 2

29. NAME *(Last, First, Middle Initial)*	30. SOCIAL SECURITY NUMBER

31. CERTIFICATION OF WITNESS

a. I certify that I have witnessed the applicant's signature above and that I have verified the data in the documents required as prescribed by my directives. I further certify that I have not made any promises or guarantees other than those listed and signed by me. I understand my liability to trial by courts-martial under the Uniform Code of Military Justice should I effect or cause to be effected the enlistment of anyone known by me to be ineligible for enlistment.

b. TYPED OR PRINTED NAME *(Last, First, Middle Initial)*	c. PAY GRADE	d. RECRUITER I.D.	e. SIGNATURE	f. DATE SIGNED *(YYYYMMDD)*

32. SPECIFIC OPTION/PROGRAM ENLISTED FOR, MILITARY SKILL, OR ASSIGNMENT TO A GEOGRAPHICAL AREA GUARANTEES

a. SPECIFIC OPTION/PROGRAM ENLISTED FOR *(Completed by Guidance Counselor, MEPS Liaison NCO, etc., as specified by sponsoring service.)* *(Use clear text English.)*

	c. APPLICANT'S INITIALS
b. I fully understand that I will not be guaranteed any specific military skill or assignment to a geographic area except as shown in Item 32.a. above and annexes attached to my Enlistment/Reenlistment Document (DD Form 4).	

33. CERTIFICATION OF RECRUITER OR ACCEPTOR

a. I certify that I have reviewed all information contained in this document and, to the best of my judgment and belief, the applicant fulfills all legal policy requirements for enlistment. I accept him/her for enlistment on behalf of the United States *(Enter Branch of Service)*

_____ and certify that I have not made any promises or guarantees other than those listed in Item 32.a. above. I further certify that service regulations governing such enlistments have been strictly complied with and any waivers required to effect applicant's enlistment have been secured and are attached to this document.

b. TYPED OR PRINTED NAME *(Last, First, Middle Initial)*	c. PAY GRADE	d. RECRUITER I.D. OR ORGANIZATION	e. SIGNATURE	f. DATE SIGNED *(YYYYMMDD)*

SECTION V - RECERTIFICATION

34. RECERTIFICATION BY APPLICANT AND CORRECTION OF DATA AT THE TIME OF ACTIVE DUTY ENTRY

a. I have reviewed all information contained in this document this date. That information is still correct and true to the best of my knowledge and belief. If changes were required, the original entry has been marked "See Item 34" and the correct information is provided below.

b. ITEM NUMBER	c. CHANGE REQUIRED

d. APPLICANT		e. WITNESS		
(1) SIGNATURE	(2) DATE SIGNED *(YYYYMMDD)*	(1) TYPED OR PRINTED NAME *(Last, First, Middle Initial)*	(2) RANK/ GRADE	(3) SIGNATURE

SECTION VI - REMARKS
(Specify item(s) being continued by item number. Continue on separate pages if necessary.)

	DD FORM 1966/4 ATTACHED? *(X one)*	YES
		NO

DD FORM 1966/3, JUL 1999

35. NAME *(Last, First, Middle Initial)*	36. SOCIAL SECURITY NUMBER

USE THIS DD FORM 1966 PAGE ONLY IF EITHER SECTION APPLIES TO THE APPLICANT'S RECORD OF MILITARY PROCESSING.

SECTION VI - PARENTAL/GUARDIAN CONSENT FOR ENLISTMENT

37. PARENT/GUARDIAN STATEMENT(S) *(Line out portions not applicable)*

a. I/we certify that *(Enter name of applicant)*

_____

has no other legal guardian other than me/us and I/we consent to his/her enlistment in the United States *(Enter Branch of Service)*

_____

I/we certify that no promises of any kind have been made to me/us concerning assignment to duty, training, or promotion during his/her enlistment as an inducement to me/us to sign this consent. I/we hereby authorize the Armed Forces representatives concerned to perform medical examinations, other examinations required, and to conduct records checks to determine his/her eligibility. I/we relinquish all claim to his/her service and to any wage or compensation for such service.

b. **FOR ENLISTMENT IN A RESERVE COMPONENT.**

I/we understand that, as a member of a reserve component, he/she must serve minimum periods of active duty for training unless excused by competent authority. In the event he/she fails to fulfill the obligations of his/her reserve enlistment, he/she may be recalled to active duty as prescribed by law. I/we further understand that while he/she is in the ready reserve, he/she may be ordered to extended active duty in time of war or national emergency declared by the Congress or the President or when otherwise authorized by law.

c. PARENT

(1) TYPED OR PRINTED NAME *(Last, First, Middle Initial)*	(2) SIGNATURE	(3) DATE SIGNED *(YYYYMMDD)*

d. WITNESS

(1) TYPED OR PRINTED NAME *(Last, First, Middle Initial)*	(2) SIGNATURE	(3) DATE SIGNED *(YYYYMMDD)*

e. PARENT

(1) TYPED OR PRINTED NAME *(Last, First, Middle Initial)*	(2) SIGNATURE	(3) DATE SIGNED *(YYYYMMDD)*

f. WITNESS

(1) TYPED OR PRINTED NAME *(Last, First, Middle Initial)*	(2) SIGNATURE	(3) DATE SIGNED *(YYYYMMDD)*

38. VERIFICATION OF SINGLE SIGNATURE CONSENT

SECTION VIII - STATEMENT OF NAME FOR OFFICIAL MILITARY RECORDS

39. NAME CHANGE.

If the preferred enlistment name (name given in Item 2) is not the same as on your birth certificate, and it has not been changed by legal procedure prescribed by state law, and it is the same as on your social security number card, complete the following:

a. NAME AS SHOWN ON BIRTH CERTIFICATE	b. NAME AS SHOWN ON SOCIAL SECURITY NUMBER CARD

c. I hereby state that I have not changed my name through any court or other legal procedure; that I prefer to use the name of

_____ by which I am known in the community as a matter of convenience

and with no criminal intent. I further state that I am the same person as the person whose name is shown in Item 2.

d. APPLICANT		e. WITNESS	
(1) SIGNATURE	(2) DATE SIGNED *(YYYYMMDD)*	(1) TYPED OR PRINTED NAME *(Last, First, Middle Initial)*	(2) PAY GRADE
		(3) SIGNATURE	

DD FORM 1966/4, JUL 1999   Page 4

RECORD OF MILITARY PROCESSING - ARMED FORCES OF THE UNITED STATES

(Read Privacy Act Statement and Instructions on back before completing this form.)

Form Approved
OMB No. 0704-0173
Expires Jul 31, 2000

The public reporting burden for this collection of information is estimated to average 20 minutes per response, including the time for reviewing instructions, searching existing data sources, gathering and maintaining the data needed, and completing and reviewing the collection of information. Send comments regarding this burden estimate or any other aspect of this collection of information, including suggestions for reducing the burden, to Department of Defense, Washington Headquarters Services, Directorate for Information Operations and Reports (0704-0173), 1215 Jefferson Davis Highway, Suite 1204, Arlington, VA 22202-4302. Respondents should be aware that notwithstanding any other provision of law, no person shall be subject to any penalty for failing to comply with a collection of information if it does not display a currently valid OMB control number.

PLEASE DO NOT RETURN YOUR FORM TO THE ABOVE ADDRESS.

A. SERVICE PROCESSING FOR	B. PRIOR SERVICE: YES / NO NUMBER OF DAYS:	C. (1) DIEUS (YYYYMMDD) (2) DIERC (YYYYMMDD)	D. SELECTIVE SERVICE CLASSIFICATION	E. SELECTIVE SERVICE REGISTRATION NO.

SECTION I - PERSONAL DATA

1. SOCIAL SECURITY NUMBER

2. NAME *(Last, First, Middle Name (and Maiden, if any), Jr., Sr., etc.)*

3. CURRENT ADDRESS *(Street, City, County, State, Country, ZIP Code)*

4. HOME OF RECORD ADDRESS *(Street, City, County, State, Country, ZIP Code)*

5. CITIZENSHIP *(X one)*
- a. U.S. AT BIRTH *(If this box is marked, also X (1) or (2).)*
  - (1) NATIVE BORN
  - (2) BORN ABROAD OF U.S. PARENT(S)
- b. U.S. NATURALIZED
- c. U.S. NON-CITIZEN NATIONAL
- d. IMMIGRANT ALIEN *(Specify)*
- e. NON-IMMIGRANT FOREIGN NATIONAL *(Specify)*

6. SEX *(X one)*
- a. MALE
- b. FEMALE

7.a. RACIAL CATEGORY
- (1) AMERICAN INDIAN/ALASKAN NATIVE
- (2) BLACK
- (3) ASIAN/PACIFIC ISLANDER
- (4) WHITE

7.b. ETHNIC CATEGORY
- (1) HISPANIC
- (2) SPECIFY ETHNIC GROUP

8. MARITAL STATUS *(Specify)*

9. NUMBER OF DEPENDENTS

10. DATE OF BIRTH *(YYYYMMDD)*

11. RELIGIOUS PREFERENCE *(Optional)*

12. EDUCATION *(Yrs/Highest Ed Gr Completed)*

13. PROFICIENT IN FOREIGN LANGUAGE *(If Yes, specify. If No, enter NONE.)*   1st   2nd

14. VALID DRIVER'S LICENSE *(X one)*   YES   NO   *(If Yes, list State, number, and expiration date)*

15. PLACE OF BIRTH *(City, State and Country)*

SECTION II - EXAMINATION AND ENTRANCE DATA PROCESSING CODES
(FOR OFFICE USE ONLY - DO NOT WRITE IN THIS SECTION - Go on to Page 2, Question 20.)

16. APTITUDE TEST RESULTS

a. TEST ID	b. TEST SCORES	AFQT PERCENTILE	GS	AR	WK	PC	NO	CS	AS	MK	MC	EI	VE

17. DEP ENLISTMENT DATA

a. DATE OF DEP ENLISTMENT (YYYYMMDD)	b. PROJ ACTIVE DUTY DATE (YYYYMMDD)	c. ES	d. RECRUITER IDENTIFICATION	e. PROGRAM ENLISTED FOR

f. T-E MOS/AFS	g. WAIVER (1)	(2)	(3)	(4)	(5)	(6)	h. PAY GRADE

18. ACCESSION DATA

a. ENLISTMENT DATE (YYYYMMDD)	b. ACTIVE DUTY SERVICE DATE (YYYYMMDD)	c. PAY ENTRY DATE (YYYYMMDD)	d. TO

e. WAIVER (1)	(2)	(3)	(4)	(5)	(6)	f. PAY GRADE	g. DATE OF GRADE (YYYYMMDD)	h. ES	i. YRS./HIGHEST ED GR COMPL

j. RECRUITER IDENTIFICATION	k. PROGRAM ENLISTED FOR	l. T-E MOS/AFS	m. PMOS/AFS	n. YOUTH	o. OA	p. TRANSFER TO (UIC)

19. SERVICE REQUIRED CODES

1	2	3	4	5	6	7	8	9	10	11	12	13	14	15	16	17	18	19	20	21	22	23	24	25
26	27	28	29	30	31	32	33	34	35	36	37	38	39	40	41	42	43	44	45	46	47	48	49	50
51	52	53	54	55	56	57	58	59	60	61	62	63	64	65	66	67	68	69	70	71	72	73	74	75	76	77	78	79	80
81	82	83	84	85	86	87	88	89	90	91	92	93	94	95	96	97	98	99	100	101	102	103	104	105	106	107	108	109	110
111	112	113	114	115	116	117	118	119	120	121	122	123	124	125	126	127	128	129	130	131	132	133	134	135	136	137	138	139	140

DD FORM 1966/1, JUL 1999   PREVIOUS EDITIONS ARE OBSOLETE.

NAME	IDENTIFICATION NUMBER	NO. OF SHEETS ATTACHED

MEASUREMENTS AND OTHER FINDINGS

20. HEIGHT	21. WEIGHT	22. COLOR HAIR	23. COLOR EYES	24. BUILD: SLENDER ☐ MEDIUM ☐ HEAVY ☐ OBESE ☐	25. TEMPERATURE

26. BLOOD PRESSURE *(Arm at heart level)*					27. PULSE *(Arm at heart level)*				
A. SITTING	SYS.	B. RECUM-BENT	SYS.	C. STANDING *(5 mins.)*	SYS.	A. SITTING	B. RECUMBENT	C. STANDING *(3 MINS)*	D. AFTER EXERCISE	E. 2 MINS. AFTER
	DIAS.		DIAS.		DIAS.					

28. DISTANT VISION		29. REFRACTION			30. NEAR VISION		
RIGHT 20/	CORR. TO 20/	BY	S.	CX	CORR. TO	BY	
LEFT 20/	CORR. TO 20/	BY	S.	CX	CORR. TO	BY	

31. HETEROPHORIA *(Specify distance)*

ESO	EXO	R.H.	L.H.	PRISM DIV.	PRISM CONV. CT	PC	PD

32. ACCOMMODATION		33. COLOR VISION *(Test used and result)*	34. DEPTH PERCEPTION *(Test used and score)*	
RIGHT	LEFT		UNCORRECTED	
			CORRECTED	

35. FIELD OF VISION		36. NIGHT VISION *(Test used and score)*	37. RED LENS TEST	38. INTRAOCULAR TENSION	
RIGHT	LEFT			RIGHT	LEFT

39. HEARING				40. AUDIOMETER									41. PSYCHOLOGICAL AND PSYCHOMOTOR *(Tests used and scores)*
RIGHT WV	/15 SV	/15		250 256	500 512	1000 1024	2000 2048	3000 2896	4000 4096	6000 6144	8000 8192		
LEFT WV	/15 SV	/15	RIGHT										
			LEFT										

42. NOTES *(Continued)* AND SIGNIFICANT OR INTERVAL HISTORY

(Use additional sheets if necessary)

43. SUMMARY OF DEFECTS AND DIAGNOSES *(List diagnoses with item numbers)*

44. RECOMMENDATIONS - FURTHER SPECIALIST EXAMINATIONS INDICATED *(Specify)*	45A. PHYSICAL PROFILE					
	P	U	L	H	E	S

46. EXAMINEE *(Check)* A. ☐ IS QUALIFIED FOR B. ☐ IS NOT QUALIFIED FOR	45B. PHYSICAL CATEGORY			
47. IF NOT QUALIFIED, LIST DISQUALIFYING DEFECTS BY ITEM NUMBER	A	B	C	E

48. TYPED OR PRINTED NAME OF PHYSICIAN	SIGNATURE
49. TYPED OR PRINTED NAME OF PHYSICIAN	SIGNATURE
50. TYPED OR PRINTED NAME OF DENTIST OR PHYSICIAN *(Indicate which)*	SIGNATURE
51. TYPED OR PRINTED NAME OF REVIEWING OFFICER OR APPROVING AUTHORITY	SIGNATURE

STANDARD FORM 88 (Rev. 10-94) BACK
USAPPC V2.00

REPORT OF MEDICAL EXAMINATION

DATE OF EXAM

1. LAST NAME - FIRST NAME - MIDDLE NAME	2. IDENTIFICATION NO.	3. GRADE AND COMPONENT OR POSITION

4. HOME ADDRESS *(Number, street or RFD, city or town, state and ZIP Code)* | 5. EMERGENCY CONTACT *(Name and address of contact)*

6. DATE OF BIRTH	7. AGE	8. SEX ☐ FEMALE ☐ MALE	9. RELATIONSHIP OF CONTACT

10. PLACE OF BIRTH

11. RACE ☐ WHITE ☐ BLACK ☐ AMERICAN INDIAN/ALASKA NATIVE ☐ HISPANIC WHITE ☐ HISPANIC BLACK ☐ ASIAN/PACIFIC ISLANDER

12a. AGENCY | 12b. ORGANIZATION UNIT | 13. TOTAL YEARS GOVERNMENT SERVICE

a. MILITARY | b. CIVILIAN

14. NAME OF EXAMINING FACILITY OR EXAMINER, AND ADDRESS | 15. RATING OR SPECIALTY OF EXAMINER

16. PURPOSE OF EXAMINATION

17. CLINICAL EVALUATION

NOR-MAL	*(Check each item in appropriate column, enter "NE" if not evaluated.)*	ABNOR-MAL	NOR-MAL	*(Check each item in appropriate column, enter "NE" if not evaluated.)*	ABNOR-MAL
	A. HEAD, FACE, NECK AND SCALP			O. PROSTATE *(Over 40 or clinically indicated)*	
	B. EARS - GENERAL *(INTERNAL CANALS)* *(Auditory acuity under items 39 and 40)*			P. TESTICULAR	
				Q. ANUS AND RECTUM *(Hemorrhoids, Fistulae) (Hemocult Results)*	
	C. DRUMS *(Perforation)*			R. ENDOCRINE SYSTEM	
	D. NOSE			S. G-U SYSTEM	
	E. SINUSES			T. UPPER EXTREMITIES *(Strength, range of motion)*	
	F. MOUTH AND THROAT			U. FEET	
	G. EYES GENERAL *(Visual acuity and refraction under items 28, 29, and 30)*			V. LOWER EXTREMITIES *(Except feet) (Strength, range of motion)*	
	H. OPHTHALMOSCOPIC			W. SPINE, OTHER MUSCULOSKELETAL	
	I. PUPILS *(Equality and reaction)*			X. IDENTIFYING BODY MARKS, SCARS, TATTOOS	
	J. OCULAR MOTILITY *(Associated parallel movements nystagmus)*			Y. SKIN, LYMPHATICS	
	K. LUNGS AND CHEST			Z. NEUROLOGIC *(Equilibrium tests under item 42)*	
	L. HEART *(Thrust, size, rhythm, sounds)*			AA. PSYCHIATRIC *(Specify any personality deviation)*	
	M. VASCULAR SYSTEM *(Varicosities, etc.)*			BB. BREASTS	
	N. ABDOMEN AND VISCERA *(Include hernia)*			CC. PELVIC *(Females only)*	

NOTES: *(Describe every abnormality in detail. Enter pertinent item number before each comment. Continue in item 42 and use additional sheets if necessary)*

18. DENTAL *(Place appropriate symbols, shown in examples, above or below number of upper and lower teeth.)*

```
        O                    /                       x              x   x   x                x   x              L
      1  2  3    Restorable  1  2  3    Non-        1  2  3  Missing  1  2  3   Replaced    1  2  3   Fixed       L
     32 31 30      Teeth    32 31 30   restorable  32 31 30  Teeth   32 31 30     by       32 31 30  Partial     E
        O                    /          Teeth       x              x   x   x   Dentures   ( x )     Dentures     F
R                                                                                                                T
I                                                                                                                L
G    1    2    3    4    5    6    7    8    9   10   11   12   13   14   15   16   E
H   32   31   30   29   28   27   26   25   24   23   22   21   20   19   18   17   F
T                                                                                   T
```

REMARKS AND ADDITIONAL DENTAL DEFECTS AND DISEASES

19. TEST RESULTS *(Copies of results are preferred as attachments)*

A. URINALYSIS: (1) SPECIFIC GRAVITY		B. CHEST X-RAY OR PPD *(Place, date, film number and result)*
(2) URINE ALBUMIN	(4) MICROSCOPIC	
(3) URINE SUGAR		
C. SYPHILIS SEROLOGY *(Specify test used and results)*	D. EKG / E. BLOOD TYPE AND RH FACTOR	F. OTHER TESTS

NSN 7540-00-634-4038

STANDARD FORM 88 (Rev.10-94)
Prescribed by GSA/ICMR FIRMR (41CFR) 201-9.202-1
USAPPC V2.00

11. FEMALES ONLY

CHECK EACH ITEM	YES	NO	DON'T KNOW	DATE OF LAST MENSTRUAL PERIOD	DATE OF LAST PAP SMEAR	DATE OF LAST MAMMO-GRAM
Treated for a female disorder						
Change in menstrual pattern						

CHECK EACH ITEM. IF "YES" EXPLAIN IN BLANK SPACE TO RIGHT. LIST EXPLANATION BY ITEM NUMBER.

ITEM	YES	NO
12. Have you been refused employment or been unable to hold a job or stay in school because of:		
a. Sensitivity to chemicals, dust, sunlight, etc.		
b. Inability to perform certain motions.		
c. Inability to assume certain positions.		
d. Other medical reasons *(If yes, give reasons.)*		
13. Have you ever been treated for a mental condition? *(If yes, specify when, where, and give details.)*		
14. Have you ever been denied life insurance? *(If yes, state reason and give details.)*		
15. Have you had, or have you been advised to have, any operation? *(If yes, describe and give age at which occurred.)*		
16. Have you ever been a patient in any type of hospital? *(If yes, specify when, where, why, and name of doctor and complete address of hospital.)*		
17. Have you consulted or been treated by clinics, physicians, healers, or other practitioners within the past 5 years for other than minor illnesses? *(If yes, give complete address of doctor, hospital, clinic, and details.)*		
18. Have you ever been rejected for military service because of physical, mental, or other reasons? *(If yes, give date and reason for rejection.)*		
19. Have you ever been discharged from military service because of physical, mental, or other reasons? *(If yes, give date, reason, and type of discharge; whether honorable, other than honorable, for unfitness or unsuitability.)*		
20. Have you ever received, is there pending, or have you ever applied for pension or compensation for existing disability? *(If yes, specify what kind, granted by whom, and what amount, when, why.)*		
21. Have you ever been arrested or convicted of a crime, other than minor traffic violations? *(If yes, provide details.)*		
22. Have you ever been diagnosed with a learning disability? *(If yes, give type, where, and how diagnosed.)*		

23. LIST ALL IMMUNIZATIONS RECEIVED

I certify that I have reviewed the foregoing information supplied by me and that it is true and complete to the best of my knowledge. I authorize any of the doctors, hospitals, or clinics mentioned above to furnish the Government a complete transcript of my medical record for purposes of processing my application for this employment or service. I understand that falsification of information on Government forms is punishable by fine and/or imprisonment.

24a. TYPED OR PRINTED NAME OF EXAMINEE	24b. SIGNATURE	24c. DATE

NOTE: HAND TO THE DOCTOR OR NURSE, OR IF MAILED MARK ENVELOPE "TO BE OPENED BY MEDICAL OFFICER ONLY."

25. PHYSICIAN'S SUMMARY AND ELABORATION OF ALL PERTINENT DATA *(Physician shall comment on all positive answers in items 7 through 11. Physician may develop by interview any additional medical history deemed important, and record any significant findings here.)*

26a. TYPED OR PRINTED NAME OF PHYSICIAN OR EXAMINER	26b. SIGNATURE	26c. DATE

STANDARD FORM 93 (REV. 6-96) **BACK**

USAPA V1.00

MEDICAL RECORD	REPORT OF MEDICAL HISTORY	DATE OF EXAM

NOTE: This information is for official and medically-confidential use only and will not be released to unauthorized persons

1. NAME OF PATIENT *(Last, first, middle)*	2. IDENTIFICATION NUMBER	3. GRADE

4a. HOME ADDRESS *(Street or RFD; City or Town; State; and ZIP Code)*	5. EXAMINING FACILITY

4b. CITY	4c. STATE	4d. ZIP CODE	

6. PURPOSE OF EXAMINATION

7. STATEMENT OF PATIENT'S PRESENT HEALTH AND MEDICATIONS CURRENTLY USED *(Use additional pages if necessary)*

a. PRESENT HEALTH	b. CURRENT MEDICATION	REGULAR OR INTERM.

c. ALLERGIES *(Include insect bites/stings and common foods)*

	d. HEIGHT	e. WEIGHT

8. PATIENT'S OCCUPATION	9. ARE YOU *(Check one)* ☐ RIGHT HANDED ☐ LEFT HANDED

10. PAST/CURRENT MEDICAL HISTORY

CHECK EACH ITEM	YES	NO	DON'T KNOW	CHECK EACH ITEM	YES	NO	DON'T KNOW	CHECK EACH ITEM	YES	NO	DON'T KNOW
Household contact with anyone with tuberculosis				Shortness of breath				Bone, joint or other deformity			
Tuberculosis or positive TB test				Pain or pressure in chest				Loss of finger or toe			
Blood in sputum or when coughing				Chronic cough				Painful or "trick" shoulder or elbow			
				Palpitation or pounding heart							
Excessive bleeding after injury or dental work				Heart trouble				Recurrent back pain or any back injury			
Suicide attempt or plans				High or low blood pressure				"Trick" or locked knee			
Sleepwalking				Cramps in your legs				Foot trouble			
Wear corrective lenses				Frequent indigestion				Nerve injury			
Eye surgery to correct vision				Stomach, liver, or intestinal trouble				Paralysis *(include infantile)*			
Lack vision in either eye				Gall bladder trouble or gallstones				Epilepsy or seizure			
Wear a hearing aid				Jaundice or hepatitis				Car, train, sea or air sickness			
Stutter or stammer				Broken bones				Frequent trouble sleeping			
Wear a brace or back support				Adverse reaction to medication				Depression or excessive worry			
Scarlet fever				Skin diseases				Loss of memory or amnesia			
Rheumatic fever				Tumor, growth, cyst, cancer				Nervous trouble of any sort			
Swollen or painful joints				Hernia				Periods of unconsciousness			
Frequent or severe headaches				Hemorrhoids or rectal disease				Parent/sibling with diabetes, cancer, stroke or heart disease			
Dizziness or fainting spells				Frequent or painful urination							
Eye trouble				Bed wetting since age 12				X-ray or other radiation therapy			
Hearing loss				Kidney stone or blood in urine				Chemotherapy			
Recurrent ear infections				Sugar or albumin in urine				Asbestos or toxic chemical exposure			
Chronic or frequent colds				Sexually transmitted disease				Plate, pin or rod in any bone			
Severe tooth or gum trouble				Recent gain or loss of weight				Easy fatigability			
Sinusitis				Eating disorder (anorexia, bulimia, etc.)				Been told to cut down or criticized for alcohol use			
Hay Fever or allergic rhinitis				Arthritis, Rheumatism or Bursitis				Used illegal substances			
Head injury											
Asthma				Thyroid trouble or goiter				Used tobacco			

NSN 7540-00-181-8638
Previous edition not usable

STANDARD FORM 93 (REV. 6/96) (EG)
Prescribed by ICMR/GSA
FIRMR (41 CFR) 201-9.202-1

USAPA V1.00

ABOUT THE AUTHOR

Scott A. Ostrow is a career military officer who started his military career as an enlisted Navy member shortly after graduating from Copiague High School (New York) in 1978. After serving in the Navy for over seven years, Scott attended Air Force Officer Training School and was commissioned as a second lieutenant in July 1986.

Scott has served as a Poseidon Missile Technician, Navy Recruiter, Air Force Missile Officer, Fighter Squadron Executive Officer, Recruiting Squadron Operations Officer and Medical Service Corps Officer (as a Reservist), and he is currently Chief of Recruiter Training with Air Force Reserve Recruiting. He holds a Bachelor of Science degree in business administration (management) from Baptist College at Charleston (now Charleston Southern University), South Carolina, and a Master of Public Administration degree from Troy State University, Alabama.

Scott was promoted to his current rank of Lieutenant Colonel in September 1999. He is married and has six children.

NOTES

NOTES

NOTES

NOTES